LATIN FOR LAWYERS

CONTAINING

I. A COURSE IN LATIN, WITH LEGAL MAXIMS AND PHRASES AS A BASIS OF INSTRUCTION.

II. A COLLECTION OF OVER ONE THOU-SAND LATIN MAXIMS, WITH ENGLISH TRANSLATIONS, EX-PLANATORY NOTES, AND CROSS-REFERENCES.

III. A VOCABULARY OF LATIN WORDS.

D1332726

THE LAWBOOK EXCHANGE, LTD.
Clark, New Jersey

ISBN 978-0-963010-64-3 (hardcover)
ISBN 978-1-61619-370-6 (paperback)

Lawbook Exchange edition 1992, 2014

The quality of this reprint is equivalent to the quality of the original work.

THE LAWBOOK EXCHANGE, LTD.
33 Terminal Avenue
Clark, New Jersey 07066-1321

*Please see our website for a selection of our other publications
and fine facsimile reprints of classic works of legal history:*
www.lawbookexchange.com

Library of Congress Catalogue Card Number 92-74408

Printed in the United States of America on acid-free paper

LATIN FOR LAWYERS

CONTAINING

I. A COURSE IN LATIN, WITH LEGAL MAXIMS AND PHRASES AS A BASIS OF INSTRUCTION.

II. A COLLECTION OF OVER ONE THOUSAND LATIN MAXIMS, WITH ENGLISH TRANSLATIONS, EXPLANATORY NOTES, AND CROSS-REFERENCES.

III. A VOCABULARY OF LATIN WORDS.

LONDON :

SWEET AND MAXWELL, LIMITED,

3 CHANCERY LANE.

TORONTO, CANADA :
THE CARSWELL CO., LTD.
19 DUNCAN STREET.

SYDNEY, N.S.W.:
LAW BOOK CO. OF AUSTRALASIA, LTD.
ELIZABETH STREET.

1915

PREFACE

THE First Part of this book consists of a course in Latin, written by E. Hilton Jackson of the American Bar, in which legal maxims and phrases are used as a basis of instruction. It has attained a wide circulation in the Law Schools of America, and has already run to a third edition. It is not designed to give a complete course in the Latin Language, and is intended chiefly to benefit law students and some of the younger members of the profession, who have not a working knowledge of Latin, by making them familiar with the fundamental principles of the language, while at the same time employing as material instruction those maxims and phrases met with daily in practice and in the leading text-books.

The maxims and phrases thus utilised comprise three hundred and eighty-five in all, in selecting which, their importance in a legal aspect has been constantly borne in mind.

These maxims have been conveniently divided into thirty-two lessons, conducting the student by a gradual and easy process from the more elementary principles of Etymology to some of the more involved constructions of Syntax.

The lessons contain references, so far as may be found serviceable to a correct translation, to the rules and principles of Etymology and Syntax, collated in a single part of this book. More of these rules and principles have been introduced than will be found indispensable to an intelligent study of the lessons, thus making the course as expansive as the inclination of the student or the discretion of the instructor may suggest.

The Second Part of the book contains a collection of nearly eleven hundred Latin Maxims, accompanied by an English translation. To all the more important maxims is added a short annotation, explanatory or illustrative of their legal aspect. For the most part these notes are abridged from *Broom's Legal Maxims*, to which useful work the reader is referred for an exhaustive treatment of the maxims. To make the book more useful for purposes of reference, cross-references are given to related maxims, and a short Subject-Index is appended.

The Third Part of the book consists of a Vocabulary of all the Latin words in Part II. together with a number of other Law-Latin words. It is hoped that this is full enough to enable the practitioner or student to translate most Latin phrases he may meet with in the Reports or other law books.

CONTENTS

PART I.

CONTENTS

PART II.

PART III.

PART I.

PRONUNCIATION

1. **ALPHABET.**—The Latin alphabet is the same as in English, except that it has no **w.**

In the classical period one form **i** served for the vowel **i** and the consonant **j,** but for convenience both forms are used in this book.

U and **v** were also denoted by the same form **v,** but the modern distinction has been retained in this book, **u** being used as a vowel.

The Liquids are **l, m, n, r.**

The Mutes, **p, b, t, d, g, c, k, q.**

The Vowels, **a, e, i, o, u, y.**

No further division of the consonants will be found serviceable in this treatise.

2. **THE ENGLISH METHOD OF PRONUNCIATION.**—Vowels usually have their long or short English sounds.

3. **LONG SOUNDS.**—Vowels have their long English sounds—**a** as in *fate*, **e** as in *mete*, **i** in *pine*, **o** in *note*, **u** in *tube*, **y** in *type*—in the following situations:

   1. In final syllables ending in a vowel, *se, si, sér-vi, sér-vo, cór-nu, mí-si.*

   2. In all syllables before a vowel or diphthong : *Dé-us, de-ó-rum, dé-œ, di-é-i, ní-hi-lum.*

1

3. In penultimate syllables before a single consonant or before a mute followed by a liquid : *Pá-ter, pá-tres, Á-thos, Ó-thrys.*

4. In unaccented syllables, not final, before a single consonant, or before a mute followed by a liquid : *Do-ló-ris, cór-po-ri, cón-su-lis, a-gríc-o-la.*

(*a*) **A** unaccented, except before consonants in final syllables, has the sound of *a* final in *America* : *mén-sa, a-cú-tus, a-má-mus.*

(*b*) **I** and **y** unaccented, in any syllable except the first and last, generally have the short sound: *nób-i-lis* (nób-e-lis), *Ám-y-cus* (Ám-e-cus).

(*c*) **I** preceded by an accented *a, e, o,* or *y,* and followed by another vowel, is a semi-vowel with the sound of *y* in *yet* : *A-chá-ia* (A-ká-ya), *Pom-pé-ius* (Pom-pé-yus), *La-tó-ia* (La-tó-ya).

(*d*) **U** has the short sound before *bl,* and the other vowels before *gl* and *tl* : *Pub-líc-o-la, Ag-lá-o-phon, Át-las.*

(*e*) **U** in *qu,* and generally in *gu* and *su,* before a vowel, has the sound of *w* : *qui* (kwi), *gua* ; *lín-gua* (lín-gwa), *lín-guis, suá-de-o* (swá-de-o).

(*f*) *Compound words.*—When the first part of a compound is entire and ends in a consonant, any vowel before such consonant has generally the *short* sound: *a* in *áb-es, e* in *réd-it, i* in *ín-it, o* in *ób-it, pród-est.* But those final syllables, which, as exceptions, have the long sound before a consonant, retain that sound in compounds : *póst-quam, hós-ce. É-ti-am* and *quó-ni-am* are generally pronounced as simple words.

4. SHORT SOUNDS.—Vowels have their short English sounds—**a** as in *fat,* **e** in *met,* **i** in *pin,* **o** in *not,* **u** in *tub,* **y** in *myth*—in the following situations :

1. In final syllables ending in a consonant : *Á-mat, á-met, réx-it, sol, cón-sul, Té-thys* ; except *post, es final,* and *os final* in plural cases : *res, dí-es, hos, á-gros.*

2. In all syllables before *x,* or any two consonants except a mute followed by a liquid : *Réx-it, bél-lum, rex-é-runt, bel-ló-rum.*

3. In all accented syllables, not penultimate, before one or more consonants : *Dóm-i-nus, pát-ri-bus.* But—

(*a*) **A, e,** or **o** before a single consonant (or a mute and a liquid), followed by *e, i,* or *y* before another vowel, has the long sound : *á-ci-es, á-cri-a, mé-re-o, dó-ce-o.*

(*b*) **U,** in any syllable not final, before a single consonant or a mute and a liquid, except *bl,* has the long sound : *Pú-ni-cus, sa-lú-bri-tas.*

(*c*) Compounds ; see **3,** f.

5. DIPHTHONGS.—Diphthongs are pronounced as follows :

Æ like *e* : *Caé-sar, Daéd-a-lus.*
Œ like *e* : *Oé-ta, Oéd-i-pus.*
Au as in author : *aú-rum.*
Eu as in neuter : *neúter.*

1. *Ei* and *oi* are seldom diphthongs, but when so used they are pronounced as in *height, coin, hei, proin.*

2. *Ui,* as a diphthong with the long sound of *i,* occurs in *cui, hui, huic.*

6.   **CONSONANTS.**—The consonants are pronounced in general as in English. Thus :

I. **C** and **G** are *soft* (like *s* and *j*) before *e, i, y, œ,* and *œ,* and *hard* in other situations : *cé-do, ci-vis, Cý-rus, caé-do, coé-pi, á-ge* (á-je), *á-gi* ; *cá-do* (ka-do), *có-go, cum, Gá-des.* But

1. *C* has the sound of *sh*—

(*a*) Before *i* preceded by an accented syllable and followed by a vowel : *só-ci-us* (só-she-us).

(*b*) Before *eu* and *yo* preceded by an accented syllable : *ca-dú-ce-us* (ca-dú-she-us), *Síc-y-on* (Sísh-y-on).

2. *Ch* is hard like *k* : *chó-rus* (kó-rus), *Chí-os* (kí-os).

3. *G* has the soft sound before *g* soft : *ág-ger.*

II. **S, T,** and **X** are generally pronounced as in the English words *son, time, expect* : *sá-cer, ti-mor, réx-i* (rék-si). But—

1. *S, T,* and *X* are aspirated before *i* preceded by an accented syllable and followed by a vowel—*s* and *t* taking the sound of *sh,* and *x* that of *ksh* : *Ál-si-um* (Ál-she-um), *ár-ti-um* (ár-she-um), *ánx-i-us* (ánk-she-us). But—

(*a*) *T* loses the aspirate (1) after *s, t,* or *x* : *Ós-ti-a, Át-ti-us, míx-ti-o* ; (2) in old infinitives in *ier* : *fléc-ti-er* ; (3) generally proper names in *tion* (*tyon*) : *Phi-lís-ti-on, Am-phíc-ty-on.*

2. *S* is pronounced like *z*—

(*a*) At the end of a word after *e, œ, au, b, m, n, r* : *spes, prœs, laus, urbs, hí-ems, mons, pars.*

(*b*) In a few words after the analogy of the corresponding English words : *Caé-sar*, Cæsar ; *caú-sa*, cause ; *mú-sa*, muse ; *mí-ser*, miser, miserable, etc.

3. *X* at the beginning of a word has the sound of *z* : *Xán-thus*.

LESSON I.

First and Second Declensions.

7. Decline **persóna, amícus, interrégnum (98), (99).**

Learn present indicative of **ésse (126).**

8.   1. Bóna ; bónus.
     2. In persónam.
     3. In Ánglia non est ínterrégnum.*
     4. Per mínas.
     5. A ménsa† et thóro.†
     6. A vínculo† matrimónii.‡
     7. Commodátum.
     8. Ab inítio.†
     9. Impérium in império.§
     10. Arbítrium est judícium.
     11. In fóro cónsciéntiæ.‖
     12. In futúro.
     13. Dámnum síne injúria.
     14. Amícus cúriæ.¶

---

* See **132**, I. p. 110.   § See **132**, XXIV. p. 111.
† See **132**, XIX. p. 111.   ‖ See **132**, VIII. p. 110.
‡ See **132**, VII. p. 110.   ¶ See **132**, X. p. 110.

9. **a** or **ab,** prep. w. abl., *from, by.*

amícus,-i, m. *friend.*

Ánglia,-æ, f. *England.*

arbítrium,-i, n. *award.*

bóna,-órum, n. *goods, property.*

bónus,-i, m. *bonus.*

commodátum,-i, n. *loan.*

consciéntia,-æ, f. *conscience.*

cúria,-æ, f. *court.*

dámnum,-i, n. *loss, damages.*

et, conj., *and.*

fórum,-i, n. *forum, court.*

futúrum,-i, n. *future.*

impérium,-i, n. *government, state.*

in, prep. w. acc., *into, to, against,* i.e. *motion* ;
     w. abl., *in, on,* i.e. *rest.*

inítium,-i, n. *beginning.*

injúria,-æ, f. *injury.*

interrégnum,-i, n. *interregnum.*

judícium,-i, n. *judgment.*

matrimónium,-i, n. *marriage, matrimony.*

ménsa,-æ, f. *board, table.*

mína,-æ, f. *threat.*

non, adv., *not.*

per, prep. w. acc., *through, by.*

persóna,-æ, f. *person.*

síne, prep. w. abl., *without.*

thórus,-i, m. *bed, couch.*

vínculum,-i, n. *bond, chain.*

LESSON II.

Adjectives of the First and Second Declensions.

10.   Decline **bónus** and **málus** (107).
Learn present indicative active of **mándo** (120).

11.   1. Málo* ánimo.†
      2. Ignorántia fácti excúsat.
      3. Mandámus.
      4. Pro bóno público.‡
      5. Mála grammática non vítiat chártam.§
      6. Arguméntum ad ignorántiam.
      7. Dóna clandestína sunt sémper suspiciósa.
      8. Térra fírma.
      9. Própter ódium delícti.
     10. Ex offício.||
     11. Injúria non excúsat injúriam.§
     12. Vía antíqua est túta.
     13. Sciénter.

12.   **ad,** prep. w. acc., *based upon, according to.*
      ánimus,-i, m. *intent, mind.*
      antíquus,-a,-um, adj., *ancient, old.*
      arguméntum,-i, n. *argument.*
      bónus,-a,-um, àdj., *good.*

---

* See **132,** IV. p. 110.   § See **132,** II. p. 110.
† See **132,** XVIII. p. 111. || See **132,** XVII. p. 111.
‡ See **132,** XVII. p. 111.

chárta,-æ, f. *writing, instrument, deed.*

clandestínus,-a,-um, adj., *secret.*

delíctum,-i, n. *offence, crime.*

dónum,-i, n. *gift.*

dum, conj., *while.*

ex, prep. w. abl., *by virtue of.*

excúso,-áre,-ávi,-átum, *excuse, condone.*

fáctum,-i, n. *fact.*

fírmus,-a,-um, adj., *firm, solid.*

grammática,-æ, f. *grammar.*

ignorántia,-æ, f. *ignorance.*

málus,-a,-um, adj., *bad, evil.*

mándo,-áre,-ávi,-átum, *command.*

ódium,-i, n. *odium.*

offícium,-i, n. *office.*

pro, prep. w. abl., *for, on behalf of.*

públicus,-a,-um, adj., *public.*

própter, prep. w. acc., *on account of.*

sciénter, adv., *with knowledge, knowingly.*

sémper, adv., *always.*

sunt, *(they) are.*

suspiciósus,-a,-um, adj., *suspicious.*

terra,-æ, f. *land.*

tútus,-a,-um, adj., *safe.*

vía,-æ, f. *way, road.*

vítio,-áre,-ávi,-átum, *vitiate, make void.*

LESSON III.

Third Declension.

13. Decline **lex, visitátio, hómo, rex, mens, con-suetúdo (100), (101), (102).**
Learn future and perfect indicative active of **mándo (120).**

14.
1. Custódia légis.
2. Impoténtia excúsat légem.
3. Visitatiónem commendámus.
4. Lex Ángliæ lex* térræ est.
5. Arguméntum ad hóminem.
6. Lex Ángliæ est lex misericórdiæ.
7. Lex dábit remédium.
8. Festinátio justítiæ† est novérca* infortúnii.
9. Aúla régis.
10. Pléne administrávit.
11. Asséntio méntium.†
12. Consuetúdo régni est lex* Ángliæ.

15. **admínistro,-áre,-ávi,-átum,** *administer.*
asséntio,-ónis, f. *assent.*
aúla,-æ, f. *hall.*
comméndo,-áre,-ávi,-átum, *commend.*
consuetúdo,-inis, f. *custom.*
Cornélia,-æ, f. *Cornelia.*
custódia,-æ, f. *custody, guard.*
de, prep. w. abl., *about, concerning.*
do,-áre, dédi, dátum, *give, furnish.*

---

* See **132**, III. p. 110.   † See **132**, IX. p. 110.

festinátio,-ónis, f. *haste.*
impoténtia,-æ, f. *inability, impotence.*
infortúnium,-i, n. *misfortune, disaster.*
justítia,-æ, f. *justice.*
lex, légis, f. *law.*
mens, méntis, f. *mind.*
misericórdia,-æ, f. *mercy, pity.*
novérca,-æ, f. *stepmother.*
pléne, adv., *fully.*
régnum,-i, n. *kingdom.*
remédium,-i, n. *remedy.*
rex, régis, m. *king.*
sicárius,-i, m. *assassin.*
visitátio,-ónis, f. *visit.*

LESSON IV.

Third Declension.

16. Decline **necéssitas, sérvitus, stipulátor (100), (101).**

Learn the present indicative active of **hábeo (121).**

17.   1. Necéssitas non hábet légem.

2. Fálsa demonstrátio non nócet.

3. Execútio légis non hábet injúriam.

4. Ínter árma léges sílent.

5. Lex dilatiónes abhórret.

6. Mísera est sérvitus, úbi lex vága aut incérta.

7. Malítia súpplet ætátem.

8. Suppréssio véri, expréssio fálsi.

9. Lex spéctat natúræ órdinem.
10. Actiónes légis.
11. Ambigúitas cóntra stipulatórem est.
12. Córam dómino rége.

18. **abhórreo,-ére,-ui, ——,** *abhor.*
áctio,-ónis, f. *action.*
aétas,-átis, f. *age.*
ambigúitas,-átis, f. *ambiguity.*
árma,-órum, n. plur. *arms.*
cóntra, prep. w. acc., *against.*
córam, prep. w. abl., *in the presence of.*
dilátio,-ónis, f. *delay.*
demonstrátio,-ónis, f. *proof.*
dóminus,-i, m. *lord, master.*
execútio,-ónis, f. *execution.*
fálsus,-a,-um, adj., *false.*
hábeo,-ére,-ui,-itum, *have.*
incértus,-a,-um, adj., *uncertain.*
ínter, prep. w. acc., *among.*
malítia,-æ, f. *malice.*
míser,-era,-erum, adj., *wretched.*
natúra,-æ, f. *nature.*
necéssitas,-átis, f. *necessity.*
nóceo,-ére,-ui,-itum, *harm, do injury.*
órdo,-inis, m. *order.*
rex,-égis, m. *king.*
sérvitus,-útis, f. *servitude, slavery.*
síleo,-ére,-ui, ——, *to be silent.*
spécto,-áre,-ávi,-átum, *look at, regard.*
stipulátor,-óris, m. *stipulator, party using.*
suppréssio,-ónis, f. *suppression.*
úbi, adv., *where.*
vágus,-a,-um, adj., *uncertain, ambiguous.*

LESSON V.

Third Declension.

19. Decline **mos, vox, cómes, júdex, jus, vis, haéres, córpus, fraus (100), (101), (102), (105).**
Learn present indicative active of **respóndeo** (like **hábeo**) **(121).**

20.
  1. Cóntra bónos móres.
  2. Vox pópuli vox Déi est.
  3. Negligéntia sémper hábet infortúniam cómitem.*
  4. Ubi jus, ibi remédium est.
  5. Ad quæstiónem fácti non respóndent júdices; ad quæstiónem júris non respóndent juratóres.
  6. Execútio est execútio júris secúndum judícium.
  7. Fraus et jus núnquam cohábitant.
  8. Lónga posséssio est pácis jus.
  9. Fálsa orthográphia síve fálsa grammática non vítiat concessiónem.
  10. Vi† et ármis.†
  11. Nam némo haéres vivéntis est.
  12. Córpus delícti.

21. **cohábito,-áre,-ávi,-átum,** *to live or dwell together.*
cómes,-itis, m. and f. *companion.*

---

* See **132**, VI. p. 110.   † See **132**, XVII. p. 111.

concéssio,-ónis, f. *grant.*

córpus,-oris, n. *body.*

delíctum,-i, n. *crime, offence.*

Déus,-i, m. *God.*

fraus,-dis, f. *fraud.*

haéres,-édis, m. *heir.*

infortúnia,-æ, f. *misfortune.*

jurátor,-óris, m. *juror.*

jus,-úris, n. *law, right.*

mos,-óris, m. *custom.*

negligéntia,-æ, f. *negligence.*

némo,-inis, c. *no one.*

núnquam, adv., *never.*

orthográphia,-æ, f. *spelling.*

posséssio,-ónis, f. *possession.*

respóndeo,-ére,-di,-spónsum, *to answer to, to respond.*

secúndum, prep. w. acc., *according to.*

síve, conj., *or.*

vis, vis, f. *force.*

vívens,-ntis, c. *a living person.*

vox,-ócis, f. *voice.*

LESSON VI.

Adjectives of the Third Declension.

22. Decline **brévis, símplex, fílius, nómen (108), (100), (101), (99).**

Learn present indicative of **indúco** (like **régo**) **(122).**

23.   1. Íra fúror brévis est.
2. Símplex commendátio non óbligat.
3. Necéssitas indúcit privilégium.
4. Fórma legális fórma essentiális.
5. Haéres est nómen légis, fílius est nómen natúræ.
6. Lex néminem cógit ad vána seu impossibília.
7. In fictióne légis, aéquitas exístit.
8. Crímen tráhit persónam.
9. Débile fundaméntum fállit ópus.
10. Lex necessitátis est lex témporis, *i.e.* instántis.

24. **aéquitas,-átis,** f. *equity.*
brévis,-e, adj., *brief, short.*
cógo,-ere, coégi, coáctum, *compel, drive.*
commendátio,-ónis, f. *recommendation.*
crímen,-inis, n. *crime.*
débilis,-e, adj., *weak.*
essentiális,-e, adj., *essential.*
exísto,-ere, éxstiti, éxstitum, *exist.*
fállo,-ere, fefélli, fálsum, *destroy.*
fíctio,-ónis, f. *fiction.*
fílius,-i, m. *son.*
fórma,-æ, f. *form.*

fúror,-óris, m. *madness.*
impossíbilis,-e, adj., *impossible.*
indúco,-ere,-dúxi,-dúctum, *induce.*
ínstans,-ntis, adj., *present.*
íra,-æ, f. *anger.*
legális,-e, adj., *legal.*
nómen,-inis, n. *name.*
óbligo,-áre,-ávi,-átum, *bind.*
ómnis,-e, adj., *all.*
ópus,-eris, n. *superstructure, work.*
privilégium,-i, n. *privilege.*
régo, ere,-réxi, réctum, *control, rule.*
seu, conj., *or.*
sólvo,-ere, sólvi, solútum, *free, release.*
témpus,-oris, n. *time.*
tráho,-ere, tráxi, tráctum, *draws (to it).*

LESSON VII.

Fourth Declension.

25. Decline **áctus, cásus** (103).
Learn present indicative active of **fácio** (like
cápio) (123).

26. 1. Ánnus lúctus.
2. In cásu extrémæ necessitátis ómnia sunt
communia.
3. Áctus légis fácit némini* injúriam.
4. Commúnis érror fácit jus.
5. Bréve judiciále non cádit pro deféctu fórmæ.

---

* See **132**, XIII. p. 110.

6. Júra natúræ sunt immutabília.
7. Lex próspicit, non réspicit.
8. Ángliæ júra in ómni cásu libertáti* dant favórem.
9. Non jus fácit sed seísina fácit stípitem.
10. Lex nil frústra fácit.
11. Excéptio próbat régulam.

27. **áctus,-us,** m. *act.*
æstimátio,-ónis, f. *estimate, value.*
ánnus,-i, m. *year.*
bréve,-is, n. *writ.*
cádo,-ere, cécidi, cásum, *fail.*
cásus,-us, m. *case, contingency.*
commúnis,-e, adj., *common.*
deféctus,-us, m. *defect, error.*
excéptio,-ónis, f. *exception.*
érror,-óris, m. *mistake, error.*
extrémus,-a,-um, adj., *dire, extreme, urgent.*
fácio,-ere, féci, fáctum, *do, make.*
fávor,-óris, m. *boon, preference.*
frústra, adv., *in vain.*
humánus,-a,-um, adj., *human.*
immutábilis,-e, adj., *unchanging, immutable.*
judiciális,-e, adj., *judicial.*
líbertas,-átis, f. *liberty.*
lúctus,-us, m. *mourning.*
mánus,-us, f. *hand, custody.*
mórtuus,-a,-um, adj., *dead.*
próbo,-áre,-ávi,-átum, *prove.*
prospício,-ere,-spéxi,-spéctum, *look forward.*
régula,-æ, f. *rule.*
respício,-ere,-spéxi,-spéctum, *look backward.*
stípes,-itis, m. *root, stock.*

* See **132,** XIII. p. 110.

LESSON VIII.

Fourth and Fifth Declensions.

28.   Decline **contráctus, res, díes** (103), (104).
Decline **fínis, ínteger, magíster** (102), (107), (99).

29.   1. Contráctus est quási áctus cóntra áctum.
2. Execútio légis est fínis et frúctus légis.
3. Res íntegra.
4. Jus ad rem ; jus in re.
5. Bóna fídes ; bóna fíde.
6. Mála fíde.
7. Díes Domínicus non est jurídicus.
8. Senátus populúsque Románus.
9. Magíster rérum úsus ; magístra rérum experiéntia.
10. Ad perpétuam réi memóriam.
11. Fractiónem diéi* non récipit lex.
12. Cúrsus cúriæ est lex cúriæ.

30.   **contráctus,-us,** m. *contract.*
cúria,-æ, f. *court.*
cúrsus,-us, m. *practice.*
díes,-éi, m. *day.*
Domínicus,-a,-um, adj., *of the Lord.*
experiéntia,-æ, f. *experience.*
fídes,-éi, f. *faith.*
fínis,-is, m. *end.*
fráctio,-ónis, f. *fraction.*

---

* See **132,** XI. p. 110.

frúctus,-us, m. *fruit.*
jurídicus,-a,-um, adj., *legal.*
magíster,-tri, m. *master.*
magístra,-æ, f. *mistress.*
memória,-æ, f. *memorial, memory.*
pars,-rtis, f. *part.*
perpétuus,-a,-um, adj., *continual.*
pópulus,-i, m. *people.*
quási, conj., *as if.*
res, réi, f. *thing, affair.*
Románus,-a,-um, adj., *Roman.*
senátus,-us, m. *senate.*
úsus,-us, m. *custom, use.*

LESSON IX.

Passive Voice.

31. Learn present indicative passive of **póndero, præsúmo, accípio, hábeo (120), (122), (121).**

32. 1. Injúria non præsúmitur.
2. Ponderántur téstes non numerántur.
3. Volúntas reputabátur pro fácto.
4. Ómnia præsumúntur cóntra spoliatórem.
5. Volúntas in delíctis non éxitus spectátur.
6. Vir et úxor in lége putántur úna persóna.
7. Útile per inútile non vitiátur.
8. Confirmátio est núlla úbi dónum præcédens* est inválidum.

---

* See **132**, IV. p. 110.

9. Úbi núllum matrimónium íbi núlla dos.
10. Res judicáta accípitur pro veritáte.
11. Ambigúitas verbórum pátens núlla verificatióne exclúditur.
12. Invíto benefícium non dátur.

33. **accípio,-ere,-cépi,-céptum,** *accept.*
benefícium,-i, n. *benefit, advantage.*
confirmátio,-ónis, f. *confirmation.*
dos, dótis, f. *dower.*
exclúdo,-ere,-clúsi,-clúsum, *explain, clear up.*
éxitus,-us, m. *end, result.*
íbi, adv., *there.*
inválidus,-a,-um, adj., *invalid, void.*
invítus,-a,-um, adj., *unwilling.*
júdico,-áre,-ávi,-átum, *adjudicate.*
número,-áre,-ávi,-átum, *count.*
núllus,-a,-um, adj., *no (one).*
pátens,-ntis, adj., *patent.*
póndero,-áre,-ávi,-átum, *weigh.*
præcédens,-ntis, adj., *precedent.*
præsúmo,-ere,-súmpsi,-súmptum, *presume.*
púto,-áre,-ávi,-átum, *regard.*
repúto,-áre,-ávi,-átum, *consider.*
spoliátor,-óris, m. *wrongdoer.*
téstis,-is, c. *witness.*
únus,-a,-um, adj., *one.*
úxor,-óris, f. *wife.*
vérbum,-i, n. *word.*
verificátio,-ónis, f. *proof.*
véritas,-átis, f. *truth.*
vir, víri, m. *husband.*
volúntas,-átis, f. *will.*

LESSON X.

34. Learn present and perfect indicative active and present imperative of **aúdio,** and the present indicative passive of **púnio (124).**
Decline **prævéniens, próhibens, álter,** like **álius (108), (109).**

35. 1. Térra tránsit cum ónere.*
      2. Lex púnit mendácium.
      3. Némo punítur pro aliéno delícto.
      4. Convéntio et módus víncunt légem.
      5. Áctio non dátur non damnificáto.
      6. Justítia est dúplex ; sevére púniens et vére prævéniens.
      7. Lex est sánctio sáncta, júbens honésta et próhibens contrária.
      8. Sémper præsúmitur pro matrimónio.
      9. Sémper præsúmitur pro legitimatióne puerórum.
   10. Lex réjicit supérflua, pugnántia, incóngrua.
   11. Aéquitas núnquam contravénit léges.
   12. Aúdi álteram pártem.

36. **aliénus,-a,-um,** adj., *another's.*
álter,-a,-um, adj., *other.*
aúdio,-íre,-ívi(-íi),-ítum, *hear.*
contrárius,-a,-um, adj., *opposite.*
contravénio,-íre,-i,-véntum, *thwart, run counter to.*

---

* See **132,** XVII. p. III.

convéntio,-ónis, f. *contract.*

cum, prep. with abl., *with, in company with.*

damnificátus,-a,-um, adj., *injured, damnified.*

dúplex,-icis, adj., *twofold.*

honéstas,-átis, f. *honesty.*

incóngruus,-a,-um, adj., *incongruous.*

júbeo,-ére, jússi, jússum, *command.*

legitimátio,-ónis, f. *legitimacy.*

mendácium,-i, n. *falsehood.*

módus,-i, m. *agreement.*

ónus,-eris, n. *incumbrance.*

pars,-rtis, f. *side.*

prævénio,-íre,-i,-véntum, *prevent by anticipating.*

prohíbeo,-ére,-ui,-itum, *prevent.*

púer,-eri, c. *child.*

púgno,-áre,-ávi,-átum, *conflict.*

púnio,-íre,-ívi(-íi),-ítum, *punish.*

rejício,-ere,-jéci,-jéctum, *refuse, reject.*

sánctio,-ónis, f. *oath.*

sánctus,-a,-um, adj., *sacred.*

sevére, adv., *severely.*

supérfluus,-a,-um, adj., *superfluous.*

tránseo,-íre,-ívi(-íi),-ítum, *pass.*

vére, adv., *truly.*

vínco,-ere, víci, víctum, *overcome.*

LESSON XI.

Perfect Passive Participle. Gerund.

37. Learn the perfect passive participle of **géro** and the gerund of **fúror (122), (120).**
Learn perfect indicative active of **cápio (123).**

38.
1. Stáre decísis.
2. De bónis non administrátis.
3. Non est informátus.
4. Ónus probándi.
5. Ánimo furándi ; ánimo testándi.
6. Mála prohíbita.
7. Jus scríptum aut non scríptum.
8. Claúsulæ inconsuétæ sémper indúcunt suspiciónem.
9. Éxtra légem pósitus est civíliter mórtuus.
10. Cépi córpus et est lánguidum.
11. Cépi córpus et parátum hábeo.
12. Res géstæ.

39. **ágo,-ere, égi, áctum,** *transact.*
cápio,-ere, cépi, cáptum, *take.*
civíliter, adv., *civilly.*
claúsula,-æ, f. *clause.*
decído,-ere,-ídi,-císum, *decide.*
decísum,-i, n. *decision.*
fúror,-ári,-átus sum, *steal.*
géro,-ere, géssi, géstum, *transact.*
indúco,-ere,-dúxi,-dúctum, *excite.*
inconsuétus,-a,-um, adj., *unusual.*

infórmo,-áre,-ávi,-átum, *inform.*
lánguidus,-a,-um, adj., *sick.*
páro,-áre,-ávi,-átum, *prepare.*
póno,-ere, pósui, pósitum, *place.*
scríbo,-ere, scrípsi, scríptum, *write.*
sto, stáre, stéti, státum, *stand, abide.*
suspício,-ónis, f. *suspicion.*
téstor,-ári,-átus sum, *make a will.*

LESSON XII.

Deponent Verbs.

40. Learn present indicative of **séquor (125), mórior.**

41.   1. Justítia* firmátur sólium.
   2. Aéquitas légem séquitur.†
   3. Lex úno óre ómnes allóquitur.
   4. Áctio personális móritur cum persóna.
   5. Lex aliquándo séquitur æquitátem.
   6. Rex núnquam móritur.
   7. Ex dólo málo áctio non óritur.
   8. Ex núdo pácto áctio non óritur.
   9. Dórmiunt léges aliquándo, núnquam moriúntur.
  10. Accessórium non dúcit, sed séquitur súum principále.
  11. Lex non óritur ex injúria.
  12. Servítia personália sequúntur persónam.

---

* See **132**, XVII. p. iii.   † See **132**, XXXV. p. 112.

42. **accessórium,-i,** n. *accessory.*
aliquándo, adv., *sometimes.*
allóquor,-lóqui,-locútus sum, *address, speak to.*
dólum,-i, n. *device.*
dórmio,-íre,-ívi(-íi),-ítum, *sleep.*
dúco,-ere, dúxi, dúctum, *lead.*
fírmo,-áre,-ávi,-átum, *strengthen.*
mórior,-i(-íri), mórtuus sum, *die.*
núdus,-a,-um, adj., *naked.*
órior,-íri, órtus sum, *arise, accrue.*
os, óris, n. *voice.*
personális,-e, adj., *personal.*
principále,-is, n. *principal.*
séquor,-i, secútus sum, *follow.*
servítia,-órum, n. plur., *services.*
sólium,-i, n. *throne.*
súus,-a,-um, poss. pron., *his.*

LESSON XIII.

The Second Periphrastic Conjugation.

43. Learn in this conjugation the present tense of **negándus ésse†** (120).

44.
1. Lex non a rége* est violánda.†
2. Justítia némini negánda est.
3. Fácultas probatiónum non est angustánda.
4. In nóvo cásu nóvum remédium apponéndum est.

---

* See **132,** XXII. p. 111.   † See **132,** XXXIV. p. 112.

5. Consuetúdo observánda est.
6. Állegans contrária non est audiéndus.
7. Állegans súam turpitúdinem non est audiéndus.
8. Mens testatóris in testaméntis spectánda est.
9. Allegátio cóntra fáctum non est admitténda.
10. Fídes servánda est.
11. Débitum in præsénti, solvéndum in futúro.
12. Generális régula generáliter est intelligénda.

45. admítto,-ere,-mísi, míssum, *admit.*
allegátio,-ónis, f. *allegation.*
állego,-áre,-ávi,-átum, *allege.*
angústo,-áre,-ávi,-átum, *restrict, limit.*
appóno,-ere,-pósui,-pósitum, *apply.*
aúdio,-íre,-ívi (íi),-ítum, *hear.*
débitum,-i, n. *debt.*
divíno,-áre,-ávi,-átum, *prophesy, forecast, foretell.*
fácultas,-átis, f. *opportunity.*
generális,-e, adj., *general.*
generáliter, adv., *generally.*
intélligo,-ere,-léxi,-léctum, *understand, interpret.*
mens,-ntis, f. *intent.*
négo,-áre,-ávi,-átum, *deny.*
praésens,-ntis, adj., *present.*
probátio,-ónis, f. *proof.*
sérvo,-áre,-ávi,-átum, *keep, preserve.*
víolo,-áre,-ávi,-átum, *disregard.*

LESSON XIV.

Deponents and Second Periphrastic Conjugation.

46. Learn present indicative of **méreor, admitténdus ésse (122).**

47.
1. Ex fácto jus óritur.
2. Ad rem lóquitur.
3. Cogitatiónis poénam némo merétur.
4. Mobília persónam sequúntur.
5. Pártus séquitur véntrem.
6. In vérbis, non vérba sed res et rátio quærénda est.
7. Fraus est odiósa et non præsuménda est.
8. In república máxime conservánda sunt júra bélli.
9. Juraméntum est indivisíbile et non est admitténdum in párte vérum et in párte fálsum.
10. Débita sequúntur persónam debitóris.
11. Ex túrpi caúsa non óritur caúsa.
12. Júdex est lex lóquens.

48. **béllum,-i,** n. *war.*

cogitátio,-ónis, f. *thought.*

consérvo,-áre,-ávi,-átum, *observe, regard.*

débitor,-óris, m. *debtor.*

ex, prep. w. abl., *from.*

indivisíbilis,-e, adj., *indivisible.*

júdex,-icis, m. *judge.*

juraméntum,-i, n. *oath.*

lóquor,-i, locútus sum, *speak.*

máxime, adv., *especially.*

méreor,-éri, méritus sum, *deserve.*

mobília,-ium, n. plur., *furniture, movables.*

odiósus,-a,-um, adj., *odious.*

pártus,-us, m. *offspring.*

poéna,-æ, f *punishment.*

quaéro,-ere, quæsívi(-íi), quæsítum, *inquire into.*

rátio,-ónis, f. *reason.*

respública,-ei,-æ, f. *republic.*

túrpis,-e, adj., *base.*

vénter,-tris, m. *womb, mother.*

vérus,-a,-um, adj., *true.*

LESSON XV.

Relative Pronouns.

49.   Decline **qui** (117).

50.   1. Qui* non ímprobat, ápprobat.

2. Némo dat qui non hábet.

3. Quod necéssitas cógit, deféndit.

4. Qui séntit cómmodum, débet et sentíre ónus, et e cóntra.

5. Qui haéret in lítera, haéret in córtice.

6. Quod ab inítio non válet, in tráctu témporis non convaléscit.

7. Érror qui non restitúitur approbátur.

8. Quod vánum et inútile est, lex non requírit.

---

* See **132,** V. p. 110.

9. Quod non appáret, non est.

10. Haéres legítimus est quem núptiæ demón-strant.

11. Páter est quem núptiæ demónstrant.

12. Fatétur fácinus qui judícium fúgit.

51. **appáreo,-ére,-ui,-itum,** *appear.*

ápprobo,-áre,-ávi,-átum, *approve,*

cómmodum,-i, n. *advantage, benefit.*

convalésco,-valéscere,-válui,—, *gather strength.*

córtex,-icis, m. and f. *bark.*

débeo,-ére,-ui,-itum, *ought.*

deféndo,-ere,-di,-sum, *defend.*

demónstro,-áre,-ávi,-átum, *indicate.*

et, adv., *also.*

fácinus,-oris, n. *crime.*

fáteor,-éri, fássus sum, *confess.*

fúgio,-ere, fúgi, fúgitum, *fly from.*

haéreo,-ére, haési, haésum, *cling to.*

ímprobo,-áre,-ávi,-átum, *blame.*

legítimus,-a,-um, adj., *legal, lawful.*

lítera,-æ, f. *letter.*

núptiæ,-árum, f. plur. *marriage.*

qui, quæ, quod, rel. pron., *who, which.*

requíro,-ere,-quisívi(-ii),-quisítum, *require.*

restítuo,-úere,-ui,-útum, *correct.*

séntio,-íre,-si,-sum, *enjoy, bear.*

vánus,-a,-um, adj., *vain.*

LESSON XVI.

Personal and Intensive Pronouns.

52.   Decline **súi** and **ípse** (115), (116).

53.   1.   Qui fácit per álium fácit per se.
2.   Qui non hábet potestátem alienándi hábet necessitátem retinéndi.
3.   Quod non hábet princípium, non hábet fínem.
4.   In cúria Dómini régis, ípse in própria persóna júra discérnit.
5.   Nihil quod inconvéniens est lícitum.
6.   In ómni re náscitur res quæ ípsa rem extérminat.
7.   In traditiónibus scriptórum, non quod díctum est sed quod géstum est inspícitur.
8.   Frústra probátur quod probátum non rélevat.
9.   Málum in se.
10.   Crímen ómnia ex se náta vítiat.
11.   Bis dat qui cíto dat.

54.   **aliéno,-áre,-ávi,-átum,** *alienate.*
bis, num. adv., *twice.*
cíto, adv., *quickly.*
díco,-ere, díxi, díctum, *say.*
discérno,-ere,-crévi,-crétum, *dispense.*
extérmino,-áre,-ávi,-átum, *destroy.*
inspício,-ere,-spéxi,-spéctum, *look into, examine.*
ípse,-a,-um, demons. pron., *himself, herself, itself.*

lícitus,-a,-um, adj., *lawful, legal.*

náscor,-i, nátus sum, *generate, arise, be born.*

nil, níhil, indecl. n., *nothing.*

potéstas,-átis, f. *power.*

princípium,-i, n. *beginning.*

próprius,-a,-um, adj., *one's own, peculiar.*

rélevo,-áre,-ávi,-átum, *be relevant.*

retíneo,-ére,-ui, reténtum, *hold.*

scríptum,-i, n. *deed.*

súi, gen. of reflex. pron., *of himself, herself, etc.*

tradítio,-ónis, f. *delivery.*

LESSON XVII.

Demonstrative and Indefinite Pronouns.

55.   Decline **is, ídem, quis, quílibet (116), (117), (118).**

56.   1.   Némo bis punítur pro eódem delícto.

2.   Cújus sólum, éjus est úsque ad coélum ; et ad ínferos.

3.   Éi incúmbit probátio qui dícit, non qui négat.

4.   Qui in útero est, pro jam náto habétur, quóties de éjus cómmodo quaéritur.

5.   Úbi éadem rátio íbi ídem lex, et de simílibus ídem est judícium.

6.   De non apparéntibus et de non existéntibus éadem est rátio.

7.   In quo quis delínquit, in éo de júre est puniéndus.

8. Jus naturále est quod ápud ómnes hómines
eándem poténtiam hábet.

9. Jus est nórma récti ; et quícquid est cóntra
nórmam récti est injúria.

10. Felónia implicátur in quálibet proditióne.

57. **ápud,** prep. w. acc., *among.*

coélum,-i, n. *sky.*

cómmodum,-i, n. *benefit.*

de, prep. w. abl., *according to.*

delínquo,-ere,-líqui,-líctum, *be wanting, offend.*

díco,-ere,-xi,-ctum, *affirm.*

felónia,-æ, f. *felony.*

hábeo,-ére,-ui,-itum, *hold, consider.*

ídem, éadem, ídem, demons. pron., *the same.*

ímplico,-áre,-ávi(-ui),-átum(-itum), *imply.*

incúmbo,-ere,-cúbui,-cúbitum, *rest upon.*

ínferus,-a,-um, adj., *belonging to the Lower World.*

injúria,-æ, f. *wrong.*

is, éa, id, demons. pron., *he, she, it, this, that.*

naturális,-e, adj., *natural.*

nórma,-æ, f. *rule.*

poténtia,-æ, f. *power.*

prodítio,-ónis, f. *treason.*

quílibet, quaélibet, quódlibet, indef. pron., *any
kind of.*

quísquis, quaéquæ, quícquid, indef. pron., *anything, something.*

rátio,-ónis, f. *rule, reason.*

réctum,-i, n. *right, truth.*

símilis,-e, adj., *like.*

sólum,-i, n. *soil.*

úsque, adv., *all the way up to.*

úterus,-i, m. *womb.*

LESSON XVIII.

Subjective and Complementary Infinitive.

58. Note present infinitives active and passive of all conjugations **(120)**, **(121)**, **(122)**, **(123)**, **(124)**.

59. 1. Cújus* est dáre, éjus est dispónere.

2. Ídem níhil dícere et insufficiénter dícere.

3. Mérito benefícium légis amíttit qui légem ípsam subvértere inténdit.

4. Némo admitténdus est inhabilitáre se ípsum.

5. Árbor dum créscit ; lígnum cum créscere néscit.

6. Fraús est celáre fraúdem.

7. Áqua cúrrit et débet cúrrere, ut cúrrere solébat.

8. Id quod commúne est, nóstrum esse dícitur.

9. Judícium non débet esse illusórium ; súum efféctum habére débet.

10. Júdicis est jus dícere, non dáre.

11. Cóntra non valéntem ágere núlla cúrrit præscríptio.

12. Némo se accusáre débet, nísi córam Déo.

60. **accúso,-áre,-ávi,-átum,** *accuse.*

amítto,-ere, amísi, amíssum, *lose.*

áqua,-æ, f. *water.*

árbor,-óris, f. *tree.*

célo,-áre,-ávi,-átum, *conceal.*

crésco,-ere, crévi, crétum, *grow.*

---

* See **132**, XII. p. 110.

cum, conj., *when.*

cúrro,-ere, cucúrri, cúrsum, *run.*

dispóno,-ere,-pósui,-pósitum, *dispose.*

efféctum,-i, n. *effect.*

illusórius,-a,-um, adj., *illusory.*

inhabílito,-áre,-ávi,-átum, *incapacitate.*

insufficiénter, adv., *insufficiently.*

inténdo,-dere,-di,-tum(-sum), *strive.*

lígnum,-i, n. *wood.*

mérito, adv., *deservedly.*

nísi, conj., *unless.*

néscio,-scíre,-scívi(-scíi),-scítum, *cease, be unable.*

nóster,-tra,-trum, poss. pron., *our, ours.*

præscríptio,-ónis, f. *prescription.*

subvérto,-ere,-ti,-sum, *overturn.*

váleo,-ére,-ui, ——, *be able to act.*

súus,-a,-um, poss. pron., *his, her, its.*

LESSON XIX.

61. Subjective and Complementary Infinitive—
   continued.

62. 1. Júdices non tenéntur exprímere caúsam sen-
téntiæ súæ.

2. Júdicis* est judicáre secúndum allegáta et
probáta.

3. Juráre est Déum in téstem vocáre ; et est áctus
divíni cúltus.

---

* See **132**, XII. p. 110.

4. Bóni júdicis* lítes dirímere est.
5. Cásus fortúitus non est spectándus et némo tenétur divináre.
6. Némo tenétur armáre adversárium cóntra se.
7. Débitor non præsúmitur donáre.
8. Némo débet esse júdex in própria caúsa.
9. Rex non débet judicáre, sed secúndum légem.
10. Scríbere est ágere.
11. Vérba débent intélligi cum efféctu.
12. Bóni júdicis* est ampliáre jurisdíctiónem.

63. **ámplio,-áre,-ávi,-átum,** *enlarge.*
ármo,-áre,-ávi,-átum, *arm.*
cásus,-us, m. *event.*
cúltus,-us, m. *worship.*
dírimo,-ímere,-émi,-émptum, *remove.*
divínus,-a,-um, adj., *divine.*
dóno,-áre,-ávi,-átum, *give.*
fortúitus,-a,-um, adj., *fortuitous.*
júdico,-áre,-ávi,-átum, *judge.*
jurisdíctio,-ónis, f. *jurisdiction.*
júro,-áre,-ávi,-átum, *swear.*
prétium,-i, n. *price.*
senténtia,-æ, f. *opinion.*
véndo,-ere, véndidi, vénditum, *sell.*

---

* See **132**, XII. p. 110.

LESSON XX.

Regular Comparison of Adjectives.

64. For comparison *vid.* (**110**).

65.
1. Fírmior et poténtior est operátio légis quam disposítio hóminis.
2. Fórtior est custódia légis quam hóminis.
3. Lex tutíssima cássis, sub clýpeo légis némo decípitur.
4. Dómus súa cuíque* tutíssimum refúgium.
5. Testaménta latíssimam interpretatiónem habére débent.
6. In criminálibus probatiónes débent esse clarióres lúce†.
7. Lex est júdicum tutíssimus dúctor.
8. Peccáta cóntra natúram sunt gravíssima.
9. Non est árctius vínculum inter hómines quam jusjurándum.
10. Arguméntum ab auctoritáte fortíssimum est in lége.
11. Ómnia delícta in apérto levióra sunt.
12. In pári delícto pótior est condítio possidéntis.

66. **apértus,-a,-um,** adj., *open.*
árctus,-a,-um, adj., *binding.*
auctóritas,-átis, f. *authority.*
cássis,-idis, f. *helmet.*

---

* See **132**, XIV. p. 110.   † See **132**, XXI. p. 111.

clárus,-a,-um, adj., *clear, plain.*
clýpeus,-i, m. *protection.*
condítio,-ónis, f. *condition.*
criminális,-e, adj., *criminal.*
decípio,-ere,-cépi,-céptum, *deceive, impose upon.*
dispositío,-ónis, f. *disposition.*
dómus,-i(-us), f. *house.*
dúctor,-óris, m. *leader.*
exércitus,-us, m. *army.*
fírmus,-a,-um, adj., *strong.*
fórtis,-e, adj., *powerful.*
grávis,-e, adj., *severe, heinous.*
hómo,-inis, c. *man.*
interpretátio,-ónis, f. *construction, interpretation.*
jusjurándum,-ris,-i, n. *oath.*
látus,-a,-um, adj., *liberal, broad.*
lux, lúcis, f. *light.*
operátio,-ónis, f. *operation.*
peccátum,-i, n. *crime.*
pótens,-ntis, adj., *powerful.*
pótis,-e, adj., *powerful.*
refúgium,-i, n. *refuge.*
vínculum,-i, n. *link.*

LESSON XXI.

Irregular Comparison of Adjectives.

67. For irregular comparison *vid.* (**111**).

68.
1. Óptima légum íntérpres est consuetúdo.
2. Léges posterióres prióres contrárias ábrogant.
3. Arguméntum ab impoténtia plúrimum válet in lége.
4. Máximus erróris pópulus magíster est.
5. Mélior est condítio possidéntis úbi neúter hábet jus.
6. Natúra vis máxima est.
7. Contemporánea exposítio est óptima et fortíssima in lége.
8. De mínimis lex non cúrat.
9. Catálla reputabántur ínter mínima in lége.
10. Conféssio, fácta in judício, ómni probatióne májor est.
11. Necéssitas pública est májor quam priváta.
12. In æquáli júre mélior est condítio possidéntis.

69. **ábrogo,-áre,-ávi,-átum,** *repeal, abrogate.*
æquális,-e, adj., *equal.*
catállum,-i, n. *chattel.*
conféssio,-ónis, f. *confession.*
contemporáneus,-a,-um, adj., *contemporaneous.*
cúro,-áre,-ávi,-átum, *bother with, care for.*
exposítio,-ónis, f. *interpretation.*

impoténtia,-æ, f. *impotence.*
intérpres,-etis, c. *interpreter.*
mágnus,-a,-um, adj., *large, great.*
máter,-tris, f. *mother.*
múltus,-a,-um, adj., *much, many.*
párvus,-a,-um, adj., *small.*
postérior,-ius, adj., *following.*
póssidens,-ntis, c. *possessor.*
prímus,-a,-um, adj., *first.*
privátus,-a,-um, adj., *private.*
públicus,-a,-um, adj., *public.*

LESSON XXII.

Irregular Comparison of Adjectives— *continued.* (111).

70.
1. Ácta exterióra índicant interióra secréta.
2. Judíciis posterióribus fídes est adhibénda.
3. Impúnitas sémper ad deterióra invítat.
4. Mors dícitur últimum supplícium.
5. Qui príor est témpore pótior est júre.
6. In júre non remóta caúsa sed próxima spectátur.
7. Sálus pópuli est supréma lex.
8. Május cóntinet mínus.
9. Última volúntas testatóris est perimplénda secúndum véram intentiónem súam.
10. Május est delíctum se ípsum occídere quam álium.

11.   Súmma rátio est quæ pro religióne fácit.

12.   Óptimus intérpres est úsus.

71. **áctum,-i,** n. *act.*

adhíbeo,-ére,-híbui,-híbitum, *give to.*

contíneo,-ére,-ui,-téntum, *contain.*

(**déterus,** not used) **detérior,-ius** and sup. adj.,
    bad.

éxterus,-a,-um, adj., *outward.*

fídes,-ei, f. *credit.*

impúnitas,-átis, f. *impunity.*

índico,-áre,-ávi,-átum, *indicate, reveal.*

inténtio,-ónis, f. *intention.*

(**ínterus,** not used) **intérior,-ius** and sup. adj.,
    within.

occído,-ere,-cídi,-císum, *kill.*

perímpleo,-ére,-évi,-étum, *carry out, execute.*

pósterus,-a,-um, adj., *following.*

própior,-ius, compar. adj., *nearer.*

quam, adv., *than.*

relígio,-ónis, f. *religion.*

remótus,-a,-um, adj., *remote.*

sálus,-útis, f. *safety.*

secrétum,i-, n. *secret.*

sémper, adv., *always.*

súperus,-a,-um, adj., *above.*

supplícium,-i, n. *punishment.*

témpus,-oris, n. *time.*

ultérior,-ius, compar. adj., *farther.*

LESSON XXIII.

Comparison of Adverbs.

72. Formation and comparison of adverbs **(112).**

73.
1. Júdex non réddit plus quam quod pétens ípse requírit.
2. Vérba chartárum fórtius accipiúntur cóntra proferéntem.
3. Plus válet únus occulátus téstis quam auríti décem.
4. Ad éa quæ frequéntius áccidunt júra adaptántur.
5. In re dúbia mágis inficiátio quam affirmátio intelligénda.
6. Múlta exercitatióne facílius quam régulis percípies.
7. Cum dúo ínter se pugnántia reperiúntur in testaméntis, últimum rátum est.
8. In testaméntis plénius testatóris intentiónem scrutámur.
9. Lex plus laudátur quándo ratióne probátur.
10. Quod príus est vérius ést : et quod príus est témpore pótius est júre.
11. Interpretáre et concordáre léges légibus est óptimus interpretándi módus.
12. Rex est májor síngulis, mínor univérsis.

74. **áccido,-ere,-cidi, ——,** *happen.*
adápto,-áre,-ávi,-átum, *suit, adapt.*

affirmátio,-ónis, f. *affirmation.*

aurítus,-i, m. *ear witness.*

concórdo,-áre,-ávi,-átum, *reconcile.*

décem, indecl. adj., *ten.*

dúbius,-a,-um, adj., *doubtful.*

dúo, dúæ, dúo, num. adj., *two.*

exercitátio,-ónis, f. *exercise, practice.*

fácile, adv., *easily.*

fréquens,-ntis, adj., *frequent.*

inficiátio,-ónis, f. *negative.*

intérpreto,-áre,-ávi,-átum, *interpret.*

laúdo,-áre,-ávi,-átum, *praise.*

módus,-i, m. *method.*

occulátus,-i, m. *eye-witness.*

percípio,-ere,-cépi,-céptum, *perceive.*

pléne, adv., *especially.*

próbo,-áre,-ávi,-átum, *support.*

prófero,-férre,-tuli,-látum, *offer.*

rátus,-a,-um, *considered.*

réddo,-ere,-didi,-ditum, *give.*

requíro,-ere,-sívi(-íi),-sítum, *ask.*

scrútor,-ári,-átus sum, *scrutinise.*

sínguli,-æ,-a, adj., *individuals.*

univérsus,-a,-um, adj., *everybody.*

LESSON XXIV.

Posse.

75. Learn the present indicative of **pósse (127).**

76.   1. Némo pótest plus júris* ad álium transférre quam ípse hábet.

2. Meliórem conditiónem súam fácere pótest mínor, deteriórem nequáquam.

3. Derivatíva potéstas non pótest ésse májor primitíva.

4. Consénsus non concúbitus fácit matrimónium ; et consentíre non póssunt ánte ánnos núbiles.

5. Júdex non pótest ésse téstis in própria caúsa.

6. Júdex non pótest injúriam síbi dátam puníre.

7. Lex non defícere pótest in justítia exhibénda.

8. In álta proditióne núllus pótest ésse accessórius sed principális solummódo.

9. Déus sólus hærédem fácere pótest, non hómo.

10. Némo pótest fácere per álium quod per se non pótest.

11. Núllus cómmodum cápere pótest de súa injúria.

77.   **accessórius,-a,-um,** adj., *accessory*.
ánnus,-i, m. *year*.
ánte, prep. w. acc., *before*.

---

* See **132,** XI. p. 110.

cápio,-ere, cépi, cáptum, *receive.*
concúbitus,-us, m. *cohabitation.*
consénsus,-us, m. *consent.*
conséntio,-tíre,-si,-sum, *consent.*
defício,-ere,-féci,-féctum, *fail.*
derivatívus,-a,-um, adj., *derived.*
exhíbeo,-ére,-ui,-itum, *mete out, dispense.*
nequáquam, adv., *never.*
núbilis,-e, adj., *marriageable.*
póssum, pósse, pótui, ——, *be able.*
potéstas,-átis, f. *power.*
primitívus,-a,-um, adj., *original.*
principális,-is, m. *principal.*
solummódo, adv., *only.*
tránsfero,-férre,-tuli,-látum, *transfer.*

LESSON XXV.

Posse, Prodésse, Deésse.

78. Learn present indicative of **prodésse** and **deésse** (128).

79.   1. Némo pótest cóntra recórdum verificáre per pátriam.

2. Qui pótest et débet vetáre, et non vétat, júbet.

3. Némo pótest mutáre consílium súum in altérius injúriam.

4. Úbi non est principális non ésse pótest accessórius.

5. Rex quod injústum est fácere non pótest.

6. Félix qui pótuit rérum cognóscere caúsas.

7. Jusjurándum ínter álios fáctum nec nocére nec prodésse débet.
8. Ómnis innovátio plus novitáte pertúrbat quam utilitáte pródest.
9. Qui non óbstat quod obstáre pótest fácere vidétur.
10. Nil fácit érror nóminis, cum de córpore cónstat.
11. Quod necessárie intellígitur id non déest.
12. Senténtia interlocutária revocári pótest, definitíva non pótest.

80. **álter,-era,-erum,** adj., *another*.
cognósco,-ere,-nóvi,-nitum, *ascertain*.
consílium,-i, n. *plan*.
cónsto,-áre,-stiti,-státum, *correspond*.
córpus,-oris, n. *body*.
désum,-ésse,-fui, ——, *be wanting*.
definitívus,-a,-um, adj., *final*.
félix,-ícis, adj., *fortunate*.
injústus,-a,-um, adj., *unjust*.
innovátio,-ónis, f. *innovation*.
interlocutárius,-a,-um, adj., *interlocutory*.
júbeo,-ére, jússi, jússum, *command*.
múto,-áre,-ávi,-átum, *change*.
nec, conj., *nor*.
necessárie, adv., *necessarily*.
nóceo,-ére,-ui,-itum, *do harm*.
nómen,-inis, n. *name*.
nóvitas,-átis, f. *novelty*.
óbsto,-áre,-stiti,-státum, *prevent*.
pátria,-æ, f. *country, jury*.
pertúrbo,-áre,-ávi,-átum, *disarrange*.
potéstas,-átis, f. *power*.

prósum, prodésse, prófui, ——, *do good.*
principále,-is, n. *principal.*
recórdum,-i, n. *record.*
revóco,-áre,-ávi,-átum, *recall.*
senténtia,-æ, f. *decree, judgment.*
utílitas,-átis, f. *utility.*
verifíco,-áre,-ávi,-átum, *verify.*
véto,-áre,-ui,-itum, *forbid.*

LESSON XXVI.

Fíeri. Íre.

81.   Learn present indicative of **fíeri** and **íre** (130).

82.   1.   Ex præcedéntibus et consequéntibus óptima fit interpretátio.

2.   Volénti non fit injúria.

3.   Mentíri est cóntra méntem íre.

4.   Lónga posséssio párit jus possidéndi et tóllit actiónem véro dómino.

5.   Interrúptio múltiplex non tóllit præscriptiónem sémel obténtam.

6.   Consénsus tóllit errórem.

7.   Súbsequens matrimónium tóllit peccátum præcédens.

8.   Poéna pótest tólli, cúlpa perénnis est.

9.   Quóties in vérbis núlla est ambigúitas íbi núlla exposítio cóntra verba expréssa fiénda est.

10.   Delegáta potéstas non pótest delegári.

11.   Mínor juráre non pótest.

12.   Ex níhilo nil fit.

83. **cónsequens,-ntis,** adj., *following.*
   cúlpa,-æ, f. *guilt, crime.*
   delegátus,-a,-um, adj., *conferred, delegated.*
   éo, íre, ívi(íi), ítum, *go.*
   exposítio,-ónis, f. *exposition.*
   éxprimo,-ere,-préssi,-préssum, *express.*
   fío, fíeri, fáctus sum, *become, be made.*
   mens,-ntis, f. *mind.*
   méntior,-íri,-ítus sum, *lie.*
   múltiplex,-icis, adj., *multiplex.*
   obtíneo,-ére,-ui,-éntum, *acquire.*
   peccátum,-i, n. *wrong, fault.*
   perénnis,-e, adj., *perpetual.*
   præcédens,-ntis, n. *precedent.*
   quóties, adv., *as often as.*
   rúo,-ere, rúi, rútum, *fall.*
   sémel, adv., *once.*
   súbsequens,-ntis, adj., *subsequent.*
   tóllo,-ere, sústuli, sublátum, *remove.*
   vólo, vélle, vólui, ——, *wish.*

LESSON XXVII.

Præférre.

84. Learn present indicative of **praéfero (131).**

85. 1. Cértum est quod cértum réddi pótest.
   2. Lex non nóvit pátrem nec mátrem ; sólam
       veritátem.
   3. Lex Ángliæ núnquam síne Parliaménto
       mutári pótest.

4. Némo pótest ésse ténens et dóminus.
5. Némo cóntra fáctum súum veníre pótest.
6. Rex non pótest peccáre.
7. Qui tácet, consentíre vidétur.
8. Benígnior senténtia in vérbis generálibus seu dúbiis est præferénda.
9. Ómne sacraméntum débet ésse de cérta sciéntia.
10. Quándo jus dómini régis et súbditi concúrrunt, jus régis præférri débet.
11. Lex cítius toleráre vult privátum dámnum quam públicum málum.
12. Filiátio non pótest probári.

86. **benígnus,-a,-um,** adj., *favourable.*
cértus,-a,-um, adj., *certain.*
cíto, adv., *quickly.*
concúrro,-ere,-cúrri,-cúrsum, *concur.*
dúbius,-a,-um, adj., *ambiguous, doubtful.*
filiátio,-ónis, f. *copulation, affiliation.*
generális,-e, adj., *general.*
málum,-i, n. *misfortune.*
nósco,-ere, nóvi, nótum, *recognise.*
Parliaméntum,-i, n. *Parliament.*
praéfero,-férre,-tuli,-látum, *prefer.*
quándo, adv., *when.*
réddo,-dere,-didi,-ditum, *make.*
sacraméntum,-i, n. *oath.*
sciéntia,-æ, f. *knowledge.*
senténtia,-æ, f. *construction.*
súbditus,-i, m. *subject.*
sólus,-a,-um, adj., *alone.*
ténens,-ntis, c. *tenant.*

tólero,-áre,-ávi,-átum, *permit.*
vénio,-íre, véni, véntum, *go.*
véritas,-átis, f. *truth.*
vídeor,-éri, vísum est, *seem, appear.*

LESSON XXVIII.

Verbs Controlling Special Cases.

87. 1. Némo prohibétur plúribus defensiónibus úti.
2. Alienátio réi præfértur júri accrescéndi.
3. Bónus júdex secúndum aéquum et bónum júdicat et æquitátem strícto júri praéfert.
4. Júra pública anteferénda privátis (júribus).
5. Jús accrescéndi onéribus præfértur.
6. Vigilántibus et non dormiéntibus júra subvéniunt.
7. Actóri incúmbit ónus probándi.
8. Assignátus útitur júre auctóris.
9. Lex succúrrit ignoránti.
10. Minátur innocéntibus qui párcit nocéntibus.
11. Res ínter álios ácta álteri nocére non débet.
12. Bóni júdicis est judícium síne dilátióne mandáre executióni.

88. **abúndans,-ntis,** adj., *abundant.*
accrésco,-ere,-évi,-étum, *increase.*
áctor,-óris, m. *plaintiff.*
aéquus,-a,-um, adj., *just.*
alienátio,-ónis, f. *alienation.*
anteféro,-férre,-tuli,-látum, w. dat., *prefer.*
assignátus,-i, m. *assignee.*

aúctor,-óris, m. *assignor.*
cautéla,-æ, f. *caution.*
deténsio,-ónis, f. *defence.*
dórmiens,-ntis, c. *sleeping person.*
ignorántia,-æ, f. *ignorance.*
incúmbo,-ere,-cúbui,-cúbitum, w. dat., *rest upon.*
ínnocens,-ntis, c. *innocent person.*
mínor,-ári,-átus sum, *threaten.*
nócens,-ntis, c. *a wrongdoer, guilty person.*
praéfero,-térre,-tuli,-látum, *prefer.*
párco,-ere, pepérci (pársi), párcitum or pársum,
    w. dat., *spare.*
prohíbeo,-ére,-ui,-itum, *prevent.*
subvénio,-íre,-i,-tum, w. dat., *come to the aid of.*
succúrro,-ere,-i,-cúrsum, w. dat., *come to the aid
    of.*
útor, úti, úsus sum, w. abl., *enjoy, use.*
vígilans,-ntis, c. *watchful person.*

LESSON XXIX.

Verbs Controlling Special Cases—*continued.*

89. 1. Quícquid plantátur sólo, sólo cédit.
2. Quod cónstat cúriæ ópere téstium non
    índiget.
3. Vérba intentióni, non e cóntra, débent
    inservíre.
4. Absolúta senténtia expositióne non índiget.
5. Inténtio inservíre débet légibus, non léges
    intentióni.

4

6. Pácta priváta júri público non derogáre
   póssunt.
7. Convéntio privatórum non pótest público
   júri derogáre.
8. Lex non fávet delicatórum vótis.
9. Némo præsúmitur ésse ímmemor súæ ætérnæ
   salútis, et máxime in artículo mórtis.
10. Fíctio cédit veritáti ; fíctio júris non est úbi
    véritas.
11. Abúndans cautéla non nócet.
12. Ædificáre in túo próprio sólo non lícet quod
    álteri nócet.
13. Némo cógitur súam rem véndere étiam jústo
    prétio.

90. **absolútus,-a,-um,** adj., *absolute.*
ac, conj., *and.*
artículus,-i, m. *point, moment.*
cédo,-ere, céssi, céssum, *pass, go.*
convéntio,-ónis, f. *convention, contract.*
delicátus,-i, m. *dainty person.*
dérogo,-áre,-ávi,-átum, *detract from.*
fáveo, favére, fávi, faútum, w. dat., *favour.*
fíctio,-ónis, f. *fiction.*
ímmemor,-oris, adj., *unmindful.*
indígeo,-ére,-ui, ——, w. gen. or abl., *be in want of.*
insérvio,-íre,-ívi(íi),-ítum, w. dat., *be subservient to.*
ópus,-eris, n. *assistance.*
páctum,-i, n. *agreement.*
plánto,-áre,-ávi,-átum, *affix, annex.*
stríctus,-a,-um, adj., *strict.*
tútus,-a,-um, adj., *safe.*
vótum,-i, n. *wish.*

LESSON XXX.

Ablative Absolute.

91. 1. Cessánte caúsa,* céssat efféctus.
2. Cessánte ratióne légis céssat ípsa lex.
3. Dúo non póssunt in sólido únam rem possidére.
4. Áctio non accrévit ínfra sex ánnos.†
5. Rátio est légis ánima ; mutáta légis ratióne mutátur et lex.
6. Reprobáta pecúnia líberat solvéntem.
7. Subláto fundaménto, cádit ópus.
8. Crescénte malítia créscere débet et poéna.
9. Légibus súmptis desinéntibus, légibus natúræ uténdum est.
10. Pendénte líte níhil innovétur.
11. Subláta caúsa, tóllitur efféctus.

92. accrésco,-ere,-évi,-étum, *accrue.*
ánima,-æ, f. *soul, life.*
césso,-áre,-ávi,-átum, *cease.*
crésco,-ere,-évi,-étum, *increase.*
désino,-ere,-íi (-ívi),-itum, *fail.*
efféctus,-us, m. *effect.*
fundaméntum,-i, n. *foundation.*
ínfra, prep., *later than.*
ínnovo,-áre,-ávi,-átum, *introduce.*
líbero,-áre,-ávi,-átum, *absolve, discharge.*

---

* See **132**, XXIII. p. III.   † See **132**, XVI. p. III.

lis, lítis, f. *suit.*
malítia,-æ, f. *malice.*
ópus,-eris, n. *structure.*
pecúnia,-æ, f. *money.*
péndeo, péndere, pepéndi, pénsum, *continue.*
réprobo,-áre,-ávi,-átum, *refuse.*
sex, indecl. num., *six.*
sólidus,-a,-um, adj., *entire.*
sólvo,-ere,-i, solútum, *free, release.*
súffero,-férre, sústuli, sublátum, *remove.*

LESSON XXXI.

Subjunctive.

93.
1. Cáveat émptor ;* cáveat vénditor.
2. Ut poéna ad paúcos, métus ad ómnes pervéniat.†
3. Respóndeat supérior.
4. Sic útere túo ut aliénum non laédas.‡
5. Qui péccat ébrius, lúat* sóbrius.
6. Interpretátio fiénda est ut res mágis váleat† quam péreat.‡
7. Núllus recédat* e cúria cancellária síne remédio.
8. Fíeri fácias ; scíre fácias.
9. Non fácias málum ut índe véniat† bónum.
10. Áctus non fácit réum nísi mens sit§ réa.
11. Cassétur* bílla.
12. Hábeas* córpus.

---

* See **132**, XXXII. p. 112.   ‡ See **132**, XXVII. p. 112.
† See **132**, XXVII. p. 112.   § See **132**, XXXIII. p. 112.

94. **bílla,-æ,** f. *writ, bill.*

cancellárius,-a,-um, *of chancery, of equity.*

cásso,-áre,-ávi,-átum, *quash.*

cáveo,-ére, cávi, caútum, *beware.*

ébrius,-a,-um, adj., *intoxicated.*

émptor,-óris, m. *buyer.*

fío, fíeri, fáctus sum, *be made.*

índe, adv., *thence.*

laédo,-ere, laédi, laésum, *injure.*

lúo,-ere, lúi, lútum, *expiate.*

málum,-i, n. *wrong.*

mens,-ntis, f. *intent.*

métus,-us, m. *fear.*

paúci,-órum, m. *few.*

pécco,-áre,-ávi,-átum, *do wrong.*

péreo,-íre,-íi(-ívi),-ítum, *fail, fall.*

pervénio,-íre,-véni,-véntum, *come upon.*

réus,-a,-um, adj., *criminal.*

réus,-i, m. *a guilty person.*

recédo,-cédere,-céssi,-céssum, *depart from.*

scío,-íre,-ívi,-ítum, *know.*

sic, adv., *so, in such a manner.*

sóbrius,-a,-um, adj., *sober.*

supérior,-óris, c. *principal.*

túus,-a,-um, poss. pron., *your, yours.*

ut, conj., *in order that.*

váleo,-ére,-ui, ——, *stand.*

vénditor,-óris, m. *purchaser.*

LESSON XXXII.

Subjunctive—*continued.*   **Accusative and Infinitive.**

95. 1. Non definítur in júre quid sit* conátus.
2. Condítio præcédens adimpléri débet priús-quam efféctus sequátur.†
3. Qui non próhibet cum prohibére póssit ‡ in cúlpa est.
4. Discrétio est discérnere per légem quid sit* jústum.
5. Dóti lex fávet; praémium pudóris est, ídeo parcátur.
6. Lex non requírit verificári quod appáret cúriæ.
7. Non decípitur qui scit se§ décipi.
8. Ínterest reipúblicæ supréma hóminum testaménta ráta habéri.
9. Lex inténdit vicínum vicíni fácta scíre.
10. Fúror contráhi matrimónium non sínit, quía consénsus ópus est.
11. Árma in armátos súmere júra sínunt.
12. Ínterest reipúblicæ res judicátas non rescíndi.

96. **adímpleo,-ére,-évi,-étum,** *fulfil.*
appáreo,-ére,-ui,-itum, *appear.*
armátus,-i, m. *an armed person.*
conátus,-us, m. *attempt.*

---

* See **132**, XXX. p. 112.   ‡ See **132**, XXIX. p. 112.
† See **132**, XXVIII. p. 112.   § See **132**, XXVI. p. 112.

cóntraho,-ere,-tráxi,-tráctum, *contract, consummate.*

cúlpa,-æ, f. *fault.*

decípio,-ere,-cépi,-céptum, *deceive.*

defínio,-íre,-ívi(-íi),-ítum, *define.*

discérno,-ere,-crévi,-crétum, *ascertain.*

discrétio,-ónis, f. *discretion.*

dos, dótis, f. *dower.*

fúror,-óris, m. *passion.*

ídeo, adv., *on that account.*

inténdo,-ere,-di,-téntum, *presume.*

íntersum,-ésse,-fui, *interest to.*

jústus,-a,-um, adj., *just.*

ópus ésse, *to be necessary.*

párco,-ere, pepérci (pársi), párcitum (pársum), *preserve.*

praémium,-i, n. *reward.*

priúsquam, conj., *before.*

púdor,-óris, m. *virtue.*

quía, conj., *because.*

quis, quæ, quid, interrog. pron., *what.*

rátus,-a,-um, adj., *regarded, confirmed.*

rescíndo,-ere,-scidi,-scíssum, *disregard.*

síno,-ere, sívi, sítum, *permit.*

súmo,-ere, súmpsi, súmptum, *to take up.*

vicínus,-i, m. *neighbour.*

NOUNS.

97. The Latin has six cases :

NAMES	ENGLISH EQUIVALENTS
Nominative,	Nominative.
Genitive,	Possessive or Objective with of.
Dative,	Objective with to or for.
Accusative,	Objective.
Vocative,	Nominative Independent.
Ablative,	Objective with from, with, by, in.

1. *Oblique Cases.*—The Genitive, Dative, Accusative, and Ablative are called the Oblique Cases.

2. *Vocative.*—The Vocative is like the Nominative, unless otherwise indicated.

98. **First Declension.—A-Stems.**

	SINGULAR	PLURAL
N.	persóna, *a person.*	persónæ, *persons.*
G.	persónæ, *of a person.*	personárum, *of persons.*
D.	persónæ, *to or for a person.*	persónis, *to or for persons.*
Ac.	persónam, *a person.*	persónas, *persons.*
Ab.	persóna, *with a person.*	persónis, *with persons.*

99.   **Second Declension.—O-Stems.**

	SINGULAR	PLURAL
N.	bónus	bóni
G.	bóni	bonórum
D.	bóno	bónis
Ac.	bónum	bónos
Ab.	bóno	bónis
N.	amícus	amíci
G.	amíci	amicórum
D.	amíco	amícis
Ac.	amícum	amícos
Ab.	amíco	amícis

(a) The Vocative singular of nouns in **-us** of the Second Declension has a special form in **-e**: **amíce.**

	SINGULAR	PLURAL
N.	dónum	dóna
G.	dóni	donórum
D.	dóno	dónis
Ac.	dónum	dóna
Ab.	dóno	dónis
N.	púer	púeri
G.	púeri	puerórum
D.	púero	púeris
Ac.	púerum	púeros
Ab.	púero	púeris
N.	magíster	magístri
G.	magístri	magistrórum
D.	magístro	magístris
Ac.	magístrum	magístros
Ab.	magístro	magístris

	SINGULAR	PLURAL
N.	fílius	fílii
G.	fíli, fílii	filiórum
D.	fílio	fíliis
Ac.	fílium	fílios
Ab.	fílio	fíliis

(a) The Vocative singular of **fílius** is **fíli.**

	SINGULAR	PLURAL
N.	consílium	consília
G.	consíli, consílii	consiliórum
D.	consílio	consíliis
Ac.	consílium	consília
Ab.	consílio	consíliis

100.   Third Declension.—Mute Stems.

	SINGULAR	PLURAL
N.	pax	páces
G.	pácis	———
D.	páci	pácibus
Ac.	pácem	páces
Ab.	páce	pácibus

N.	rex	réges
G.	régis	régum
D.	régi	régibus
Ac.	régem	réges
Ab.	rége	régibus

N.	cómes	cómites
G.	cómitis	cómitum
D.	cómiti	comítibus
Ac.	cómitem	cómites
Ab.	cómite	comítibus

	SINGULAR	PLURAL
N.	cáput	cápita
G.	cápitis	cápitum
D.	cápiti	capítibus
Ac.	cáput	cápita
Ab.	cápite	capítibus
N.	aétas	ætátes
G.	ætátis	ætátum
D.	ætáti	ætátibus
Ac.	ætátem	ætátes
Ab.	ætáte	ætátibus
N.	fraus	fraúdes
G.	fraúdis	fraúdum
D.	fraúdi	fraúdibus
Ac.	fraúdem	fraúdes
Ab.	fraúde	fraúdibus
N.	haéres	hærédes
G.	hærédis	hærédum
D.	hærédi	hærédibus
Ac.	hærédem	hærédes
Ab.	hæréde	hærédibus
N.	sérvitus	servitútes
G.	servitútis	servitútum
D.	servitúti	servitútibus
Ac.	servitútem	servitútes
Ab.	servitúti	servitútibus
N.	dos	dótes
G.	dótis	dótium
D.	dóti	dótibus
Ac.	dótem	dótes
Ab.	dóte	dótibus

101.   **Liquid Stems.**

SINGULAR	PLURAL
N.	visitátio	visitatiónes
G.	visitatiónis	visitatiónum
D.	visitatióni	visitatiónibus
Ac.	visitatiónem	visitatiónes
Ab.	visitatióne	visitatiónibus
N.	mos	móres
G.	móris	mórum
D.	móri	móribus
Ac.	mórem	móres
Ab.	móre	móribus
N.	páter	pátres
G.	pátris	pátrum
D.	pátri	pátribus
Ac.	pátrem	pátres
Ab.	pátre	pátribus
N.	consuetúdo	consuetúdines
G.	consuetúdinis	consuetúdinum
D.	consuetúdini	consuetudínibus
Ac.	consuetúdinem	consuetúdines
Ab.	consuetúdine	consuetudínibus
N.	stipulátor	stipulatóres
G.	stipulatóris	stipulatórum
D.	stipulatóri	stipulatóribus
Ac.	stipulatórem	stipulatóres
Ab.	stipulatóre	stipulatóribus
N.	hómo	hómines
G.	hóminis	hóminum
D.	hómini	homínibus
Ac.	hóminem	hómines
Ab.	hómine	homínibus

	SINGULAR	PLURAL
N.	jus	júra
G.	júris	júrum
D.	júri	júribus
Ac.	jus	júra
Ab.	júre	júribus

N.	os	óra
G.	óris	———
D.	óri	óribus
Ac.	os	óra
Ab.	óre	óribus

N.	córpus	córpora
G.	córporis	córporum
D.	córpori	corpóribus
Ac.	córpus	córpora
Ab.	córpore	corpóribus

N.	nómen	nómina
G.	nóminis	nóminum
D.	nómini	nomínibus
Ac.	nómen	nómina
Ab.	nómine	nomínibus

102.   **Stems in I.**

	SINGULAR	PLURAL
N.	téstis	téstes
G.	téstis	téstium
D.	tésti	téstibus
Ac.	téstem	téstes
Ab.	téste	téstibus

	SINGULAR	PLURAL
N.	principále	principália
G.	principális	principálium
D.	principáli	principálibus
Ac.	principále	principália
Ab.	principáli	principálibus

N.	mens	méntes
G.	méntis	méntium
D.	ménti	méntibus
Ac.	méntem	méntes
Ab.	ménte	méntibus

N.	pars	pártes
G.	pártis	pártium
D.	párti	pártibus
Ac.	pártem, -im	pártes
Ab.	párte	pártibus

103.   **Fourth Declension.—U-Stems.**

	SINGULAR	PLURAL
N.	áctus	áctus
G.	áctus	áctuum
D.	áctui	áctibus
Ac.	áctum	áctus
Ab.	áctu	áctibus

104.   **Fifth Declension.—E-Stems.**

	SINGULAR	PLURAL
N.	díes	díes
G.	diéi	diérum
D.	diéi	diébus
Ac.	díem	díes
Ab.	díe	diébus

	SINGULAR	PLURAL
N.	res	res
G.	réi	rérum
D.	réi	rébus
Ac.	rem	res
Ab.	re	rébus

105.   Special Paradigms.

	SINGULAR	PLURAL
N.	déus	déi, díi, di
G.	déi	deórum, déum
D.	déo	déis, díis, dis
Ac.	déum	déos
Ab.	déo	déis, díis, dis

N.	dómus	dómus
G.	dómus	dómuum, domórum
D.	dómui, dómo	dómibus
Ac.	dómum	dómos, dómus
Ab.	dómo, dómu	dómibus

N.	vis	víres
G.	vis	vírium
D.	vi	víribus
Ac.	vim	víres
Ab.	vi	víribus

106.   Compound Nouns.

	SINGULAR	PLURAL
N.	respública	respúblicæ
G.	reipúblicæ	rerumpublicárum
D.	reipúblicæ	rebuspúblicis
Ac.	rempúblicam	respúblicas
Ab.	república	rebuspúblicis

ADJECTIVES.

107. First and Second Declensions.

SINGULAR

	Masculine	Feminine	Neuter
N.	bónus	bóna	bónum
G.	bóni	bónæ	bóni
D.	bóno	bónæ	bóno
Ac.	bónum	bónam	bónum
Ab.	bóno	bóna	bóno

PLURAL

N.	bóni	bónæ	bóna
G.	bonórum	bonárum	bonórum
D.	bónis	bónis	bónis
Ac.	bónos	bónas	bóna
Ab.	bónis	bónis	bónis

SINGULAR

N.	míser	mísera	míserum
G.	míseri	míseræ	míseri
D.	mísero	míseræ	mísero
Ac.	míserum	míseram	míserum
Ab.	mísero	mísera	mísero

PLURAL

N.	míseri	míseræ	mísera
G.	miserórum	miserárum	miserórum
D.	míseris	míseris	míseris
Ac.	míseros	míseras	mísera
Ab.	míseris	míseris	míseris

SINGULAR

N.	ínteger	íntegra	íntegrum
G.	íntegri	íntegræ	íntegri
D.	íntegro	íntegræ	íntegro
Ac.	íntegrum	íntegram	íntegrum
Ab.	íntegro	íntegra	íntegro

PLURAL

	Masculine	Feminine	Neuter
N.	íntegri	íntegræ	íntegra
G.	integrórum	integrárum	integrórum
D.	íntegris	íntegris	íntegris
Ac.	íntegros	íntegras	íntegra
Ab.	íntegris	íntegris	íntegris

108.   THIRD DECLENSION.

SINGULAR

	Masculine and Feminine	Neuter
N.	símplex	símplex
G.	símplicis	símplicis
D.	símplici	símplici
Ac.	símplicem	símplex
Ab.	símplici, -e	símplici, -e

PLURAL

N.	símplices	simplícia
G.	simplícium	simplícium
D.	simplícibus	simplícibus
Ac.	símplices, -is	simplícia
Ab.	simplícibus	simplícibus

SINGULAR

N.	præcédens	præcédens
G.	præcedéntis	præcedéntis
D.	præcedénti	præcedénti
Ac.	præcedéntem	præcédens
Ab.	præcedénte, -i	præcedénte, -i

PLURAL

N.	præcedéntes	præcedéntia
G.	præcedéntium	præcedéntium
D.	præcedéntibus	præcedéntibus
Ac.	præcedéntes, -is	præcedéntia
Ab.	præcedéntibus	præcedéntibus

5

SINGULAR

Masculine and Feminine	Neuter
N.	brévis	bréve
G.	brévis	brévis
D.	brévi	brévi
Ac.	brévem	bréve
Ab.	brévi	brévi

PLURAL

	Masculine and Feminine	Neuter
N.	bréves	brévia
G.	brévium	brévium
D.	brévibus	brévibus
Ac.	bréves, -is	brévia
Ab.	brévibus	brévibus

109.   Irregular Adjectives.

SINGULAR

	Masculine	Feminine	Neuter
N.	álius	ália	áliud
G.	alíus	alíus	alíus
D.	álii	álii	álii
Ac.	álium	áliam	áliud
Ab.	álio	ália	álio

PLURAL

	Masculine	Feminine	Neuter
N.	álii	áliæ	ália
G.	aliórum	aliárum	aliórum
D.	áliis	áliis	áliis
Ac.	álios	álias	ália
Ab.	áliis	áliis	áliis

SINGULAR

	Masculine	Feminine	Neuter
N.	únus	úna	únum
G.	uníus	uníus	uníus
D.	úni	úni	úni
Ac.	únum	únam	únum
Ab.	úno	úna	úno

110.   Comparison of Adjectives.

In Latin, as in English, there are three degrees of comparison—the positive, the comparative, and the superlative.

Positive	Comparative	Superlative
fírmus	fírmior	firmíssimus
fórtis	fórtior	fortíssimus
símplex	simplícior	simplicíssimus

(a) Observe that the comparative is formed from the stem of the positive by dropping the stem vowel, if there be one, and adding **-ior ;** the superlative by adding **-issimus.**

(b) The comparative of all adjectives except **plus,** *more,* is declined like **firmior (113) ;** the superlative like **bonus.**

111.   Irregular Comparison.

Positive	Comparative	Superlative
éxterus	extérior	extrémus, éxtimus
ínferus	inférior	ínfimus, ímus
pósterus	postérior	postrémus, póstumus
súperus	supérior	suprémus, súmmus
[præ, pro, *before*]	príor	prímus
[própe, *near*]	própior	próximus
[última, *beyond*]	ultérior	últimus
bónus	mélior, mélius	óptimus
mágnus	májor, május	máximus
múltus	———, plus	plúrimus
párvus	mínor, mínus	mínimus

112.   Formation and Comparison of Adverbs.

Formation—Models.

ADJECTIVE	STEM	ADVERB
fírmus, *firm.*	fírmo —	fírme, *firmly.*
míser, *wretched.*	mísero —	mísere, *wretchedly.*

(*a*) Observe that adverbs from adjectives with o-stems are formed by changing the **o** into **e**.

fórtis, *brave.*	fórti —	fórtiter, *bravely.*
fréquens, *frequent.*	frequénti —	frequénter, *frequently.*

(*b*) Observe that adverbs are formed from adjectives with i-stems by adding **ter** to the stem.

(*c*) Observe that stems **-nti** drop **ti** before **ter**.

ADJECTIVE	ADVERB
múltus, *much.*	múltum, *much.*
fácilis, *easy.*	fácile, *easily.*
brévis, *brief.*	bréve, *briefly.*

(*d*) The accusative singular neuter of the adjective is sometimes used as an adverb.

cítus, *quick.*	cíto, *quickly.*
prímus, *first.*	prímo, *at first.*

(*e*) The ablative singular neuter of the adjective is sometimes used as an adverb.

Comparison.

Positive	Comparative	Superlative
fírme	fírmius	firmíssime
mísere	misérius	misérrime
felíciter	felícius	felicíssime
béne	mélius	óptime
mále	péjus	péssime
múltum	plus	plúrimum
———	mágis	máxime

(*a*) Observe that the comparative of the adverb is the same as the neuter accusative singular of the comparative of the adjective ; and that the superlative is formed from the superlative of the adjective by changing, as in the positive, the final **o** of the stem to **e.**

(*b*) If the adjective is irregular in comparison, the adverb is also irregular.

113.   Declension of Comparatives.

SINGULAR

Masculine and Feminine	Neuter
N.	fírmior	fírmius
G.	firmióris	firmióris
D.	firmióri	firmióri
Ac.	firmiórem	fírmius
Ab.	firmióre, -i	firmióre, -i

PLURAL

	Masculine and Feminine	Neuter
N.	firmióres	firmióra
G.	firmiórum	firmiórum
D.	firmióribus	firmióribus
Ac.	firmióres, -is	firmióra
Ab.	firmióribus	firmióribus

SINGULAR

		Neuter
N.	———	plus
G.	———	plúris
D.	———	———
Ac.	———	plus
Ab.	———	plúre

PLURAL

	Masculine and Feminine	Neuter
N.	plúres	plúra
G.	plúrium	plúrium
D.	plúribus	plúribus
Ac.	plúres, -is	plúra
Ab.	plúribus	plúribus

114.   **Numerals.**

	CARDINALS	ORDINALS
1.	únus,-a,-um	prímus,-a,-um
2.	dúo, dúæ, dúo	secúndus (or álter)
3.	tres, tría	tértius
4.	quáttuor	quártus
5.	quínque	quíntus
6.	sex	séxtus
7.	séptem	séptimus
8.	ócto	octávus
9.	nóvem	nónus
10.	décem	décimus

PRONOUNS.

115.   **Reflexive.**

	SINGULAR	PLURAL
N.	———	———
G.	súi	súi
D.	síbi	síbi
Ac.	se, sése	se, sése
Ab.	se, sése	se, sése

116.   **Demonstrative.**

	SINGULAR			PLURAL		
N.	hic	hæc	hoc	hi	hæ	hæc
G.	húius	húius	húius	hórum	hárum	hórum
D.	huic	huic	huic	his	his	his
Ac.	hunc	hanc	hoc	hos	has	hæc
Ab.	hoc	hac	hoc	his	his	his
N.	ílle	ílla	íllud	ílli	íllæ	ílla
G.	illíus	illíus	illíus	illórum	illárum	illórum
D.	ílli	ílli	ílli	íllis	íllis	íllis
Ac.	íllum	íllam	íllud	íllos	íllas	ílla
Ab.	íllo	ílla	íllo	íllis	íllis	íllis

	SINGULAR			PLURAL		
N.	is	éa	id	éi, íi	éæ	éa
G.	éius	éius	éius	eórum	eárum	eórum
D.	éi	éi	éi	éis, íis	éis, íis	éis, íis
Ac.	éum	éam	id	éos	éas	éa
Ab.	éo	éa	éo	éis, íis	éis, íis	éis, íis

	SINGULAR		
N.	ídem	éadem	ídem
G.	eiúsdem	eiúsdem	eiúsdem
D.	eídem	eídem	eídem
Ac.	eúndem	eándem	ídem
Ab.	eódem	eádem	eódem

	PLURAL		
N.	{ eídem / iídem	eaédem	éadem
G.	eorúndem	earúndem	eorúndem
D.	{ eísdem / iísdem	{ eísdem / iísdem	{ eísdem / iísdem
Ac.	eósdem	eásdem	éadem
Ab.	{ eísdem / iísdem	{ eísdem / iísdem	{ eísdem / iísdem

	SINGULAR			PLURAL		
N.	ípse	ípsa	ípsum	ípsi	ípsæ	ípsa
G.	ipsíus	ipsíus	ipsíus	ipsórum	ipsárum	ipsórum
D.	ípsi	ípsi	ípsi	ípsis	ípsis	ípsis
Ac.	ípsum	ípsam	ípsum	ípsos	ípsas	ípsa
Ab.	ípso	ípsa	ípso	ípsis	ípsis	ípsis

117.   Relative.

	SINGULAR			PLURAL		
N.	qui	quæ	quod	qui	quæ	quæ
G.	cúius	cúius	cúius	quórum	quárum	quórum
D.	cui	cui	cui	quíbus	quíbus	quíbus
Ac.	quem	quam	quod	quos	quas	quæ
Ab.	quo	qua	quo	quíbus	quíbus	quíbus

118.   Interrogative.

	SINGULAR			PLURAL		
N.	quis	quæ	quid	qui	quæ	quæ
G.	cúius	cúius	cúius	quórum	quárum	quórum
D.	cui	cui	cui	quíbus	quíbus	quíbus
Ac.	quem	quam	quid	quos	quas	quæ
Ab.	quo	qua	quo	quíbus	quíbus	quíbus

119.   Indefinite.

SINGULAR

N.	áliquis	áliqua	áliquid, áliquod
G.	alicúius	alicúius	alicúius
D.	álicui	álicui	álicui
Ac.	áliquem	áliquam	áliquid, áliquod
Ab.	áliquo	áliqua	áliquo

PLURAL

N.	áliqui	áliquæ	áliqua
G.	aliquórum	aliquárum	aliquórum
D.	aliquíbus	aliquíbus	aliquíbus
Ac.	áliquos	áliquas	áliqua
Ab.	aliquíbus	aliquíbus	aliquíbus

SINGULAR

N.	quídam	quaédam	quíddam, quóddam
G.	cuiúsdam	cuiúsdam	cuiúsdam
D.	cuídam	cuídam	cuídam
Ac.	quéndam	quándam	quíddam, quóddam
Ab.	quódam	quádam	quódam

PLURAL

N.	quídam	quaédam	quaédam
G.	quorúndam	quarúndam	quorúndam
D.	quibúsdam	quibúsdam	quibúsdam
Ac.	quósdam	quásdam	quaédam
Ab.	quibúsdam	quibúsdam	quibúsdam

NOTE.—**Quisquis,** "*whoever*" or "*whatever*," is called from its signification a general relative. It is rare except in the forms **quisquis, quidquid (quicquid).**

REGULAR VERBS.

120.   **First Conjugation.—A-Verbs.**

Mándo, *I command.*

PRINCIPAL PARTS
mándo, mandáre, mandávi, mandátus

Active Voice.

INDICATIVE MOOD—PRESENT TENSE

I command.

Singular	Plural
mándo	mandámus
mándas	mandátis
mándat	mándant

IMPERFECT

I was commanding, or *I commanded.*

mandábam	mandabámus
mandábas	mandabátis
mandábat	mandábant

FUTURE

I shall or *will command.*

mandábo	mandábimus
mandábis	mandábitis
mandábit	mandábunt

PERFECT

I have commanded, or *I commanded.*

mandávi	mandávimus
mandavísti	mandavístis
mandávit	mandavérunt, *or* -re

PLUPERFECT

I had commanded.

mandáveram	mandaverámus
mandáveras	mandaverátis
mandáverat	mandáverant

FUTURE PERFECT
I shall have commanded, etc.

mandávero	mandavérimus
mandáveris	mandavéritis
mandáverit	mandáverint

SUBJUNCTIVE—PRESENT
May I command ; let him command.

mándem	mandémus
mándes	mandétis
mándet	mándent

IMPERFECT
I should command ; he would command.

mandárem	mandarémus
mandáres	mandarétis
mandáret	mandárent

PERFECT
I may have commanded, or *I have commanded.*

mandáverim	mandavérimus
mandáveris	mandavéritis
mandáverit	mandáverint

PLUPERFECT
I should have commanded ; he would have commanded.

mandavíssem	mandavissémus
mandavísses	mandavissétis
mandavísset	mandavíssent

IMPERATIVE—PRESENT
mánda, *command thou.*

mandáte, *command ye.*

FUTURE
mandáto, *thou shalt command.*

mandáto, *he shall command.*

mandatóte, *ye shall command.*

mandánto, *they shall command.*

INFINITIVE

Pres. mandáre, *to command.*

Perf. mandavísse, *to have commanded.*

Fut. mandatúrus ésse, *to be about to command.*

PARTICIPLES

Pres. mándans,-ántis, *commanding.*

Fut. mandatúrus,-a,-um, *about to command.*

GERUND

N. ⸻

G. mandándi, *of commanding.*

D. mandándo, *for commanding.*

Ac. mandándum, *commanding.*

Ab. mandándo, *by commanding.*

SUPINE

Ac. mandátum, *to command.*

Ab. mandátu, *to command, be commanded.*

Passive Voice.

INDICATIVE—PRESENT TENSE

I am commanded, etc.

mándor	mandámur
mandáris, *or* -re	mandámini
mandátur	mandántur

IMPERFECT

I was commanded, etc.

mandábar	mandabámur
mandabáris, *or* -re	mandabámini
mandabátur	mandabántur

FUTURE

I shall be commanded, etc.

mandábor	mandábimur
mandáberis, *or* -re	mandabímini
mandábitur	mandabúntur

PERFECT

I have been (was) commanded, etc.

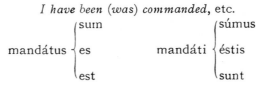

mandátus { sum / es / est   mandáti { súmus / éstis / sunt

PLUPERFECT

I had been commanded, etc.

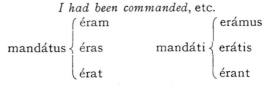

mandátus { éram / éras / érat   mandáti { erámus / erátis / érant

FUTURE PERFECT

I shall have been commanded, etc.

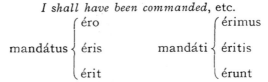

mandátus { éro / éris / érit   mandáti { érimus / éritis / érunt

SUBJUNCTIVE—PRESENT

May I be commanded ; let him be commanded.

mánder	mandémur
mandéris, *or* -re	mandémini
mandétur	mandéntur

IMPERFECT

I should be commanded ; he would be commanded.

mandárer	mandarémur
mandaréris, *or* -re	mandarémini
mandarétur	mandaréntur

PERFECT

I may have been commanded, etc.

mandátus { sim / sis / sit   mandáti { símus / sítis / sint

PLUPERFECT

I should have been commanded, etc.

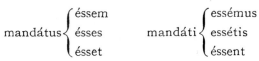

mandátus { éssem / ésses / ésset   mandáti { essémus / essétis / éssent

IMPERATIVE—PRESENT

mandáre, *be thou commanded.*
mandámini, *be ye commanded.*

FUTURE

mandátor, *thou shalt be commanded.*
mandátor, *he shall be commanded.*

---

mandántor, *they shall be commanded.*

INFINITIVE

Pres. mandári, *to be commanded.*
Perf. mandátus ésse, *to have been commanded.*
Fut. mandátum íri, *to be about to be commanded.*

PARTICIPLES

Ger. mandándus,-a,-um, *to be commanded.*
Perf. mandátus,-a,-um, *commanded, having been commanded.*

121.   Second Conjugation.—E-Verbs.

Hábeo, *I hold.*

PRINCIPAL PARTS

hábeo, habére, hábui, hábitus.

Active Voice.

INDICATIVE MOOD—PRESENT TENSE

I hold.

Singular	Plural
hábeo	habémus
hábes	habétis
hábet	hábent

IMPERFECT

I was holding, or *I held.*

habébam	habebámus
habébas	habebátis
habébat	habébant

FUTURE

I shall or *will hold.*

habébo	habébimus
habébis	habébitis
habébit	habébunt

PERFECT

I have held, or *I held.*

hábui	habúimus
habuísti	habuístis
hábuit	habuérunt, *or* -re

PLUPERFECT

I had held.

habúeram	habuerámus
habúeras	habuerátis
habúerat	habúerant

FUTURE PERFECT

I shall or *will have held.*

habúero	habuérimus
habúeris	habuéritis
habúerit	habúerint

SUBJUNCTIVE—PRESENT

May I hold; let him hold.

hábeam	habeámus
hábeas	habeátis
hábeat	hábeant

IMPERFECT

I should hold; he could hold.

habérem	haberémus
habéres	haberétis
habéret	habérent

PERFECT

I may have held, or *I have held.*

habúerim	habuérimus
habúeris	habuéritis
habúerit	habúerint

PLUPERFECT

I should have held; he would have held.

habuíssem	habuissémus
habuísses	habuissétis
habuísset	habuíssent

IMPERATIVE—PRESENT

hábe, *have thou.*

habéte, *have ye.*

FUTURE

habéto, *thou shalt hold.*

habéto, *he shall hold.*

habetóte, *ye shall hold.*

habénto, *they shall hold.*

INFINITIVE

Pres. habére, *to hold.*

Perf. habuísse, *to have held.*

Fut. habitúrus ésse, *to be about to hold.*

PARTICIPLES

Pres. hábens,-éntis, *holding.*

Fut. habitúrus,-a,-um, *about to hold.*

GERUND

Gen. habéndi, *of holding.*
Dat. habéndo, *for holding.*
Ac. habéndum, *holding.*
Ab. habéndo, *by holding.*

SUPINE

Ac. hábitum, *to hold.*
Ab. hábitu, *to hold, to be held.*

Passive Voice.

INDICATIVE MOOD—PRESENT TENSE

I am held.

hábeor	habémur
habéris, *or* -re	habémini
habétur	habéntur

IMPERFECT

I was held.

habébar	habebámur
habebáris, *or* -re	habebámini
habebátur	habebántur

FUTURE

I shall or *will be held.*

habébor	habébimur
habéberis, *or* -re	habebímini
habébitur	habebúntur

PERFECT

I have been held, or *I was held.*

hábitus { sum / es / est   hábiti { súmus / éstis / sunt

PLUPERFECT

I had been held.

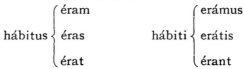

hábitus { éram, éras, érat   hábiti { erámus, erátis, érant

FUTURE PERFECT

I shall or *will have been held.*

hábitus { éro, éris, érit   hábiti { érimus, éritis, érunt

SUBJUNCTIVE—PRESENT

May I be held; let him be held.

hábear	habeámur
habeáris, *or* -re	habeámini
habeátur	habeántur

IMPERFECT

I should be held; he would be held.

habérer	haberémur
haberéris, *or* -re	haberémini
haberétur	haberéntur

PERFECT

I may have been held.

hábitus { sim, sis, sit   hábiti { símus, sítis, sint

PLUPERFECT

I should have been held.

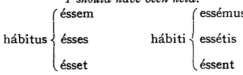

hábitus { éssem, ésses, ésset   hábiti { essémus, essétis, éssent

6

IMPERATIVE—PRESENT

habére, *be thou held.*
habémini, *be ye held.*

FUTURE

habétor, *thou shalt be held.*
habétor, *he shall be held.*

———

habéntor, *they shall be held.*

INFINITIVE

Pres. habéri, *to be held.*
Perf. hábitus ésse, *to have been held.*
Fut. hábitum íri, *to be about to be held.*

PARTICIPLES

Ger. habéndus,-a,-um, *to be held.*
Perf. hábitus,-a,-um, *held, having been held.*

12¡2. **Third Conjugation.—E-Verbs.**

Régo, *I rule.*

PRINCIPAL PARTS

régo, régere, réxi, réctus.

Active Voice.

INDICATIVE MOOD—PRESENT TENSE

I rule.

Singular	Plural
régo	régimus
régis	régitis
régit	régunt

IMPERFECT

I was ruling, or I ruled.

regébam	regebámus
regébas	regebátis
regébat	regébant

FUTURE

I shall or *will rule.*

régam	regémus
réges	regétis
réget	régent

PERFECT

I have ruled, etc.

réxi	réximus
rexísti	rexístis
réxit	rexérunt, *or* -re

PLUPERFECT

I had ruled, etc.

réxeram	rexerámus
réxeras	rexerátis
réxerat	réxerant

FUTURE PERFECT

I shall have ruled, etc.

réxero	rexérimus
réxeris	rexéritis
réxerit	réxerint

SUBJUNCTIVE—PRESENT

May I rule; let him rule.

régam	regámus
régas	regátis
régat	régant

IMPERFECT

I should rule; he would rule.

régerem	regerémus
régeres	regerétis
régeret	régerent

PERFECT

I may have ruled, or *I have ruled.*

réxerim	rexérimus
réxeris	rexéritis
réxerit	réxerint

PLUPERFECT

I should have ruled; he would have ruled.

rexíssem	rexissémus
rexísses	rexissétis
rexísset	rexíssent

IMPERATIVE—PRESENT

rége, *rule thou.*

régite, *rule ye.*

FUTURE

régito, *thou shalt rule.*

régito, *he shall rule.*

regitóte, *ye shall rule.*

regúnto, *they shall rule.*

INFINITIVE

Pres. régere, *to rule.*

Perf. rexísse, *to have ruled.*

Fut. rectúrus ésse, *to be about to rule.*

PARTICIPLES

Pres. régens,-éntis, *ruling.*

Fut. rectúrus,-a,-um, *about to rule.*

GERUND

N. ———

G. regéndi, *of ruling.*

D. regéndo, *for ruling.*

Ac. regéndum, *ruling.*

Ab. regéndo, *by ruling.*

SUPINE

Ac. réctum, *to rule.*

Ab. réctu, *to rule, to be ruled.*

Passive Voice.

INDICATIVE—PRESENT TENSE

I am ruled, etc.

régor	régimur
régeris, *or* -re	regímini
régitur	regúntur

IMPERFECT

I was ruled, etc.

regébar	regebámur
regebáris, *or* -re	regebámini
regebátur	regebántur

FUTURE

I shall be ruled, etc.

régar	regémur
regéris, *or* -re	regémini
regétur	regéntur

PERFECT

I have been ruled, etc.

réctus	sum	récti	súmus
	es		éstis
	est		sunt

PLUPERFECT

I had been ruled, etc.

réctus	éram	récti	erámus
	éras		erátis
	érat		érant

FUTURE PERFECT

I shall have been ruled, etc.

réctus	éro	récti	érimus
	éris		éritis
	érit		érunt

SUBJUNCTIVE—PRESENT

May I be ruled ; let him be ruled.

régar	regámur
regáris, *or* -re	regámini
regátur	regántur

IMPERFECT

I should be ruled ; he would be ruled.

régerer	regerémur
regeréris, *or* -re	regerémini
regerétur	regeréntur

PERFECT

I may have been ruled, or *I have been ruled.*

	sim		símus
réctus	sis	récti	sítis
	sit		sint

PLUPERFECT

I should have been ruled, etc.

	éssem		essémus
réctus	ésses	récti	essétis
	ésset		éssent

IMPERATIVE—PRESENT

régere, *be thou ruled.*
regímini, *be ye ruled.*

FUTURE

régitor, *thou shalt be ruled.*
régitor, *he shall be ruled.*

———

regúntor, *they shall be ruled.*

INFINITIVE

Pres. régi, *to be ruled.*
Perf. réctus ésse, *to have been ruled.*
Fut. réctum íri, *to be about to be ruled.*

PARTICIPLES

Ger. regéndus,-a,-um, *to be ruled.*

Perf. réctus,-a,-um, *ruled, having been ruled.*

123.   **Third Conjugation.**

Verbs of the third conjugation in **io** have some forms of the present stem like the fourth conjugation. Before **a, o, u,** and **i** they retain the **i** of the stem, but lose it elsewhere, except in the gerund and participle.

Cápio, *I take.*

PRINCIPAL PARTS

cápio,   cápere,   cépi,   cáptus.

Active Voice.

INDICATIVE MOOD—PRESENT TENSE

I take.

Singular	Plural
cápio	cápimus
cápis	cápitis
cápit	cápiunt

IMPERFECT

I was taking; I took.

capiébam	capiebámus
capiébas	capiebátis
capiébat	capiébant

FUTURE

I shall or will take.

cápiam	capiémus
cápies	capiétis
cápiet	cápient

PERFECT

I have taken, or *I took.*

cépi	cépimus
cepísti	cepístis
cépit	cepérunt

PLUPERFECT

I had taken.

céperam	ceperámus
céperas	ceperátis
céperat	céperant

FUTURE PERFECT

I shall or *will have taken.*

cépero	cepérimus
céperis	cepéritis
céperit	céperint

SUBJUNCTIVE—PRESENT

May I take; let him take.

cápiam	capiámus
cápias	capiátis
cápiat	cápiant

IMPERFECT

I should take; he would take.

cáperem	caperémus
cáperes	caperétis
cáperet	cáperent

PERFECT

I may have taken, or *I have taken.*

céperim	cepérimus
céperis	cepéritis
céperit	céperint

PLUPERFECT

I should have taken ; he would have taken.

cepíssem	cepissémus
cepísses	cepissétis
cepísset	cepíssent

IMPERATIVE—PRESENT

cápe, *take thou.*
cápite, *take ye.*

FUTURE

cápito, *thou shalt take.*
cápito, *he shall take.*
capitóte, *ye shall take.*
capiúnto, *they shall take.*

INFINITIVE

Pres. cápere, *to take.*
Perf. cepísse, *to have taken.*
Fut. captúrus ésse, *to be about to take.*

PARTICIPLES

Pres. cápiens,-iéntis, *taking.*
Fut. captúrus,-a,-um, *about to take.*

GERUND

N. ———
G. capiéndi, *of taking.*
D. capiéndo, *for taking.*
Ac. capiéndum, *taking.*
Ab. capiéndo, *by taking.*

SUPINE

Ac. cáptum, *to take.*
Ab. cáptu, *to take, to be taken.*

Passive Voice.

INDICATIVE—PRESENT TENSE
I am taken, etc.

cápior	cápimur
cáperis	capímini
cápitur	capiúntur

IMPERFECT
I was taken, etc.

capiébar	capiebámur
capiebáris	capiebámini
capiebátur	capiebántur

FUTURE
I shall be taken, etc.

cápiar	capiémur
capiéris	capiémini
capiétur	capiéntur

PERFECT
I have been taken, etc.

cáptus { sum / es / est }   cápti { súmus / éstis / sunt }

PLUPERFECT
I had been taken, etc.

cáptus { éram / éras / érat }   cápti { erámus / erátis / érant }

FUTURE PERFECT

I shall have been taken.

cáptus { éro / éris / érit   cápti { érimus / éritis / érunt

SUBJUNCTIVE—PRESENT

May I be taken; let him be taken.

cápiar	capiámur
capiáris	capiámini
capiátur	capiántur

IMPERFECT

I should be taken; he would be taken.

cáperer	caperémur
caperéris	caperémini
caperétur	caperéntur

PERFECT

I may have been taken; I have been taken.

cáptus { sim / sis / sit   cápti { símus / sítis / sint

PLUPERFECT

I should have been taken, etc.

cáptus { éssem / ésses / ésset   cápti { essémus / essétis / éssent

IMPERATIVE—PRESENT

cápere, *be thou taken.*
capímini, *be ye taken.*

FUTURE

cápitor, *thou shalt be taken.*
cápitor, *he shall be taken.*
capiúntor, *they shall be taken.*

INFINITIVE

Pres. cápi, *to be taken.*
Perf. cáptus ésse, *to have been taken.*
Fut. cáptum íri, *to be about to be taken.*

124.   Fourth Conjugation.—I-Verbs.

Aúdio, *I hear.*

PRINCIPAL PARTS

aúdio,   audíre,   audívi,   audítus.

Active Voice.

INDICATIVE MOOD—PRESENT TENSE
I hear.

Singular	Plural
aúdio	audímus
aúdis	audítis
aúdit	aúdiunt

IMPERFECT
I was hearing, or *I heard.*

audiébam	audiebámus
audiébas	audiebátis
audiébat	audiébant

FUTURE
I shall or *will hear.*

aúdiam	audiémus
aúdies	audiétis
aúdiet	aúdient

PERFECT

I have heard, or *I heard.*

audívi	audívimus
audivísti	audivístis
audívit	audivérunt, *or* -ére

PLUPERFECT

I had heard.

audíveram	audiverámus
audíveras	audiverátis
audíverat	audíverant

FUTURE PERFECT

I shall or *will have heard.*

audívero	audivérimus
audíveris	audivéritis
audíverit	audíverint

SUBJUNCTIVE—PRESENT

May I hear; let him hear.

aúdiam	audiámus
aúdias	audiátis
aúdiat	aúdiant

IMPERFECT

I should hear; he would hear.

audírem	audirémus
audíres	audirétis
audíret	audírent

PERFECT

I may have heard, or *I have heard.*

audíverim	audivérimus
audíveris	audivéritis
audíverit	audíverint

PLUPERFECT

I should have heard; he would have heard.

audivíssem	audivissémus
audivísses	audivissétis
audivísset	audivíssent

IMPERATIVE—PRESENT

aúdi, *hear thou.*
audíte, *hear ye.*

FUTURE

audíto, *thou shalt hear.*
audíto, *he shall hear.*
auditóte, *ye shall hear.*
audiúnto, *they shall hear.*

INFINITIVE

Pres. audíre, *to hear.*
Perf. audivísse, *to have heard.*
Fut. auditúrus ésse, *to be about to hear.*

PARTICIPLES

Pres. aúdiens,-éntis, *hearing.*
Fut. auditúrus,-a,-um, *about to hear.*

GERUND

Gen. audiéndi, *of hearing.*
Dat. audiéndo, *for hearing.*
Acc. audiéndum, *hearing.*
Ab. audiéndo, *by hearing.*

SUPINE

Acc. audítum, *to hear.*
Ab. audítu, *to hear, to be heard.*

Passive Voice.

INDICATIVE MOOD—PRESENT TENSE

I am heard.

aúdior	audímur
audíris, *or* -re	audímini
audítur	audiúntur

IMPERFECT

I was heard.

audiébar	audiebámur
audiebáris, *or* -re	audiebámini
audiebátur	audiebántur

FUTURE

I shall or *will be heard.*

aúdiar	audiémur
audiéris, *or* -re	audiémini
audiétur	audiéntur

PERFECT

I have been heard, or *I was heard.*

audítus $\begin{cases} \text{sum} \\ \text{es} \\ \text{est} \end{cases}$ audíti $\begin{cases} \text{súmus} \\ \text{éstis} \\ \text{sunt} \end{cases}$

PLUPERFECT

I had been heard.

audítus $\begin{cases} \text{éram} \\ \text{éras} \\ \text{érat} \end{cases}$ audíti $\begin{cases} \text{erámus} \\ \text{erátis} \\ \text{érant} \end{cases}$

FUTURE PERFECT
I shall or *will have been heard.*

audítus { éro / éris / érit   audíti { érimus / éritis / érunt

SUBJUNCTIVE—PRESENT
May I be heard ; let him be heard.

aúdiar	audiámur
audiáris, *or* -re	audiámini
audiátur	audiántur

IMPERFECT
I should be heard; he would be heard.

audírer	audirémur
audiréris, *or* -re	audirémini
audirétur	audiréntur

PERFECT
I may have been heard.

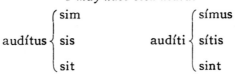

audítus { sim / sis / sit   audíti { símus / sítis / sint

PLUPERFECT
I should have been heard.

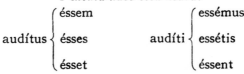

audítus { éssem / ésses / ésset   audíti { essémus / essétis / éssent

IMPERATIVE—PRESENT
audíre, *be thou heard.*
audímini, *be ye heard.*

FUTURE

audítor, *thou shalt be heard.*
audítor, *he shall be heard.*

———— ————

audiúntor, *they shall be heard.*

INFINITIVE

Pres. audíri, *to be heard.*
Perf. audítus ésse, *to have been heard.*
Fut. audítum íri, *to be about to be heard.*

PARTICIPLES

Pres. ——————
Ger. audiéndus,-a,-um, *to be heard.*
Perf. audítus,-a,-um, *having been heard.*

125.   Deponent Verbs.

Séquor, *I follow.*

PRINCIPAL PARTS

séquor	séqui	secútus

INDICATIVE MOOD—PRESENT TENSE

I follow.

Singular	Plural
séquor	séquimur
séqueris, *or* -re	sequímini
séquitur	sequúntur

IMPERFECT

I was following, or *I followed.*

sequébar	sequebámur
sequebáris, *or* -re	sequebámini
sequebátur	sequebántur

7

FUTURE

I shall or *will follow.*

séquar	sequémur
sequéris, *or* -re	sequémini
sequétur	sequéntur

PERFECT

I have followed, or *I followed.*

secútus { sum / es / est   secúti { súmus / éstis / sunt

PLUPERFECT

I had followed.

secútus { éram / éras / érat   secúti { erámus / erátis / érant

FUTURE PERFECT

I shall or *will have followed.*

secútus { éro / éris / érit   secúti { érimus / éritis / érunt

SUBJUNCTIVE—PRESENT

May I follow; let him follow.

séquar	sequámur
sequáris, *or* -re	sequámini
sequátur	sequántur

IMPERFECT

I should follow; he would follow.

séquerer	sequerémur
sequeréris, *or* -re	sequerémini
sequerétur	sequeréntur

PERFECT
I may have followed, or *I have followed.*

secútus { sim   secúti { símus
         sis   sítis
         sit   sint

PLUPERFECT
I should have followed.

secútus { éssem   secúti { essémus
         ésses   essétis
         ésset   éssent

IMPERATIVE—PRESENT
séquere, *follow thou.*
sequímini, *follow ye.*

FUTURE
séquitor, *thou shalt follow.*
séquitor, *he shall follow.*
sequúntor, *they shall follow.*

INFINITIVE
Pres. séqui, *to follow.*
Perf. secútus ésse, *to have followed.*
Fut. secutúrus ésse, *to be about to follow.*

PARTICIPLES
Pres. séquens, -éntis, *following.*
Fut. secutúrus,-a,-um, *about to follow.*
Perf. secútus,-a,-um, *having followed.*
Ger. sequéndus,-a,-um, *to be followed.*

GERUND
Gen. sequéndi, *of following.*
Dat. sequéndo, *for following.*
Ac. sequéndum, *following.*
Ab. sequéndo, *by following.*

SUPINE

Ac. secútum, *to follow.*
Ab. secútu, *to follow, to be followed.*

It will be observed that *séquor* is conjugated like the passive of the third conjugation. Deponents in their conjugations follow the passive voice of the conjugation to which they belong. It will be noted, however, from the conjugation of *séquor*, that the present participle, future participle, gerund, supine, and gerundive are added from the corresponding active conjugations.

126.   **Irregular Verbs.**

Sum, *I am.*

PRINCIPAL PARTS

sum,	ésse,	fúi,	futúrus.

INDICATIVE MOOD—PRESENT TENSE

Singular	Plural
sum	súmus
es	éstis
est	sunt

IMPERFECT

éram	erámus
éras	erátis
érat	érant

FUTURE

éro	érimus
éris	éritis
érit	érunt

PERFECT

fúi	fuérimus
fuísti	fuéritis
fúit	fúerint

PLUPERFECT

fúeram	fuerámus
fúeras	fuerátis
fúerat	fúerant

FUTURE PERFECT

fúero	fuérimus
fúeris	fuéritis
fúerit	fúerint

SUBJUNCTIVE—PRESENT

sim	símus
sis	sítis
sit	sint

IMPERFECT

éssem	essémus
ésses	essétis
ésset	éssent

PERFECT

fúerim	fuérimus
fúeris	fuéritis
fúerit	fúerint

PLUPERFECT

fuíssem	fuissémus
fuísses	fuissétis
fuísset	fuíssent

IMPERATIVE—PRESENT

es
éste

FUTURE

ésto
ésto
estóte
súnto

INFINITIVE

Pres. ésse
Perf. fuísse
Fut. futúrus ésse

PARTICIPLE

Fut. futúrus,-a,-um

127. Póssum, pósse, pótui, *to be able.*

INDICATIVE—PRESENT TENSE

Singular	Plural
póssum	possúmus
pótes	potéstis
pótest	póssunt

IMPERFECT

póteram	poterámus

FUTURE

pótero	potérimus

PERFECT

pótui	potúimus

PLUPERFECT

potúeram	potuerámus

FUTURE PERFECT

potúero	potuérimus

SUBJUNCTIVE—PRESENT

póssim	possímus
póssis	possítis
póssit	póssint

IMPERFECT

póssem	possémus

PERFECT

potúerim	potuérimus

PLUPERFECT

potuíssem	potuissémus

INFINITIVE

Pres. pósse
Perf. potuísse

128. Prósum, prodésse, prófui, profutúrus, *to benefit.*

INDICATIVE—PRESENT TENSE

Singular	Plural
prósum	prósumus
pródes	pródestis
pródest	prósunt

IMPERFECT

próderam	proderámus

FUTURE

pródero	prodérimus

PERFECT

prófui	profúimus

PLUPERFECT

profúeram	profuerámus

FUTURE PERFECT

profúero	profuérimus

SUBJUNCTIVE—PRESENT

prósim	prosímus
prósis	prosítis
prósit	prósint

IMPERFECT

prodéssem	prodessémus

PERFECT

profúerim	profuérimus

PLUPERFECT

profuíssem	profuissémus

IMPERATIVE—PRESENT

pródes	prodéste

FUTURE

prodésto	prodestóte

INFINITIVE

Pres. prodésse
Perf. profuísse
Fut. profutúrus ésse

PARTICIPLE

Fut. profutúrus,-a,-um

129. Vólo, vélle, vólui, *to be willing, wish.*

INDICATIVE—PRESENT TENSE

Singular	Plural
vólo	volúmus
vis	vúltis
vult	vólunt

IMPERFECT

volébam	volebámus

FUTURE

vólam	volémus

PERFECT

vólui	volúimus

PLUPERFECT

volúeram	voluerámus

FUTURE PERFECT

volúero	voluérimus

SUBJUNCTIVE—PRESENT

vélim	velímus
vélis	velítis
vélit	vélint

IMPERFECT

véllem	vellémus

PERFECT

volúerim	voluérimus

PLUPERFECT

voluíssem	voluissémus

INFINITIVE

Pres. vélle
Perf. voluísse

PARTICIPLE

Pres. vólens

130. Éo, íre, ívi(íi), itúrus, *to go.*

INDICATIVE—PRESENT TENSE

Singular	Plural
éo	ímus
is	ítis
it	éunt

IMPERFECT

íbam	ibámus

FUTURE

íbo	íbimus

PERFECT

ívi(íi)	ívimus

PLUPERFECT

íveram	iverámus

FUTURE PERFECT

ívero	ivérimus

SUBJUNCTIVE—PRESENT

éam	eámus

IMPERFECT

írem	irémus

PERFECT

íverim	ivérimus

PLUPERFECT

ivíssem	ivissémus

IMPERATIVE—PRESENT

i	íte

FUTURE

íto	itóte
íto	eúnto

INFINITIVE

Pres. íre
Perf. ivísse
Fut. itúrus ésse

PARTICIPLES

Pres. íens, eúntis
Fut. itúrus,-a,-um

GERUND

Gen. eúndi
Dat. eúndo
Ac. eúndum
Ab. eúndo

SUPINE

Ac. ítum
Ab. ítu

fío, fíeri, fáctus sum (supplies passive to facio, *make*), *to be made, become.*

INDICATIVE—PRESENT TENSE

fío	fímus
fis	fítis
fit	fíunt

IMPERFECT

fiébam	fiebámus

FUTURE

fíam	fiémus

PERFECT

fáctus sum	fácti súmus

PLUPERFECT

fáctus éram	fácti erámus

FUTURE PERFECT

fáctus éro   fácti érimus

SUBJUNCTIVE—PRESENT

fíam   fiámus

IMPERFECT

fíerem   fierémus

PERFECT

fáctus sim   fácti símus

PLUPERFECT

fáctus éssem   fácti essémus

IMPERATIVE—PRESENT

fi   fíte

INFINITIVE

Pres. fíeri
Perf. fáctus ésse
Fut. fáctum íri

PARTICIPLES

Perf. fáctus,-a,-um
Ger. faciéndus,-a,-um

131.   féro, férre, túli, látus, *to bear, carry, endure.*

Active Voice.

INDICATIVE—PRESENT TENSE

Singular	Plural
féro	férimus
fers	fértis
fert	férunt

IMPERFECT

ferébam   ferebámus

FUTURE

féram   ferémus

PERFECT

túli   túlimus

PLUPERFECT

túleram   tulerámus

FUTURE PERFECT

túlero   tulérimus

SUBJUNCTIVE—PRESENT

féram   ferámus

IMPERFECT

férrem   ferrémus

PERFECT

túlerim   tulérimus

PLUPERFECT

tulíssem   tulissémus

IMPERATIVE—PRESENT

fer   férte

FUTURE

férto   fertóte
férto   ferúnto

INFINITIVE

Pres. férre
Perf. tulísse
Fut. latúrus ésse

PARTICIPLES

Pres. férens
Fut. latúrus,-a,-um

GERUND

Gen. feréndi
Dat. feréndo
Ac. feréndum
Ab. feréndo

SUPINE

Ac. látum
Ab. látu

Passive Voice.

INDICATIVE MOOD—PRESENT TENSE

féror	férimur
férris	ferímini
fértur	ferúntur

IMPERFECT

ferébar	ferebámur

FUTURE

férar	ferémur

PERFECT

látus sum	láti súmus

PLUPERFECT

látus éram	láti erámus

FUTURE PERFECT

látus éro	láti érimus

SUBJUNCTIVE—PRESENT

férar	ferámur

IMPERFECT

férrer	ferrémur

PERFECT

látus sim	láti símus

PLUPERFECT

látus éssem	láti essémus

IMPERATIVE—PRESENT

férre	ferímini

FUTURE

fértor	————
fértor	ferúntor

INFINITIVE

Pres. férri
Perf. látus ésse
Fut. látum íri

PARTICIPLES

Perf. látus,-a,-um
Ger. feréndus,-a,-um

132.   RULES OF SYNTAX.

I. The subject of a Finite Verb is in the Nominative Case.

II. The object of a Transitive Verb is in the Accusative Case.

III. A Predicate Noun after a neuter or passive verb takes the same case as the subject.

IV. Adjectives, Adjective Pronouns, and Participles agree with their nouns in Gender, Number, and Case.

V. A Pronoun agrees with its antecedent in Gender and Number, but its Case depends upon the construction of the clause in which it stands.

VI. A Noun joined to another noun denoting the same person or thing is in the same case by Apposition.

VII. A Noun limiting another noun denoting a different person or thing is in the Genitive.

VIII. The Possessive Genitive denotes the Author, or the Possessor.

IX. The Subjective Genitive denotes the Subject or Agent of the action or feeling.

X. The Objective Genitive denotes the Object toward which the action or feeling is directed.

XI. The Partitive Genitive denotes the Whole of which a part is taken.

XII. A Noun predicated of another noun denoting a different person or thing, is put in the Predicate Genitive.

XIII. The Indirect Object of an action is in the Dative.

XIV. After **sum** and similar verbs, the possessor is expressed by the Dative, the thing possessed being the subject of the verb.

XV. The subject of the Infinitive is in the Accusative.

XVI. Duration of Time and Extent of Space are expressed by the Accusative.

XVII. Source and Cause are denoted by the Ablative with or without a preposition ; Accompaniment is denoted by the Ablative, generally with the preposition **cum ;** Means and Instrument are denoted by the Ablative alone.

XVIII. Manner is denoted by the Ablative with the preposition **cum,** unless the noun is modified by an adjective or a genitive, in which case the Ablative alone is used.

XIX. That of which anything is deprived, or from which it is removed or separated, is expressed by the Ablative.

XX. The Ablative of Specification is used with Nouns, Adjectives, and Verbs, to denote *in what respect* anything is true.

XXI. The Comparative is followed by the Ablative when **quam** (than) is not expressed.

XXII. The Voluntary Agent of a verb in the passive voice is in the Ablative with **a** or **ab.**

XXIII. A noun and a participle, or a noun and an adjective, or two nouns, may be put in the Ablative to denote the time, cause, or other attendant circumstances of an action. This is called the Ablative Absolute. It corresponds with the Nominative Absolute in English.

XXIV. Place where is expressed by the Ablative with **in.**

XXV. After verbs of Motion, Place to which is expressed by the Accusative, Place from which by the Ablative; names of Towns, without a preposition; other nouns take **ad** or **in** with the Accusative, and **ab, de,** or **ex** with the Ablative.

XXVI. Verbs of Declaring, Thinking, Believing, Knowing take after them an Infinitive with a subject Accusative.

XXVII. Clauses denoting Purpose or Result take the Subjunctive after **ut.**

XXVIII. Clauses introduced by **priusquam** take the Subjunctive when they involve an idea of purpose.

XXIX. **Cum** Causal (since), or Concessive (although), takes the Subjunctive ; **Cum** Temporal (when) generally takes the Indicative in the Present and Perfect Tenses.

XXX. The Indirect Question has its verb in the Subjunctive.

XXXI. In Indirect Discourse **(Oratio Obliqua)** the verb of the Principal clauses is in the Infinitive, and the verbs of the Subordinate clauses are in the Subjunctive.

XXXII. The Subjunctive is used to express a command, or an exhortation. In this sense it is used chiefly in the first and second persons singular, and the first and third persons plural of the Present Tense.

XXXIII. Clauses introduced by **nisi** express condition, and take the Indicative to represent the supposed case as real ; and the Subjunctive to represent it as possible.

XXXIV. The Active Periphrastic Conjugation, formed by combining the Future Active Participle with **sum,** denotes an intended or future action ; the Passive Periphrastic Conjugation formed by combining the Gerundive with **sum,** denotes necessity or duty.

XXXV. Deponent Verbs are passive in form and active in meaning.

PART II.—LATIN MAXIMS

LAW, like moral philosophy or politics, has its maxims which sum up in a pregnant sentence some leading principle or axiom of law ; so called, says Coke, " quia maxima est ejus dignitas et certissima auctoritas atque quod maxime omnibus probetur." The merit of the maxim is twofold. It is a useful generalisation of law wherein every student who would become his gown may note, as Wingate says, how the same key opens many locks, or, to put it in another way, how all the cases are reducible to a few theses. The other merit of the maxim lies in its epigrammatic form. Like the proverb, it embodies " the wisdom of many and the wit of one."

These qualities of the maxim—its sententiousness and its epigrammatic point—have made it at all times a favourite form of legal currency, tendered and accepted generally—or, to take another metaphor, a portable armoury of legal weapons. Nowhere more than in its maxims does the robust good sense of the common law of England display itself; and does not one of those very maxims warn the critic that no one ought to be wiser than the laws ?—" Neminem oportet legibus esse sapientiorem."

The maxims of English law, like the rules of the common law, derive their source and sanction from an immemorial antiquity, from frequent judicial recognition, and from the *imprimatur* of the sages of our law. One writer, indeed— Wingate—has gone so far as to describe them as " prime

8

emanations of the Eternal Wisdom." Their usefulness may be said to increase, rather than to diminish, as the law grows more complex and involved, for they bring back the mind to first principles.

Maxims touch, if they do not cover, the whole field of law —the theory of the King's sovereignty, the office of a judge, the first principles of law, public policy, marriage, infancy, crime, evidence, the interpretation of statutes and legal instruments, and many other matters.—*Encyclopædia of the Laws of England* (2nd ed.), vol. ix. p. 100.

1. *Ab abusu ad usum non valet consequentia.*—A conclusion as to the use of a thing from its abuse is invalid.

> In *Stockdale* v. *Hansard* (9 A. & E. 116) Lord Denman observed that this maxim cannot apply '' where an abuse is directly charged and offered to be proved.''

2. *Absoluta sententia expositore non indiget* (2 Inst. 533).—An absolute sentence requires no exposition. (See Maxim 436.)

3. *Abundans cautela non nocet* (11 Co. 6).—Abundant caution does no injury.

4. *Accessorium non ducit, sed sequitur suum principale* (Finch, Law, 128).—The accessory right does not lead, but follows its principal.

> Rent is incident to the reversion, and by a grant of the reversion the rent will pass. The law relative to contracts and mercantile transactions likewise presents many examples of the rule; thus, where framed pictures are sent by a carrier, the frames as well as the pictures are within the Carriers Act, 1830, s. 1. Again, the obligation of the surety is accessory to that of the principal, and is extinguished by the release or discharge of the latter; but the converse does not hold. (See next

maxim.) So, likewise, interest of money is accessory to the principal, and must, in legal language, follow its nature. (See Maxims 929, 1020a, 827, 554, 746).

5. *Accessorium non trahit principale.*—The accessory does not bring the principal. (See Maxim 4.)

6. *Accessorius sequitur naturam sui principalis* (3 Inst. 139).—An accessory follows the nature of its principal. (See Maxim 4.)

7. *Accusare nemo se debet, nisi coram Deo* (Hawke, 222). —No one is compelled to accuse himself, except before God. (See Maxim 659.)

8. *Accusator post rationabile tempus non est audiendus, nisi se bene de omissione excusaverit* (Moor. 817).—An accuser is not to be heard after a reasonable time unless he can account satisfactorily for the delay. (See Maxim 1062.)

9. *A communi observantiâ non est recedendum et minimè mutandæ sunt quæ certam interpretationem habent* (Wing. Max. 756).—Common observance is not to be departed from, and things which have a certain meaning are to be changed as little as possible.

10. *Acta exteriora indicant interiora secreta* (8 Co. 146).— External actions show internal secrets.
> The law, in some cases, judges of a man's previous intentions by his subsequent acts; and on this principle it was resolved in a well-known case, that, if a man abuse an authority given him by the law, he becomes a trespasser *ab initio*, but that if he abuse an authority given him by the party, he does not (*The Six Carpenters' Case*, 8 Rep. 290).

11. *Actio personalis moritur cum personâ* (Noy, Max. 20). —A personal right of action dies with the person.
> This rule of the common law has been encroached upon by various statutes, but it still applies to such actions as for libel, slander, false imprisonment, or other personal injury. The general rule of the common law is, that

if an injury were done either to the person or to the property of another for which unliquidated damages only could be recovered in satisfaction, the action died with the person to whom, or by whom, the wrong was done (*Wheatley* v. *Lane*, 1 Wms. Saund. 216a, n. 1).

12. *Actio non accrevit infra sex annos.*—The action has not accrued within six years.

13. *Actio non datur non damnificato* (Jenk. Cent. 69).—An action is not given to him who is not injured.
    The injury here referred to must be such as the law makes actionable, otherwise the party is *non damnificatus,* and the maxim *Damnum sine injuria* applies. (See Maxims 170, 1028, 521).

14. *Actio quælibet it suâ viâ* (Jenk. Cent. 77).—Every kind of action proceeds in its own way.

15. *Actionum genera maxime sunt servanda* (Lofft's Rep. 460).—The correct form of action should be followed.

16a. *Actor sequitur forum rei* (Branch, Max. 4).—The plaintiff follows the Court.

16b. *Actore non probante absolvitur reus* (Hob. 103).— When the plaintiff does not prove his case the defendant is acquitted.

17. *Actori incumbit onus probandi* (Hob. 103).—The burden of proof lies on a plaintiff. (See Maxim 217.)

18. *Actus curiæ neminem gravabit* (Jenk. Cent. 118).—An act of the Court shall prejudice no one.
    This maxim " is founded upon justice and good sense, and affords a safe and certain guide for the administration of the law " (12 C. B. 415). As long as there remains a necessity, in any stage of the proceedings in an action, for an appeal to the authority of the Court, or any occasion to call upon it to exercise its jurisdiction, the Court has, even if there has been some express

arrangement between the parties, an undoubted right, and is, moreover, bound to interfere, if it perceives that its own process or jurisdiction is about to be used for purposes which are not consistent with justice (*Wade* v. *Simeon*, 13 M. & W. 647; *Cumber* v. *Wane*, 1 Sm. L.C.). (See Maxim 239.)

19. *Actus Dei nemini facit injuriam* (5 Co. 87).—The act of God is prejudicial to no one.

Duties are either imposed by law or undertaken by contract, and the ordinary rule of law is that when the law creates a duty, and the party is disabled from performing it, without any default of his own, by the act of God, the law excuses him, but when a party by his own contract creates a duty upon himself he is bound to make it good, notwithstanding any accident by inevitable necessity (*Paradine* v. *Jane*, Aleyn, 26). (See next maxim.)

20. *Actus Dei nemini nocet* (Lofft, 102).—The act of God does injury to no one.

The above general rule must be applied with due caution (Ld. Raym. 433). Thus where, after the indictment and arraignment, the jury charged, and evidence given on a trial for a capital offence, one of the jurymen became incapable through illness of proceeding to verdict, the Court of oyer and terminer discharged the jury, charged a fresh jury with the prisoner, and convicted him, although it was argued that *actus Dei nemini nocet*, and that the sudden illness was a Godsend, of which the prisoner ought to have the benefit (*R.* v. *Edwards*, 13 R. R. 601).

21. *Actus inceptus cujus perfectio pendet ex voluntate partium revocari potest; si autem pendet ex voluntate tertiæ personæ vel ex contingenti, revocari non potest* (Bac. Max. Reg. 20).—An act already begun, the completion of which depends on the will of the parties, may be recalled; but if it depend on the consent of a third person, or on a contingency, it cannot.

22. *Actus judiciarius coram non judice irritus habetur, de ministeriali autem à quocunque provenit ratum esto* (Lofft's Rep. 458).—A judicial act done in excess of authority is not binding; otherwise as to a ministerial act.

23. *Actus legis nemini est damnosus* (5 Co. 81).—An act in law shall prejudice no man.

> A distinction has often been drawn, in accordance with this maxim, between the act of the law and the act of a party. If a person abuse an authority given by the law he becomes a trespasser *ab initio,* as if he had never had that authority, which is not the case where an authority given by a party is abused (*Six Carpenters' Case,* 8 Rep. 290); and this distinction has been ascribed to the principle that the law wrongs no man. (Maxim 24.)

24. *Actus legis nemini facit injuriam* (5 Co. 116).—The act of law operates an injury to no man. (See previous maxim.)

25. *Actus legitimi non recipiunt modum* (Hob. 153).— Legal actions do not admit a limitation.

26. *Actus non facit reum, nisi mens sit rea* (3 Inst. 107).— The act itself does not constitute guilt unless done with a guilty intent.

> " The intent and the act must both concur to constitute the crime " (7 T. R. 514). Two leading cases on this maxim of our criminal law are *R.* v. *Prince* (44 L. J. M.C. 122) and *R.* v. *Tolson* (58 L. J. M.C. 97), and the judgments delivered therein should be consulted upon the general relation of *mens rea* to crime. As a general rule of our law, a guilty mind is an essential ingredient of crime, and this rule ought to be borne in mind in construing all penal statutes. Yet the law will sometimes imply the intent from the act. (See Maxim 10.) (See Stroud on *Mens Rea.*)

27. *Ad ea quæ frequentius accidunt jura adaptantur* (2 Inst. 137).—The laws are adapted to those cases which most frequently occur.

Laws cannot be so worded as to include every case which may arise, but it is sufficient if they apply to those things which most frequently happen. The maxim was forcibly applied by Lord Blackburn in *Dixon* v. *Caledonian R. Co.* (5 App. Cas. 838); and two other judgments of Lord Blackburn's (*Clarke* v. *Wright*, 6 H. & N. 862, and *Dalton* v. *Angus*, 6 App. Cas. 818) demonstrate that it has force, not only as a canon of construction of statute law, but also as a principle of the common law. (See Maxims 467, 905, 93.)

28. *Adjournamentum est ad diem dice're seu diem dare* (4 Inst. 27).—An adjournment is to appoint a day or to give a day.

29. *Ad officium justiciariorum spectat, unicuique coram eis placitanti justitiam exhibere* (2 Inst. 451).—It is the duty of justices to administer justice to everyone seeking it from them.

30. *Ad proximum antecedens fiat relatio, nisi impediatur sententia* (Jenk. Cent. 180).—The antecedent has relation to that which next follows unless thereby the meaning of the sentence would be impaired.

Relative words must ordinarily be referred to the last antecedent, where the intent upon the whole deed or instrument does not appear to the contrary, and where the matter itself does not hinder it, the last antecedent being the last word which can be made an antecedent so as to have a meaning (*E. Counties R. Co.* v. *Marriage*, 9 H.L. Cas. 32; Finch, Law, 8; 1 A. & E. 445). But although this general proposition is true in strict grammatical construction, yet there are numerous examples in the best writers to show that the context often requires a deviation from the rule, and that the relative may refer to nouns which go before the last antecedent, and either take from it or give to it some qualification (*Beer* v. *Santer*, 10 C. B. N.S. 435).

31. *Ad quæstionem facti non respondent judices; ad quæstionem juris non respondent juratores* (Co. Litt. 295).—

To questions of fact judges do not answer : to questions of law the jury do not answer.

Two instances must suffice to show the application of this maxim. Thus, there are two requisites to the validity of a deed : (1) that it be sufficient in law, on which the Court decides; (2) that certain matters of fact, as sealing and delivery, be duly proved, on which it is the province of the jury to determine (*Jenkin* v. *Peace*, 6 M. & W. 576); and where interlineations or erasures are apparent on the face of a deed it is now the practice to leave it to the jury to decide whether the rasing or interlining was done before the delivery (*Alsager* v. *Close*, 10 M. & W. 576).

Again, it is the duty of the Court to construe all written instruments as soon as the true meaning of any words of art or commercial phrases used therein have been ascertained as facts by the jury; and it is the duty of the jury to take the construction from the Court (*Simpson* v. *Holliday*, L. R. 1 H.L. 320). (See Maxim 242.)

32. *Ædificare in tuo proprio solo non licet quod alteri noceat* (3 Inst. 201).—It is not permitted to build upon one's own land what may be injurious to another. (See Maxim 973.)

So an action lies if, by an erection on his own land, a man causes a nuisance by obstructing another's ancient lights and windows. (See Maxims 414, 973.)

33. *Ædificatum solo, solo cedit* (Co. Litt. 4a).—That which is built upon the land goes with the land. (See Maxim 854.)

34. *Æquitas est correctio legis generaliter latæ, quâ parte deficit* (Plow. 375).—Equity is a correction of the law, when too general, in the part where it is defective.

35. *Æquitas est perfecta quædam ratio quæ jus scriptum interpretatur et emendat; nulla scriptura comprehensa, sed sola ratione consistens* (Co. Litt. 24).—Equity is a sort of perfect reason which interprets and amends written law; comprehended in no code, but consistent with reason alone. (See Maxim 504.)

36. *Æquitas est quasi equalitas* (Co. Litt. 24).—Equity is as it were equality.

> Equity favours true equality both of rights and liabilities dividing burdens and benefits in equal shares. Hence its leaning to tenancy in common, instead of joint-tenancy, when the purchase-money has been advanced in unequal shares and in mortgages. On the same principle it divides burden and benefit equally between co-sureties, the right of contribution between co-sureties being founded on equity, not on contract; it being equitable that the burden should be borne by all alike.

37. *Æquitas nunquam contravenit leges.*—Equity never counteracts the laws.

> It is the function of equity rather to supplement the law by affording full relief, as in case of specific performance of contract, where the law gives only partial relief in damages.

38. *Æquitas sequitur legem* (Gilb. 136).—Equity follows law.

> This maxim is true in a very narrow and restricted sense in two meanings: first, equity follows the law in the sense of obeying it and conforming to its general rules and policy; and secondly, in applying legal rules to equitable estates. Thus, in the interpretation of statutes, and in the construction of wills and other legal instruments, this maxim applies. (See Maxim 492.)

39. *Æquum et bonum est lex legum* (Hob. 224).—That which is equal and good is the law of laws.

40. *Affectus punitur licet non sequatur effectus* (9 Co. 57a).—The intention is punished, though the consequence does not follow. (See Maxims 26, 372.)

41. *Affinitas dicitur, cùm duæ cognationes, inter se divisæ, per nuptias copulantur, et altera ad alterius fines accidit* (Co. Litt. 157).—It is called affinity when two families, divided from one another, are united by marriage, and one of them approaches the confines of another.

42. *Affirmanti non neganti incumbit probatio* (Halk. Max. 9).—The proof lies upon him who affirms, not upon him who denies.

> The onus of proving negligence lies upon him who alleges it, and to establish a case to be left to the jury he must prove the negligence charged affirmatively, by adducing reasonable evidence of it (18 App. Cas. 45; 3 H. & C. 601). (See Maxim 217.)

43. *Agentes et consentientes, pari pœná plectentur* (5 Co. 80).—The parties acting, and the parties consenting, are liable to the same punishment.

44. *Alienatio licet prohibeatur, consensu tamen omnium in quorum favorem prohibita est potest fieri* (Co. Litt. 98).— Although alienation be prohibited, yet by the consent of all those in whose favour it is prohibited it may take place; for it is in the power of every man to renounce a law made in his own favour. (See Maxim 749*b*.)

45. *Alienatio rei prefertur juri accrescendi* (Co. Litt. 185*a*). —Alienation of property is favoured by the law rather than accumulation.

> Commonly used in connection with the right of survivorship between joint tenants, which is defeated by a disposition of his share by one of the joint-tenants during the life of the other.

> Not only will our Courts oppose the creation of a perpetuity by deed, but they will likewise frustrate the attempt to create it by will (*Cadell* v. *Palmer*, 10 Bing. 142). The rule is well established that, although an estate may be rendered inalienable during the existence of a life or of any number of lives in being, and twenty-one years after, or, possibly, even for nine months beyond the twenty-one years, in case the person ultimately entitled to the estate should, at the time of its accruing to him, be an infant *en ventre sa mère*, yet that all attempts to postpone the enjoyment of the fee for a longer period are void (*Thellusson* v. *Woodford*, 8 R. R. 119). (See Maxim 464.)

46. *Aliquid conceditur ne injuria remaneat impunita, quod alias non concederetur* (Co. Litt. 197).—Something is conceded, which otherwise would not be conceded, lest an injury should remain unpunished.

47. *Aliquis non debet esse judex in propriâ causâ, quia non potest esse judex et pars.*—A person ought not to be judge in his own cause, because he cannot act as judge and party. (See *Dimes* v. *Grand Junction R. Co.*, 3 H.L. C. 759; *R.* v. *Rand*, L. R. 1 Q.B. 230). (See Maxims 635, 645.)

48. *Aliud est celare, aliud tacere.*—To conceal is one thing, to be silent another. (See *Carter* v. *Boehm*, 3 Burr. 1910; 2 C. & P. 341; Maxim 98.)

49. *Aliud est possidere, aliud esse in possessione* (Hob. 163). —It is one thing to possess, another to be in possession.

50. *Allegans contraria non est audiendus* (Jenk. Cent. 16). —He who alleges contrary things is not to be heard.

> A man shall not be permitted to " blow hot and cold " with reference to the same transaction, or insist, at different times, on the truth of each of two conflicting allegations, according to the promptings of his private interest (*Wood* v. *Dwarris*, 11 Exch. 493).

> The doctrine of estoppel, at any rate by deed and *in pais*, is in great measure a development of the principle expressed in this maxim. Indeed the author of Smith's Leading Cases seems to connect estoppel by record also with the present maxim. He defines estoppel generally as a conclusive admission, or something which the law treats as equivalent to an admission. (See Maxim 53.)

51. *Allegans suam turpitudinem non est audiendus* (4 Inst. 279).—A person alleging his own infamy is not to be heard.

> The meaning is that no one shall be heard in a Court of justice to allege his own turpitude as a foundation of a right or claim; not that a man shall not be heard who testifies to his own turpitude, however much his testimony may be discredited by his character (*In re Hallett*, 13 Ch. D. 696). (See Maxim 247.)

52. *Allegari non debuit quod probatum non relevat* (1 Chan. Cas. 45).—That which, if proved, would not be relevant, ought not to be heard.

53. *Allegatio contra factum non est admittenda.*—An allegation contrary to a deed is not admissible.

> A rule of evidence which excludes all untrue statements; but if the doctrine of estoppel applies, a party will not be allowed to prove even what is true. (For estoppel, see Maxims 50, 644, 630.)

54. *Alterius circumventio alii non præbet actionem.*—The defrauding of one person does not afford an action to another (Dig. 50, 17, 49).

55. *Alternativa petitio non est audienda* (5 Co. 40).—An alternative petition is not to be heard.

56. *Ambigua responsio contra proferentem est accipienda.* —An ambiguous answer is to be taken against him who offers it.

57. *Ambiguitas verborum latens verificatione suppletur, nam quod ex facto oritur ambiguum verificatione facti tollitur* (Bac. Max. Reg. 23).—Latent ambiguity of words may be supplied by evidence; for ambiguity arising upon the deed is removed by proof of the deed.

> A latent ambiguity in a written instrument is where the writing appears on the face of it certain and free from ambiguity, but the ambiguity is introduced by evidence of something extrinsic, or by some collateral matter outside the instrument. With respect to *ambiguitas latens* the rule is that, inasmuch as the ambiguity is raised by extrinsic evidence, so it may be removed in the same manner (*Way* v. *Hearn*, 13 C. B. N.S. 305). The rule may be applied to mercantile instruments with a view to ascertain the intention, though not to vary the contract of the parties (*Smith* v. *Jeffryes*, 15 M. & W. 561). (See as to this and the next maxim, Wigram on the *Admission of Extrinsic Evidence in Aid of the Interpretation of Wills* (5th ed.).)

58. *Ambiguitas verborum patens nullâ verificatione excluditur* (Bac. Max. 25).—A patent ambiguity cannot be cleared up by extrinsic evidence.

> *Patens ambiguitas* is an ambiguity apparent on the face of the instrument itself. *Ambiguitas patens,* said Lord Bacon, cannot be holpen by averment, and the reason is, because the law will not couple and mingle matter of speciality, which is of the higher account, with matter of averment, which is of the lower account in law, for that were to make all deeds hollow, and subject to averment; and so, in effect, to make that pass without deed which the law appoints shall not pass but by deed.

59. *Ambulatoria est voluntas defuncti usque ad vitæ supremum exitum* (Dig. 34, 4, 4).—The will of a deceased person is ambulatory until the latest moment of life. (See Maxim 752.)

60. *Angliæ jura in omni casu libertati dant favorem* (Fortesc. c. 42).—The laws of England in every case are favourable to liberty.

61. *Animo furandi* (Co. 3rd Inst. 107).—With an intention of stealing.

> In order to constitute larceny, the thief must take the property *animo furandi;* for when the taking of property is lawful, although it may afterwards be converted *animo furandi* to the taker's use, it is not larceny.

62. *Animo testandi.*—With the intention of making a will.

> *Animus testandi* is required to make a valid will. An idiot can make no will, for he can have no intention.

63. *Animus hominis est anima scripti* (3 Bulst. 67).—Intention is the soul of an instrument.

> The governing maxim on interpretation of deeds.

64. *A non posse ad non esse sequitur argumentum necessarie negative, licet non affirmative* (Hob. 336).—An argument follows necessarily in the negative from the not possible to the not being, though not in the affirmative.

If a thing is impossible, an argument in the negative may
be deduced—viz. that it has no existence; but an argument in the affirmative cannot be deduced—viz. that if
a thing is possible, it is in existence.

65. *Applicatio est vita regulæ* (2 Bulst. 79).—Application is
the life of a rule.

66. *Arbitrium est judicium* (Jenk. Cent. 137).—An award
is a judgment.

67. *Arbor dum crescit; lignum cum crescere nescit* (2 Bul.
82).—A tree is so called whilst growing, but wood when it
ceases to grow.

68. *Argumentum ab impossibili plurimum valet in lege*
(Co. Litt. 92).—An argument deduced from an impossibility
greatly avails in law.   (See Maxim 352.)

69. *Argumentum ab auctoritate fortissimum est in lege*
(Co. Litt. 254).—An argument from authority is most powerful
in law.

70. *Argumentum ab inconvenienti plurimum valet in lege*
(Co. Litt. 66).—An argument from inconvenience avails much
in law.
> Arguments of inconvenience are sometimes of great value
> upon the question of intention. If there be in any
> instrument equivocal expressions, and great incon-
> venience must necessarily follow from one construction,
> it is strong to show that such construction is not
> according to the true intention of the grantor; but where
> there is no equivocal expression in the instrument, and
> the words used admit only of one meaning, arguments
> of inconvenience prove only want of foresight in the
> grantor (*Glyn* v. *E. & W. India Dock Co.*, 7 App. Cas.
> 591; *Bottomley's Case*, 16 Ch. D. 686).

71. *Argumentum a communiter accidentibus in jure fre-
quens est* (Gothofred ad D. 44, 2, 6).—An argument from
things commonly happening is frequent in law.

72. *Argumentum a divisione est fortissimum in jure* (6 Rep. 60).—An argument from division is most powerful in law.

73. *Argumentum à majori ad minus negativè non valet; valet è converso* (Jenk. Cent. 281).—An argument from the greater to the less is of no force negatively; affirmatively it is.

74. *Argumentum à simili valet in lege* (Co. Litt. 191).—An argument from a like case avails in law.

75. *Arma in armatos sumere jura sinunt* (2 Jus. 574).—The laws permit to take arms against armed persons.

76. *Assensio mentium.*—The meeting of minds—*i.e.* mutual consent.

> Mutual assent, which is the meeting of the minds of both parties to a contract, is vital to the existence of a contract.

77. *Assignatus utitur jure auctoris* (Hal. Max. 14).—That which is assigned takes with it for its use the rights of the assignor.

> This maxim applies generally to all property, real and personal, and refers to assigns by act of parties, as where the assignment is by deed; and to assigns by operation of law, as in the case of an executor. All rights of the assignor in the thing assigned must pass from him to the assignee by virtue of the assignment, for *duo non possunt in solido unam rem possidere.* It should be observed, also, that the thing assigned takes with it all the liabilities attached to it in the hands of the assignor at the time of the assignment, except in cases for the encouragement of commerce, such as sales in market overt, negotiation of promissory notes, bills of exchange, etc. (See Maxims 631, 649.)

78. *Aucupia verborum sunt judice indigna* (Hob. 343).—Verbal quibbles are unworthy of a Judge.

79. *Audi alteram partem.*—Hear the other side. It has long been a received rule that no one is to be condemned, punished,

or deprived of property in any judicial proceeding, unless he
has had an opportunity of being heard (16 C. B. N.S. 416;
Harper v. *Carr*, 4 R. R. 441).

80. *A verbis legis non est recedendum* (5 Co. 118).—From
the words of the law there is not any departure.

> A Court of law will not make any interpretation contrary
> to the express letter of a statute. " Nothing is more
> unfortunate than a disturbance of the plain language of
> the Legislature by the attempt to use equivalent words "
> (*Everard* v. *Poppleton*, 5 Q.B. 184).

81. *Benedicta est expositio quando res redimitur à destruc-
tione* (4 Co. 25).—Blessed is the exposition by which anything
is saved from destruction.

82. *Benignæ faciendæ sunt interpretationes, propter sim-
plicitatem laicorum, ut res magis valeat quam pereat; et verba
intentioni, non è contra, debent inservire* (Co. Litt. 36).—
Liberal constructions of written documents are to be made,
because of the simplicity of the laity, and with a view to carry
out the intention of the parties and uphold the document; and
words ought to be made subservient, not contrary, to the
intention.

> This maxim is in some cases restricted by the operation
> of technical rules, which for the sake of uniformity
> ascribe definite meanings to particular expressions; and
> in other cases it receives, when applied to particular
> instruments, certain qualifications which are imposed for
> wise and beneficial purposes; but, notwithstanding these
> restrictions and qualifications, the above maxim is
> undoubtedly the most important and comprehensive
> which can be used for determining the true construction
> of written instruments (*Baker* v. *Tucker*, 3 H.L. Cas.
> 116; 1 Bulst. 175; Jenk. Cent. 260).

83. *Benignior sententia in verbis generalibus seu dubiis est
præferenda* (4 Co. 15).—The most favourable construction is
to be placed on general or doubtful expressions.

> This maxim proceeds upon the principle of carrying into
> effect, as far and as nearly as possible, the intention of

the testator, and if there be a general and also a particular intention apparent on the will, and the particular intention cannot take effect, the words shall be so construed as to give effect to the general intention. This is the *cy-près* doctrine which is carried into efficient operation by the Courts of equity.

84. *Bonæ fidei possessor in id tantum quod ad se pervenerit, tenetur.*—A possessor in good faith is only liable for that which he himself has obtained.

85. *Bona fides non patitur, ut bis idem exigatur.*—Good faith does not suffer the same thing to be exacted twice.

86. *Boni judicis est ampliare jurisdictionem* (Chan. Prac. 329).—A good judge will, when necessary, extend the limits of his jurisdiction.

This maxim, as above worded and literally rendered, is erroneous. Lord Mansfield suggested that for the word *jurisdictionem, justitiam* should be substituted. The true maxim of our law is " to amplify its remedies, and, without usurping jurisdiction, to apply its rules, to the advancement of substantial justice." The principle upon which our Courts act is, to enforce the performance of contracts not injurious to society, and to administer justice to a party who can make his claim to redress appear, by enlarging the legal remedy, if necessary, in order to do justice; for the common law is the birthright of the subject (1 Burr. 304; *Russell* v. *Smyth*, 9 M. & W. 818; 4 T. R. 344). But if, in the presumed exercise of discretion, a judge has decided in a manner absolutely unreasonable and opposed to justice, his error will be corrected on appeal (*R.* v. *Mayor of Maidenhead*, 51 L. J. Q.B. 448; *Hunt* v. *Chambers*, 51 L. J. Ch. 683; *Wigney* v. *Wigney*, 7 P. D. 182).

87. *Boni judicis est judicium sine dilatione mandare executioni* (Co. Litt. 289*b*).—It is the duty of a good judge to order judgment to be executed without delay.

9

88. *Boni judicis est lites dirimere* (4 Co. 15).—It is the duty of a good judge to prevent litigation. (See Maxims 89, 183, 412.)

89. *Bonus judex secundum æquum et bonum judicat, et æquitatem stricto juri præfert* (Co. Litt. 24).—A good judge decides according to justice and right, and prefers equity to strict law.

> " I commend the judge," observed Lord Hobart, " that seems fine and ingenious, so it tend to right and equity ; and I condemn them that either out of pleasure to show a subtle wit will destroy, or out of incuriousness or negligence will not labour to support, the act of the party by the art or act of the law " (Hob. 125).

90. *Breve judiciale non cadit pro defectu formæ* (Jenk. Cent. 43).—A judicial writ fails not through defect of form.

91. *Carcer ad homines custodiendos, non ad puniendos, dari debet* (Co. Litt. 260).—A prison should be assigned to the custody, not the punishment of persons.

92. *Casus fortuitus non est sperandus; et nemo tenetur divinare* (4 Co. 66).—A fortuitous event is not to be foreseen ; and no person is bound to divine it.

> This is another way of saying *nemo tenetur ad impossibile*, for to foresee a fortuitous or unlooked-for event is impossible, and this the law requires of no one. This maxim, however, would not excuse anyone from liability resulting reasonably from one's act, although such liability was not foreseen by the party himself.

93. *Casus omissus et oblivioni datus dispositioni communis juris relinquitur* (5 Co. 37).—A case omitted and consigned to oblivion is left to the disposal of the common law.

> " A *casus omissus*," observed Buller, J., " can in no case be supplied by a Court of law, for that would be to make laws " (*Jones* v. *Smart*, 1 T. R. 52). (See Maxim 27.)

94. *Catalla reputantur inter minima in lege* (Jenk. Cent. 28). —Chattels are considered in law among the minor things.

95. *Causa proxima non remota spectatur* (Bac. Max. Reg. 1).—The immediate, not the remote cause, is to be considered. (See Maxim 384.)

96. *Causæ dotis, vitæ, libertatis, fisci, sunt inter favorabilia in lege* (Jenk. Cent. 284).—Causes of dower, life, liberty, revenue, are among the favourable things in law.

97. *Causa ecclesiæ publicis causis æquiparatur; et summa est ratio quæ pro religione facit* (Co. Litt. 341).—The cause of the Church is equal to public causes; and for the best of reasons —it is the cause of religion.

98. *Caveat emptor; qui ignorare non debuit quod jus alienum emit* (Hob. 99).—Let a purchaser beware; no one ought in ignorance to buy that which is the right of another.

As the maxim applies, with certain specific restrictions, not only to the quality of, but also to the title to, land which is sold, the purchaser is generally bound to view the land and to enquire after and inspect the title-deeds, at his peril if he does not.

Upon a sale of goods the general rule with regard to their nature or quality is *caveat emptor,* so that, in the absence of fraud, the buyer has no remedy against the seller for any defect in the goods not covered by some condition or warranty, expressed or implied. It is beyond all doubt that, by the general rules of law there is no warranty of quality arising from the bare contract of sale of goods, and that where there has been no fraud, a buyer, who has not obtained an express warranty, takes all risk of defect in the goods, unless there are circumstances beyond the mere fact of sale from which a warranty may be implied (*Springwell* v. *Allen,* Alleyn, 91). (See Maxim 48.)

99. *Caveat venditor.*—Let the seller beware.

This maxim of the civil law expresses a doctrine the reverse of the rule of *caveat emptor* of the common law. It applies to executory sales, to contracts for goods to be manufactured or produced, or to sales where the buyer has no opportunity to inspect the article purchased.

100. *Certa debet esse intentio, et narratio, et certum fundamentum, et certa res quæ deducitur in judicium* (Co. Litt. 303a).—The intention, the count, and the foundation, ought to be certain, and so ought the thing to be which is brought for judgment.

101. *Certum est quod certum reddi potest* (9 Co. 47).— That is certain which is able to be rendered certain.

This maxim, which sets forth a rule of logic as well as a rule of law, is peculiarly applicable in construing a written instrument. For instance, although every estate for years must have a certain beginning and a certain end, " albeit there appear no certainty of years in the lease, yet if by reference to a certainty it may be made certain, it sufficeth " (Co. Litt. 45b). Again, the word " certain " must, in a variety of cases, where a contract is entered into for the sale of goods, refer to an indefinite quantity at the time of the contract made, and must mean a quantity which is to be ascertained according to the above maxim (*Wildman* v. *Glossop*, 1 B. & A. 12). (See also *Palmer* v. *Moxon*, 2 M. & S. 50; *Gordon* v. *Whitehouse*, 18 C. B. 747; *R.* v. *Wooldale*, 6 Q.B. 549; *Barber* v. *Butcher*, 8 Q.B. 863; *L. C. & D. R. Co.* v. *S. E. R. Co.*, 63 L. J. Ch. 93.)

102. *Cessante causâ, cessat effectus* (Co. Litt. 70).—When the cause ceases, the effect ceases. (See next maxim.)

103. *Cessante ratione legis, cessat ipsa lex* (Co. Litt. 70).— The reason of the law ceasing, the law itself ceases.

This finds familiar illustration in the protection from all civil process given to a foreign Ambassador whilst in the exercise of the duties of his office; to Members of Parliament during the sitting of Parliament; to judges exercising their judicial functions; to barristers attending the Courts of law and equity, and others; the reason being that such protection is necessary for the performance by them of their respective duties; but the moment they cease to be so acting the protection so afforded them also ceases. This maxim is also applicable to property, and finds illustration in the case of a proprietor who is responsible for the due performance of rights and duties respecting his property so long as he is owner thereof; but so soon as the property passes from him the incidents connected therewith which the law attaches thereto also pass. (See Maxims 102, 524, 917, 918, 1027.)

104. *Cessante statu primitivo, cessat derivativus* (8 Co. 34).—The original estate ceasing, that which is derived from it ceases.

The exceptions to this rule have been said to create some of the many difficulties which present themselves in the investigation of titles (1 Preston, Abs. 245). (See *London Loan Co.* v. *Drake*, 6 C. B. N.S. 798.)

105. *Charta de non ente non valet* (Co. Litt. 36a).—A charter concerning a thing not in existence is of no avail.

106. *Chartarum super fidem, mortuis testibus, ad patriam, de necessitudine, recurrendum est* (Co. Litt. 36).—The witnesses being dead, it must be referred, as to the truth of charters, out of necessity, to the country—*i.e.* a jury.

107. *Chirographum apud debitorem repertum præsumitur solutum* (Halk. 20).—A deed or bond found with the debtor is presumed to be paid.

108. *Circuitus est evitandus; et boni judicis est lites dirimere, ne lis ex lite oriatur* (5 Co. 31).—Circuity is to be avoided; and it is the duty of a good judge to determine litigations, lest one lawsuit arise out of another.

109. *Clausula generalis de residuo non ea complectitur, quæ non ejusdem sint generis cum iis quæ speciatim dicta fuerint* (Lofft, 419).—A general clause of residuum does not comprehend those things which may not be of the same kind with those which have been specially expressed.

110. *Clausula generalis non refertur ad expressa* (8 Co. 154).—A general clause does not refer to things expressed.

111. *Clausula quæ abrogationem excludit ab initio non valet* (Bac. Max. Reg. 19).—A clause which excludes abrogation avails not from the beginning.

112. *Clausula vel dispositio inulilis per presumptionem vel causam remotam ex post facto non fulcitur* (Bac. Max. Reg. 21).—An unnecessary clause or disposition is not upheld by a remote presumption or a cause arising after the event.

Lord Bacon explains *clausula vel dispositio inutilis* '' when the act or words do work or express no more than the law by intendment would have supplied,'' and such a clause or disposition is not supported by any subsequent matter '' which may induce an operation of those idle words or acts.''

113. *Clausulæ inconsuetæ semper inducunt suspicionem* (3 Co. 81).—Unusual clauses always excite suspicion. (See *Twyne's Case*, 3 Co. Rep. 80, and Maxim 201.)

114. *Clerici non ponentur in officiis* (Co. Litt. 96).—The clergy should not be placed in temporal offices.

115. *Cogitationis pœnam nemo meretur* (2 Inst. Jur. Civ. 658).—No man deserves punishment for a thought.

It is laid down by Lord Mansfield that, so long as an act rests in bare intention it is not punishable, yet when an act is done the law judges not only of the act itself but of the intent with which it was done. (See Maxims 1071, 1072.)

116. *Cohæredes sunt quasi unum corpus, propter unitatem juris quod habent* (Co. Litt. 163).—Co-heirs are deemed as one person on account of the unity of right which they possess.

117. *Commercium jure gentium commune esse debet, et non in monopolium et privatum paucorum quæstum convertendum* (3 Inst. 56).—Commerce, by the law of nations, ought to be common, and not converted to monopoly and the private gain of a few.

118. *Communis error facit jus* (4 Inst. 240).—Common error sometimes passes current as law.

The above maxim must be applied with very great caution. " It has sometimes been said," observed Lord Ellenborough, " *communis error facit jus*; but I say *communis opinio* is evidence of what the law is—not where it is an opinion merely speculative and theoretical, floating in the minds of persons; but where it has been made the groundwork and substratum of practice " (*Isherwood* v. *Oldknow*, 16 R. R. 305). (See also Lord Denman's remarks in *O'Connell* v. *R.*, and *per* Pollock, C.B., 2 H. & N. 139. See Maxim 572.)

119. *Compromissarii sunt judices* (Jenk. Cent. 128).— Arbitrators are judges.

120. *Conditio beneficialis quæ statum construit, benignè, secundum verborum intentionem, est interpretanda; odiosa, autem, quæ statum destruit, strictè, secundum verborum proprietatem, accipienda* (8 Co. 90).—A beneficial condition, which creates an estate, ought to be construed favourably, according to the intention of the words; but a condition which destroys an estate is odious, and ought to be construed strictly according to the letter of the words.

121. *Conditio præcedens adimpleri debet priusquam sequatur effectus* (Co. Litt. 201a).—A condition precedent must be fulfilled before the effect can follow.

In case of a conditional contract the condition precedent must happen before either party becomes bound by the contract.

122. *Conditiones quælibet odiosæ; maxime autem contra matrimonium et commercium* (Lofft, 644).—Some conditions are odious, but chiefly those which are against commerce or marriage.

123. *Confessio facta in judicio omni probatione major est* (Jenk. Cent. 102).—A confession made in judicial proceedings is of greater force than all proof.

124. *Confessus in judicio pro judicato habetur, et quodam-modo suâ sententiâ damnatur* (11 Co. 30).—A person confessing a judgment is deemed as adjudged, and in a manner is condemned by his own sentence.

125. *Confirmare est id quod prius infirmum fuit firmare* (Co. Litt. 295b).—To confirm is to make strong that which was before not strong.

126. *Confirmare nemo potest priusquam jus ei acciderit* (10 Co. 48).—No person can confirm a right before the right shall come to him.

127. *Confirmatio est nulla ubi donum præcedens est invalidum* (Co. Litt. 295b).—There is no confirmation where the preceding gift is invalid.

> An illegal act cannot be rendered valid by a subsequent confirmation. Thus, a lease for twenty years fraudulently executed by a life tenant cannot be confirmed by the remainderman or reversioner.

128. *Confirmatio omnes supplet defectus, licet id quod actum est ab initio non valuit* (Co. Litt. 295b).—Confirmation supplies all defects, though that which had been done was not valid from its beginning.

129. *Consensus non concubitus facit matrimonium; et consentire non possunt ante annos nubiles* (6 Co. 22).— Consent, and not coition, constitutes marriage; and the parties are not able to consent before marriageable years. (See Maxim 739.)

> By the law of England marriage is considered in the light of a contract, to which, with some exceptions, the ordinary principles which govern contracts in general must be applied; and the leading principle is that embodied in the above maxim: *concubitus* may take place for the mere gratification of present appetite, but marriage requires an agreement of the parties looking to the *consortium vitæ* (2 Hagg. Consist. 62). If infants intermarry while under the age of discretion, which is

fourteen years for a boy and twelve for a girl, the marriage is voidable. If a person above and a person under the age of discretion intermarry, the former, as well as the latter, may elect to avoid the marriage when the latter reaches that age; for in contracts of matrimony both parties must be bound, or neither. At the common law, if the parties be of the age of discretion, no consent but their own is necessary to make their marriage valid. Under the Marriage Acts the consent of a parent or guardian is usually required for the marriage of an infant who is not a widower or widow; but though a person whose consent is required can take steps to prevent the marriage, yet, if the marriage takes place, the absence of the consent does not invalidate it.

130. *Consensus tollit errorem* (Co. Litt. 126).—Consent takes away error.
    The acquiescence of a party who might take advantage of an error obviates its effect. On this maxim depends the important doctrine of waiver—that is, the passing by of a thing—a doctrine which is of wide application both in the science of pleading and in those practical proceedings which are to be observed in the progress of a cause from the first issuing of a writ to the ultimate signing of judgment and execution. (See Maxims 225, 869.)

131. *Consentientes et agentes pari pœnâ plectentur* (5 Co. 80).—Those consenting and those perpetrating are embraced in the same punishment.

132. *Constitutiones tempore posteriores potiores sunt his quæ ipsas præcesserunt* (D. 1, 4, 4).—Later laws prevail over those which preceded them.

133. *Constructio legis non facit injuriam* (Co. Litt. 183a).— The construction of law does not work any injury.

134. *Consuetudo debet esse certa; nam incerta pro nullis habentur* (Dav. 33).—A custom should be certain, for uncertain things are held as nothing.

135. *Consuetudo est optimus interpres legum* (2 Inst. 18).—
Custom is the best expounder of the laws. (See Maxims 772,
139.)

136. *Consuetudo et communis assuetudo vincit legem
non scriptam, si sit specialis; et interpretatur legem scriptam,
si lex sit generalis* (Jenk. Cent. 273).—Custom and common
usage overcome the unwritten law, if it be special; and interpret
the written law if it be general.

137. *Consuetudo ex certâ causâ rationabili usitata privat
communem legem* (Litt. § 169).—A custom grounded on a
certain reasonable cause supersedes the common law.

> In proof whereof may be instanced the customs of gavel-
> kind and borough-English, which are directly contrary
> to the general law of descent; or the custom of Kent,
> which is opposed to the general law of escheat.

138. *Consuetudo, licet sit magnæ auctoritatis, nunquam
tamen præjudicat manifestæ veritati* (4 Co. 18).—A custom,
though it be of great authority, should never, however, be
prejudicial to manifest truth.

139. *Consuetudo manerii et loci observanda est* (4 Co. 21).—
The custom of a manor and place is to be observed.

> A custom may be defined to be a usage which has obtained
> the force of law, and is, in truth, the binding law within
> a particular district or at a particular place, of the
> persons and things which it concerns. There are several
> requisites to the validity of a custom : it must be certain,
> reasonable in itself, have existed from time immemorial,
> have continued without any interruption, have been
> peaceably enjoyed and acquiesced in, be compulsory,
> be consistent with other local customs; while customs in
> derogation of the common law must be strictly
> construed; and if it is sought to attach a usage or custom
> to a written contract it must not be inconsistent
> therewith. (See Maxims 772, 773.)

140. *Consuetudo neque injuria oriri neque tolli potest*
(Lofft, 340).—Custom can neither arise from, nor be taken
away by, injury.

141. *Consuetudo regni Angliæ est lex Angliæ* (Jenk. Cent. 119).—The custom of England is the law of England.

142. *Consuetudo semel reprobata non potest amplius induci* (Dav. 33).—Custom once disallowed cannot be again alleged.

143. *Contemporanea expositio est optima et fortissima in lege* (2 Inst. 11).—A contemporaneous exposition is the best and strongest in law.

> However general the words of an ancient grant may be, it is to be construed by evidence of the manner in which the thing granted has always been possessed and used; for so the parties thereto must be supposed to have intended; so where the words of an instrument are ambiguous, the Court may call in aid acts done under it as a clue to the intention. Upon the same principle depends the great authority which, in construing an old statute, is attributed to the construction put upon it by judges who lived at or soon after the time when the statute was made, as being best able to determine the intention of the Legislature from their knowing the circumstances to which the statute related. (See Maxim 249.)

144. *Contra negantem principia non est disputandum* (Co. Litt. 343).—Against a man denying principles there is no disputing.

145. *Contra non valentem agere nulla currit præscriptio.*—No prescription runs against a person unable to bring an action.

> For instance, in the case of a debt, it only begins to run from the time when the creditor has a right to institute his suit, because no delay can be imputed to him before that time.

146. *Contractus est quasi actus contrà actum* (2 Co. 15).—A contract is, as it were, act against act.

147. *Contrectatio rei alienæ, animo furandi, est furtum*
(Jenk. Cent. 132).—The touching of property not one's own,
with an intention to steal, is theft.

148. *Conventio et modus vincunt legem* (2 Co. Rep. 73).
—A contract and agreement overcome the law. (See
Maxim 590.)

149. *Conventio privatorum non potest publico juri derogare*
(Wing. 746).—A convention of private persons cannot detract
from public right.   (See Maxims 148, 779.)

150. *Copulatio verborum indicat acceptationem in eodem
sensu* (Bac. iv. 26).—The coupling of words shows that they
are to be taken in the same sense.

151. *Corpus delicti.*—The body—*i.e.* the gist—of the offence.
The *corpus delicti* in murder has two components—death
as the result, and criminal agency of another as the
means.   Where there is direct proof of the one, the
other may be established by circumstantial evidence.

152. *Corpus humanum non recipit æstimationem* (Hob. 59).
—A human body is not susceptible of appraisement.

153. *Crescente malitiâ crescere debet et pœna* (2 Inst. 479).
—Vice increasing, punishment ought also to increase.

154. *Crimen læsæ majestatis omnia alia crimina excedit-
quoad pœnam* (3 Inst. 210).—The crime of treason exceeds all
other crimes as to its punishment.   (See Maxim 941.)

155. *Cui licet quod majus non debet quod minus est non
licere* (4 Co. 23).—He who has authority to do the more
important act shall not be debarred from doing that of less
importance.   (See Maxim 684.)

156. *Cuicunque aliquis quid concedit concedere videtur et
id sine quo res ipsa esse non potuit* (11 Co. 52).—The grantor
of anything to another grants that also without which the thing
granted would be useless.
   Where a man, having a close surrounded with his land,
   grants the close, the grantee shall have a way over the

land as incident to the grant (1 Wms. Saund. 323). If a man lease his land and all the mines therein, when there are no open mines, the lessee may dig for the minerals (5 Rep. 12*a*); by the grant of the fish in a man's pond is granted power to come upon the banks and fish for them (Shep. Touch. 89). If trees be excepted in a lease, the lessor has power, as incident to the exception, to enter the land demised at any reasonable times to fell and remove the trees, and the like law holds good of a demise by parol (11 Rep. 52*a*; 7 Exch. 77). (See Maxim 844.)

157. *Cuilibet in suâ arte perito est credendum* (Co. Litt. 125).—Whosoever is skilled in his profession is to be believed. Almost all the injuries which one individual may receive from another, and which lay the foundation of actions, involve questions peculiar to the trades and conditions of the parties; and in these cases the jury must, according to the above maxim, attend to the witnesses, and decide according to their number, professional skill, and means of knowledge. Respecting matters, then, of science or trade, and others of the same description, persons of skill may not only speak as to facts, but are even allowed to give their opinions in evidence, which is contrary to the general rule that the opinion of a witness is not evidence. But, although a skilled witness may be examined as to mercantile usage, or as to the meaning of a term of art, he cannot be asked to construe a written document (*Kirkland* v. *Nisbet*, 3 Macq. 766), for *ad quæstionem legis respondent judices.*

158. *Cujus est dare ejus est disponere* (Wing. Max. 53).— Whose is to give, his is to dispose. This maxim sets forth the principle on which the old feudal system of feoffment depended, but it must now be received with considerable caution. In another form (Maxim 591) it is still applicable to modern grants; the bargainer of an estate may, since the land moves from him, annex such conditions as he pleases to the estate bargained, provided that they are not illegal, repugnant,

or impossible; so may he, by insertion of special coven-
ants in a conveyance of demise, reserve to himself rights
of easement and other privileges in the land so conveyed
or demised, and thus surrender the enjoyment of it only
partially, and not absolutely, to the feoffee or tenant.

159. *Cujus est instituere ejus est abrogare.*—" We say, in
general, he that institutes may also abrogate, most especially
when the institution is not only by, but for, himself. If the
multitude, therefore, do institute, the multitude may abrogate;
and they themselves, or those who succeed in the same right,
can only be fit judges of the performance of the ends of the
institution " (Sidney on *Government*, p. 15).

160. *Cujus est solum ejus est usque ad cœlum, et ad inferos*
(Co. Litt. 4).—Whose is the soil, his is also that which is above
and below it.

Land, in its legal signification, has an indefinite extent
upwards, so that by a conveyance of land all buildings,
growing timber and water, erected and being thereupon, likewise pass. From the above maxim it follows
that a person has no right to erect a building on his own
land which interferes with the due enjoyment of adjoining premises, and occasions damage thereto, either by
overhanging them or by the flow of water from the roof
and eaves upon them. If a landowner allows the
branches of his trees to overhang his boundary, his
neighbour has a right of action for actual damage caused
thereby; and the neighbour is entitled to cut the
branches back, whether or not they cause damage.

In law land extends also downwards, so that whatever is
in a direct line between the surface and the centre of
the earth belongs to the owner of the surface; and if a
man grants all his lands, he grants thereby all his mines,
woods, waters, and houses, as well as his fields and
meadows. (See Maxims 32, 973.)

161. *Culpâ caret, qui scit, sed prohibere non potest* (D. 50,
17, 50).—He is free from fault who knows but cannot prevent.

162. *Culpa est immiscere se rei ad se non pertinenti* (D. 50, 17, 36).—It is a fault for a man to meddle in a matter not pertaining to him.

163. *Cum duo inter se pugnantia reperiuntur in testamento ultimum ratum est* (Co. Litt. 112).—Where two clauses in a will are repugnant one to the other, the last in order shall prevail.

> This maxim must in its application be restricted by, and made subservient to, that general principle which requires that the testator's intention shall, if possible, be ascertained and carried into effect. It is well settled that where there are two repugnant clauses in a will the last prevails, as being the most indicative of the intent; for unless the principle were recognised of adopting one clause and rejecting the other, both would be necessarily void.

164. *Cum in testamento ambigue aut etiam perperam scriptum est, benigne interpretari debet et secundum id quod credibile est cogitatum credendum est* (D. 34, 5, 24).—Where an ambiguous, or even erroneous, expression occurs in a will, it should be construed liberally and in accordance with the testator's probable meaning.

165. *Cum par delictum est duorum semper oneratur petitor* (D. 50, 17, 154).—When both parties are in fault the plaintiff must always fail, and the cause of the person in possession be preferred.

166. *Curia Parliamenti suis propriis legibus subsistit* (4 Inst. 50).—The Court of Parliament is governed by its own peculiar laws.

167. *Cursus curiæ est lex curiæ* (3 Buls. 53).—The practice of the Court is the law of the Court.

> An inveterate practice in the law generally stands upon principles that are founded in justice and convenience. Hence, if any necessary proceeding be informal, or be not done within the time limited for it, or in the manner prescribed by the practice of the Court, it may some-

times be set aside for irregularity. Anything required to be done by the law of the land must be noticed by a Court of appellate jurisdiction, but such a Court does not of necessity regard the practice of an inferior one. In matters of practice and procedure, as in matters of discretion, the practice of the House of Lords has been not to interfere with the decisions of Courts below, unless perfectly satisfied that they are based upon erroneous principles. (See Maxims 189, 1060.)

168. *Custos statum hæredis in custodiâ existentis meliorem, non deteriorem, facere potest* (7 Co. 7).—A guardian can make the estate of an existing heir under his guardianship better, but not worse.

169. *Damnum sentit dominus.*—The lord suffers the damage.
> This expresses the general rule applicable to the case of the accidental destruction of goods contracted to be sold : in the absence of any agreement to the contrary the loss usually falls upon the buyer or the seller according as the property in the goods has or has not passed. (But see Maxim 594.)

170. *Damnum sine injuria esse potest* (Halk. Max. 12).— There may be damage or injury inflicted without any act of injustice.
> For such damage no action can be maintained. The maxim *Ubi jus ibi remedium* does not apply, for there is no *jus*, no legal right to demand that the act which causes the damage shall not be done, and therefore there is no *remedium*. (See Maxims 13, 521, 1028.)

171. *Debile fundamentum fallit opus* (Noy, Max. 20).— A weak foundation destroys the superstructure.
> This maxim is familiarly illustrated in the case of a will void by reason of its not being duly attested according to statute provisions.

172. *Debita sequuntur personam debitoris* (Halk. Max. 13). —Debts follow the person of the debtor.

173. *Debitum et contractus sunt nullius loci* (7 Co. 3).—
Debt and contract are of no place.

> This refers to the common law rule respecting *venue*,
> which had to be laid truly in all actions except those of a
> transitory nature.

174. *Debitor non præsumitur donare* (Jur. Civ.)—A debtor
is not presumed to give.

> This maxim has reference to the law of satisfaction.

175. *Debitorum pactionibus creditorum petitio nec tolli nec
minui potest* (1 Pothier, 108).—The rights of creditors can
neither be taken away nor diminished by agreements among
the debtors.

176. *Deficiente uno sanguine non potest esse hæres*
(3 Co. 41).—One blood being wanting, he cannot be heir.

> But see 3 & 4 Wm. IV. c. 106, s. 9, and 33 & 34 Vict. c. 23,
> s. 1.

177. *De fide et officio judicis non recipitur quæstio; sed de
scientiâ, sive error sit juris sive facti* (Bac. Max. Reg. 17).—Of
the good faith and intention of a judge a question cannot be
entertained; but it is otherwise as to his knowledge, whether
the error be one of law or fact.

> It is a general rule that no action will lie against a judge
> for any act done by him in the exercise of his judicial
> functions, provided such act, though done mistakenly,
> were within the scope of his jurisdiction; but his errors
> may be corrected by appellate tribunals in all cases
> where the law allows of an appeal.

178. *De gratiâ speciali, certâ scientiâ, et mero motu; talis
clausula non valet in his in quibus præsumitur principem esse
ignorantem* (1 Co. Rep. 53).—The clause, "Of our special
grace, certain knowledge, and mere motion," is of no avail
where it may be presumed that the prince was ignorant.

> Thus the Crown cannot by grant of lands create in them a
> new estate of inheritance, or give them a new descendible
> quality, and the power of the Crown is similarly
> restricted as regards the grant of a peerage or honour.

10

179. *Delegata potestas non potest delegari* (2 Inst. 597).—
A delegated power cannot be delegated.

> This rule applies wherever the authority involves a trust
> or discretion in the agent for the exercise of which he
> is selected; but does not apply where it involves no
> matter of discretion, and it is immaterial whether the act
> be done by one person or another, and the original agent
> remains responsible to the principal. (See Maxims 4,
> 186, 859.)

180. *Delegatus non potest delegare* (*Ibid.*).—A delegate
cannot delegate. (See Maxim 1061.)

181. *Delicatus debitor est odiosus in lege* (2 Bulst. 148).—
A luxurious debtor is odious in law.

182. *Deliberandum est diu quod statuendum est semel*
(12 Co. 74).—That which is to be resolved once for all, should
be long deliberated upon.

183. *De minimis non curat lex* (Cro. Eliz. 353).—Of trifles
the law does not concern itself.

> Courts of justice generally do not take trifling and
> immaterial matters into account, except under peculiar
> circumstances, such as the trial of a right, or where
> personal character is involved; they will not, for
> instance, take notice of the fraction of a day, except in
> cases where there are conflicting rights, for the deter-
> mination of which it is necessary that they should do
> so. (See Maxim 88.)

184. *De morte hominis nulla est cunctatio longa* (Co.
Litt. 134).—Concerning the death of a man no delay is long.

185. *De non apparentibus, et non existentibus, eadem est
ratio* (5 Co. 6).—Of things which do not appear and things
which do not exist, the rule in legal proceedings is the same.

> What is not in evidence is presumed to be non-existent.
> This maxim applies where a party seeks to rely upon
> any deeds or writings which are not produced in Court,

and the loss of which is not accounted for or supplied in the manner which the law prescribes; for in this case they should be treated, as against such party, as if non-existent. (See Maxims 896, 337.)

186. *Derivativa potestas non potest esse major primitivâ* (Noy Wing. 66).—The power derived cannot be greater than that from which it is derived. (See Maxim 4.)

187. *Designatio justiciariorum est à rege; jurisdictio vero ordinaria à lege* (4 Inst. 74).—The appointment of justices is by the king; but ordinary jurisdiction is by the law.

188. *Designatio unius est exclusio alterius, et expressum facit cessare tacitum* (Co. Litt. 210a).—The appointment of one is the exclusion of another, and that which is expressed makes that understood to cease.

189. *De similibus idem est judicium* (7 Co. 18).—In like cases the judgment is the same. (See Maxims 366, 497.)

190. *Deus solus hæredem facere potest non homo* (Co. Litt. 7).—God alone, and not man, can make an heir.
   The word " heir " in legal understanding signifies him to whom lands, tenements, or hereditaments, by the act of God and right of blood, descend; and he only is heir who is *ex justis nuptiis procreatus*. (See Maxims 321-327, 792.)

191. *Dies Dominicus non est juridicus* (Co. Litt. 135).— The Lord's Day (Sunday) is not juridical, or a day for legal proceedings.
   The judges cannot sit on a Sunday, that day being exempt from all legal business by the common law. By the Lord's Day Act, if a man, in the exercise of his ordinary calling, make a contract on a Sunday, that contract is void, so as to prevent a party, who was privy to what made it illegal, from suing upon it, but not so as to defeat a claim made upon it by an innocent party.

192. *Discretio est discernere per legem quid sit justum* (10 Co. 140).—Discretion is to know through law what is just.

"Discretion, when applied to a court of justice, means sound discretion guided by law. It must be governed by rule, not by humour; it must not be arbitrary, vague and fanciful, but legal and regular." (Lord Mansfield, 2 Burr. 25, 39.)

193. *Distinguenda sunt tempora; distingue tempora, et concordabis leges* (1 Co. 24).—Times are to be distinguished; distinguish times, and you will make the laws agree.

194. *Divinatio, non interpretatio est, quæ omnino recedit a literâ* (Bac. Max. Reg. 3).—It is guessing, not interpretation, which altogether departs from the letter.

195. *Dolo malo pactum se non servabit* (D. 2, 14, 7).— A pact made with malicious intent will not be upheld.

196. *Dolosus versatur in generalibus* (2 Co. 34).—A deceiver deals in general terms.

197. *Dolus circuitu non purgatur* (Bac. Max. Reg. 1).— Fraud is not purged by circuity.

"*Dolus* here means any *wrongful* act tending to the damage of another" (6 E. & B. 948).

198. *Dolus et fraus una in parte sanari debent* (Noy, Max. 45).—Deceit and fraud should always be remedied.

199. *Dominium non potest esse in pendenti* (Halk. 39).— Lordship cannot be in suspense.

200. *Domus sua cuique est tutissimum refugium* (5 Co. 91). —To every one his house is his surest refuge; or, every man's house is his castle.

If thieves come to a man's house to rob or murder him, and he or his servants kill any of the thieves in defence of himself and his house, this is not felony.

When any house is recovered by action, the sheriff may
break the house, and deliver the possession to the plaintiff; for after judgment it is not the house of the
defendant.

In all cases where the king is party (as where a felony or
misdemeanour has been committed), the sheriff may
break the party's house to execute the king's process,
if otherwise he may not enter.

In all cases when the door is open the sheriff may enter
the house and do execution, at the suit of any subject.
(See *Seymayne's Case*, 1 Smith's L.C.)

201. *Dona clandestina sunt semper suspiciosa* (3 Co. 81).—
Clandestine gifts are always suspicious. (See Maxim 113.)

202. *Donari videtur, quod nullo jure cogente conceditur*
(D. 50, 17, 82).—A thing is said to be given when it is yielded
otherwise than by virtue of a right.

203. *Donatio non præsumitur* (Jenk. Cent. 109).—A gift is
not presumed.

204. *Donatio perficitur possessione accipientis* (Jenk.
Cent. 109).—A gift is perfected by the possession thereof by
the donee.

205. *Donationum alia perfecta, alia incepta et non perfecta;
ut si donatio lecta fuit et concessa, ac traditio nondum fuerit
subsecuta* (Co. Litt. 56).—Some gifts are perfect, others
incipient or not perfect; as if a gift were chosen and granted,
but delivery had not then followed.

206. *Donator nunquam desinit possidere antequam dona-
tarius incipiat possidere* (Dyer, 281).—He who gives never
ceases to possess before that the receiver begins to possess.

207. *Dormiunt aliquando leges, nunquam moriuntur* (2 Inst.
161).—The laws sometimes sleep, never die.

For example, a state of war sometimes suspends contracts
and the Statute of Limitations.

208. *Doti lex favet; præmium pudoris est, ideò parcatur* (Co. Litt. 31).—The law favours dower; it is the reward of chastity, therefore is to be preserved. (See Maxims 991, 1031*b*.)

So strong is this maxim in its operation that dower, when it once attaches, cannot be defeated except by the consent of the wife, or by divorce *a vinculo*.

209. *Duo non possunt in solido unam rem possidere* (Co. Litt. 368).—Two persons cannot possess one thing in entirety. (See Maxim 77.)

210. *Duo sunt instrumenta ad omnes res aut confirmandas aut impugnandas—ratio et auctoritas* (8 Co. 16).—There are two instruments either to confirm or impugn all things—reason and authority.

211. *Eadem mens præsumitur regis quæ est juris, et quæ esse debet, præsertim in dubiis* (Hob. 154).—The mind of the king is presumed to be in conformity with the law, and with what it should be, especially in doubtful cases.

The law will not suppose that the king meant either an unwise or an injurious action, but declares that he was deceived in his grant; and thereupon such grant becomes void upon the supposition of deception either by or upon those agents whom the Crown has thought proper to employ.

212. *Ea quæ commendandi causâ in venditionibus dicuntur si palam appareant venditorem non obligant* (D. 18, 1, 43).— Those things which are said for the sake of commendation in sales, if they are plainly apparent, do not bind the seller.

The maxim, *caveat emptor*, applies as a rule in cases where the seller affirms that the subject-matter of the sale has not a defect, if there is a visible defect and one obvious to the senses.

213. *Ea quæ raro accidunt, non temere in agendis negotiis computantur* (D. 50, 17, 64).—Those things which seldom happen are not rashly to be taken into account in transacting business.

214. *Ecclesia ecclesiæ decimas solvere non debet* (Cro. Eliz. 479).—A church ought not to pay tithes to a church.

215. *Ecclesia meliorari non deteriorari potest* (2 Eden, 313). —The church can make its condition better, but not worse.

216. *Ecclesia non moritur* (2 Inst. 3).—The Church does not die.

217. *Ei incumbit probatio qui dicit, non qui negat.*—The proof lies upon him who affirms, not upon him who denies.
> The rule is adopted because the negative does not admit of the direct and simple proof of which the affirmative is capable. (See Maxims 17, 42.)

218. *Ei qui affirmat, non ei qui negat, incumbit probatio.*— See previous maxim.

219. *Ejus nulla culpa est cui parere necesse sit* (D. 50, 17, 169).—He who is bound to obey is in no fault.
> As where the proper officer executes a criminal, or where an officer of justice, in the legal exercise of a particular duty, kills a person who resists. (See Maxim 491.)

220. *Electio semel facta non patitur regressum* (Co. Litt. 146a).—Election once made cannot be recalled.

221. *Eodem ligamine quo ligatum est dissolvitur* (Co. Litt. 212b).—A bond is released by the same formalities with which it is contracted.
> Although the obligor of a bond cannot, at the day appointed, pay a less sum in satisfaction of the whole, yet if the obligee then receive a part and give his acquittance under seal for the whole, this will be a good discharge (15 M. & W. 34). (See Maxims 609, 671.)

222. *Eodem modo quo quid constituitur, eodem modo destruitur* (6 Co. 53).—In the same way in which anything is constituted, it may be destroyed. (See Maxims 910, 450.)

223. *Episcopus alterius mandato quam regis non tenetur obtemperare* (Co. Litt. 134).—A bishop need not obey any mandate save the king's.

224. Error fucatus nudâ veritate in multis est probabilior; et sæpenumero rationibus vincit veritatem error (2 Co. 73).— Painted error appears in many things more probable than naked truth; and again and again conquers truth by reasoning.

225. Error qui non resistitur, approbatur (Doct. and Stud. c. 70).—An error which is not resisted, is approved.

Thus, one who enables another to commit a fraud is answerable. A person who has a title to property offered at auction, and, knowing his title, stands by and encourages the sale, or does not forbid it, will be bound by the sale. (See Maxims 130, 869, 870.)

226. Errores ad sua principia referre, est refellere (3 Inst. 15).—To refer errors to the principles, is to refute them.

227. Eventus est qui ex causâ sequitur; et dicitur eventus quia ex causis evenit (9 Co. 81).—An event is that which follows from the cause; and is called an event, because it results from causes.

228. Eventus varios res nova semper habet (Co. Litt. 379). —A new matter always induces various events.

229. Ex antecedentibus et consequentibus fit optima interpretatio (2 Inst. 317).—From that which goes before, and from that which follows, is derived the best interpretation.

The law will judge of a deed or other instrument consisting of divers parts or clauses by looking at the whole; and will give to each part its proper office, so as to ascertain and carry out the intention of the parties (Hob. 275). Thus in the case of a bond with a condition, the latter may be read and taken into consideration, in order to explain the obligatory part of the instrument. In construing a statute the intention of the law-giver and the meaning of the law are to be ascertained by viewing the whole and every part of the Act.

230. Exceptio ejus rei cujus petitur dissolutio nulla est (Jenk. Cent. 37).—There is no exception of that thing of which the dissolution is sought.

231. *Exceptio nulla est versus actionem quæ exceptionem perimit* (Jenk. Cent. 106).—There is no exception against an action which entirely destroys an exception.

232. *Exceptio probat regulam de rebus non exceptis* (11 Co. 41).—An exception proves the rule concerning things not excepted.

233. *Exceptio semper ultima ponenda est* (9 Co. 53).—An exception is always to be put last.

234. *Excessivum in jure reprobatur. Excessus in re qualibet jure reprobatur communi* (Co. 44).—Prolixity in law is reprehended. Prolixity in any fact is reprehended at common law.

235. *Excusat aut extenuat delictum in capitalibus quod non operatur idem in civilibus* (Bac. Max. Reg. 15).—A wrong, in capital cases, is excused or palliated, which would not be so treated in civil cases.

236. *Ex diuturnitate temporis omnia præsumuntur esse rite et solennitur acta* (Jenk. Cent. 185).—From lapse of time, all things are presumed to have been done rightly and regularly.

This maxim applies as well where matters are in contest between private persons as to matters public in their nature. Deeds, wills, and other attested documents which are more than thirty years old, and are produced from the proper custody, prove themselves, and the testimony of the subscribing witness may be dispensed with. The law will presume strongly in favour of the validity of a marriage, especially where a great length of time has elapsed since its celebration. It will also presume in favour of honesty and against fraud, and this presumption acquires weight from the length of time during which a transaction has subsisted.

237. *Ex dolo malo non oritur actio* (Cowp. 341).—From fraud a right of action does not arise.

A Court of law will not lend its aid to enforce the performance of a contract which appears to have been entered into by both the contracting parties for the express purpose of carrying into effect that which is prohibited by the law of the land, or is founded upon an immoral consideration. (See Maxims 259, 732.)

238. *Executio est finis et fructus legis* (Co. Litt. 289b).— Execution is the end and fruit of the law. (See Maxim 240.)

239. *Executio juris non habet injuriam* (2 Inst. 482).—The execution of the process of the law does no injury.
   If an action be brought in a Court which has jurisdiction upon insufficient grounds or against the wrong party, no injury is thereby done for which an action can be maintained; he is not to be esteemed a wrong-doer who merely avails himself of his legal rights. On the other hand, if an individual, under colour of the law, does an illegal act, or if he abuses the process of the Court to make it an instrument of oppression or extortion, this is a fraud upon the law, by the commission of which liability will be incurred. (See Maxim 18.)

240. *Executio est executio juris secundum judicium* (3 Inst. 212).—Execution is the execution of the law according to the judgment. (See Maxim 238.)

241. *Exempla illustrant, non restringunt, legem* (Co. Litt. 240).—Copies (of instruments) make the law clearer and do not destroy it.

242. *Ex facto jus oritur* (2 Inst. 49).—The law becomes operative after the fact.

243. *Ex maleficio non oritur contractus.*—A contract cannot arise out of an illegal act. (See Maxim 237.)

244. *Ex multitudine signorum colligitur identitas vera* (Bac. Works, vol. 4, p. 73).—True identity is collected from a number of signs.

245. *Ex non scripto jus venit quod usus comprobavit* (I. 1, 2, 9).—Law arises from custom which use has sanctioned.

246. *Ex nudo pacto non oritur actio* (Plow. Com. 305).—
From a nude contract—*i.e.* a contract without consideration—
an action does not arise.

" A consideration of some sort or another is so necessary
to the forming of a contract, that a *nudum pactum*, or
agreement to do or pay something on one side, without
any compensation on the other, will not at law support
an action; and a man cannot be compelled to perform
it " (2 Bl. Com. 445). Where indeed a promise is made
under seal, the solemnity of that mode of delivery is
held to import, at law, that there was a sufficient
consideration for the promise, so that the plaintiff is
not in this case required to prove a consideration; nor
can the deed be impeached by merely showing that it
was made without consideration, unless proof be given
that it originated in fraud.

247. *Ex pacto illicito non oritur actio.*—No action arises
out of an illicit bargain. (See Maxims 51, 237, 246.)

248. *Expedit reipublicæ ne sua re quis male utatur* (I. 1,
8, 2).—It is for the public good that no one should use his
property badly. (See Maxim 973.)

249. *Ex præcedentibus et consequentibus est optima interpretatio* (1 Rol. Rep. 375).—The best interpretation is made
from that which precedes and follows. (See Maxim 229.)

250. *Expressa nocent, non expressa non nocent* (D. 50, 17,
195).—Things expressed harm, things not expressed do not.

251. *Expressa non prosunt quæ non expressa proderunt*
(4 Co. 73).—Things expressed do no good, which, not
expressed, do no harm.

252. *Expressio eorum quæ tacitè insunt nihil operatur*
(Co. Litt. 210).—The expressing of those things which are
tacitly implied, is inoperative.

For instance, if land be let to two persons for the term of
their lives, this creates a joint tenancy; and the words

" and the survivor of them," if added, are mere surplusage, because by law the term would go to the survivor.

253. *Expressio unius personæ vel rei, est exclusio alterius* (Co. Litt. 210).—The express mention of one person or thing is the exclusion of another.

> Great caution is necessary in dealing with this maxim, for it is not of universal application, but depends upon the intention of the party as discoverable upon the face of the instrument or of the transaction; thus, where general words are used in a written instrument, it is necessary, in the first instance, to determine whether those general words are intended to include other matters besides such as are specifically mentioned, or to be referable exclusively to them, in which latter case only can the above maxim be properly applied. Where, moreover, an expression, which is *prima facie* a word of qualification, is introduced, the true meaning of the word can only be ascertained by an examination of the whole instrument, reference being had to the ordinary rules of construction.

254. *Expressum facit cessare tacitum* (Co. Litt. 183).— What is expressed makes what is silent to cease. (See Maxim 253.)

255. *Extortio est crimen quando quis colore officii extorquet quod non est debitum, vel supra debitum, vel ante tempus quod est debitum* (10 Co. 102).—Extortion is a crime, when, by colour of office, any person extorts that which is not due, or above due, or before the time when it is due.

256. *Extra legem positus est civiliter mortuus* (Co. Litt. 130a).—An outlaw is civilly dead.

257. *Extra territorium jus dicenti impune non paretur* (10 Co. 77).—The sentence of one adjudicating beyond his jurisdiction cannot be obeyed with impunity.

258. *Extraneus est subditus qui extra terram, i.e. potestatem regis, natus est* (7 Co. 16).—A foreigner is one who is born out of the territory—that is, the government—of the king.

259. *Ex turpi causâ non oritur actio* (Cowp. 343).—An action does not arise from a base cause. (See Maxim 237.)

260. *Facta tenent multa quæ fieri prohibentur* (12 Co. 125). —Deeds contain many things which are prohibited to be done.

261. *Factum à judice quod ad ejus officium non spectat, non ratum est* (10 Co. 76).—An action of a judge, which relates not to his office, is of no force.

262. *Facultas probationum non est angustanda* (4 Inst. 279).—The opportunity of proof is not to be narrowed. (See Maxim 652.)

263. *Falsa demonstratio non nocet* (6 T. R. 676).—A false description does not vitiate a document.

This rule signifies that where the description is made up of more than one part, and one part is true, but the other false, there, if the part which is true describes the subject with sufficient legal certainty, the untrue part will be rejected and will not vitiate the devise: the characteristic of cases within the rule being, that the description, so far as it is false, applies to no subject at all, and, so far as it is true, applies to one only. The rule has sometimes been stated to be that " if there be an adequate and sufficient description, with convenient certainty of what was meant to pass, a subsequent erroneous addition will not vitiate it " (4 Exch. 604). (See Maxims 557, 578, 663, 860.)

264. *Falsa demonstratione legatum non perimitur* (I. 2, 20, 30).—A legacy will not fail from a false description.

265. *Falsa orthographia, sive falsa grammatica non vitiat concessionem* (9 Co. 48).—False spelling or false grammar does not vitiate a grant. (See Maxim 557.)

266. *Falsus in uno, falsus in omnibus.*—False in one, false in all.

 This maxim may properly be applied in those cases only where a witness speaks to a fact with reference to which he cannot be presumed liable to mistake.

267. *Fatetur facinus qui judicium fugit* (3 Inst. 14).—He who flees judgment confesses his guilt.

268. *Favorabiliores rei potius quam actores habentur* (D. 50, 17, 125).—The condition of the defendant is to be favoured rather than that of the plaintiff.

269. *Favorabiliores sunt executiones aliis processibus quibuscunque* (Co. Litt. 289).—Executions are more preferred than all other processes whatever.

270. *Felonia implicatur in quálibet proditione* (3 Inst. 15). —Felony is implied in every treason.

271. *Felonia, ex vi termini, significat quodlibet capitale crimen felleo animo perpetratum* (Co. Litt. 391).—Felony, by force of the term, signifies some capital crime perpetrated with a malignant mind.

272. *Feodum est quod quis tenet ex quâcunque causâ, sive sit tenementum sive reditus* (Co. Litt. 1).—A fee is that which anyone holds, from whatever cause, whether it be a tenement or a rent.

273. *Feodum simplex quia feodum idem est quod hæreditas, et simplex idem est quod legitimum vel purum, et sic feodum simplex idem est quod hæreditas, legitima vel hæreditas pura* (Litt. § 1).—A fee-simple, so called because fee is the same as inheritance, and simple is the same as legitimate or pure ; and thus fee-simple is the same as a legitimate or pure inheritance.

274. *Feodum taliatum, i.e. hæreditas in quandam certitudinem limitata* (Litt. § 13).—Fee-tail—that is, an inheritance within a certain limit.

275. *Fere secundum promissorem interpretamur* (D. 45, 1, 99).—We generally infer in favour of the promissor.

> *Promissor* signified the person who contracted the obligation.

276. *Festinatio justitiæ est noverca infortunii* (Hob. 97).—Hasty justice is the stepmother of misfortune.

277. *Fiat justitia, ruat cœlum* (Dyer, 385).—Let right be done, though the heavens fall.

278. *Fictio cedit veritati: fictio juris non est ubi veritas* (11 Co. 51).—Fiction yields to truth: where there is truth, fiction of law does not exist.

279. *Fictio legis inique operatur alicui damnum vel injuriam* (3 Co. 36).—A legal fiction does not properly work loss or injury. (See Maxim 380.)

280. *Fictio legis neminem lædit* (3 Co. 36a).—A legal fiction must injure no one.

> Fictions are only to be made for necessity, and to avoid mischief.

281. *Filiatio non potest probari* (Co. Litt. 126).—Affiliation cannot be proved.

> When the mother is or has been married, her husband is presumed to be the father of the children born during the coverture, or within a competent time afterwards, whether they were conceived during the coverture or not.   (See Maxims 792, 966, 967b.)

282. *Finis rei attendendus est* (3 Inst. 51).—The end of a thing is to be attended to.

283. *Finis finem litibus imponit* (3 Co. 78).—The end puts an end to litigations.

284. *Finis unius diei est principium alterius* (2 Buls. 305).—The end of one day is the beginning of another.

285. *Firmior et potentior est operatio legis quàm dispositio hominis* (Co. Litt. 102).—The operation of the law is firmer and more powerful than the will of man.

Thus an agreement entered into between two persons cannot, in general, affect the rights of a third party; so, if it be agreed between A and B that B shall discharge a debt due from A to C, such an agreement cannot prevent C from suing A for its recovery. (See Maxim 292.)

286. *Flumina et portus publica sunt, ideoque jus piscandi omnibus commune est.*—Navigable rivers and ports are public; therefore the right of fishing there is common to all.

287. *Felix qui potuit rerum cognoscere causas* (Co. Litt. 231).—Happy is he who can apprehend the causes of things.

288. *Feminæ non sunt capaces de publicis officiis* (Jenk. Cent. 237).—Women are not able to hold public offices.

289. *Forma legalis forma essentialis* (10 Co. 100).—Legal form is an essential form. (See Maxims 167, 919.)

290. *Forma non observata infertur adnullatio actus* (12 Co. 7).—Form not being observed, a nullity of the act is inferred.

291. *Fortior est custodia legis quam hominis* (2 Rol. Rep. 325).—The custody of the law is stronger than that of man.

292. *Fortior et potentior est dispositio legis quam hominis* (Co. Litt. 234).—The will of the law is more resolute and more powerful than that of man. (See Maxim 285.)

293. *Fractionem diei non recipit lex* (Lofft, 572).—The law does not regard the fraction of a day. (See Maxim 183.)

294. *Frater fratri uterino non succedet in hæreditate paternâ* (*Fort. de Laud*, by Amos, 15).—A brother shall not succeed a brother by the mother's side in the paternal inheritance.

The law, however, was entirely altered by the Inheritance Act, 1833, s. 9, which enables the half-blood to inherit after any relation in the same degree of the whole blood and his issue, where the common ancestor is a male, and next after the common ancestor where a female, so that the brother of the half-blood on the part of the father shall inherit next after the sisters of the whole blood on the part of the father and their issue, and the brother of the half-blood on the part of the mother shall inherit next after the mother.

295. *Fraus est celare fraudem* (1 Vern. 270).—It is fraud to conceal fraud. (See Maxims 130, 869, 336.)

296. *Fraus est odiosa et non præsumenda* (Cro. Car. 550). —Fraud is hateful and not to be presumed.

297. *Fraus et dolus nemini patrocinari debent* (3 Co. 78b). —Fraud and deceit ought not to benefit anyone. (See Maxims 732, 891.)

298. *Fraus et jus nunquam cohabitant* (Wing. 680).—Fraud and justice never dwell together. (See Maxim 469.)

299. *Frequentia actus multum operatur* (4 Co. 78).—The frequency of an act operates much.

300. *Frustrà fit per plura, quod fieri potest per pauciora* (Jenk. 61).—That is uselessly done by more (words) which may be done by fewer.

301. *Frustrà legis auxilium quærit qui in legem committit* (2 Hale P.C. 386).—He who offends against the law vainly seeks the help of the law.

302. *Frustrà probatur quod probatum non relevat* (Halk. Max. 50).—It is useless to prove that which, being proved, would not avail.

303. *Furiosi nulla voluntas est* (D. 50, 17, 5).—A madman has no free will.

> There must be as an essential ingredient in a criminal offence some blameworthy condition of mind, and such condition of mind cannot justly be imputed to madmen who are under a natural disability of distinguishing between good and evil.

11

304. *Furiosus absentis loco est* (D. 50, 17, 124).—
A madman is like a man who is absent.

305. *Furiosus solo furore punitur* (Co. Litt. 247).—
A madman is only punished by his madness.

306. *Furiosus stipulare non potest, nec aliquid negotium agere, qui non intelligit quid agit* (4 Co. 126).—A madman, who knows not what he does, cannot make a bargain, nor transact any business.

307. *Furtum est contrectatio rei alienæ fraudulenta, cum animo furandi, invito illo domino cujus res illa fuerat* (3 Inst. 107).—A theft is the fraudulent handling of another's property with an intention of stealing, the proprietor, whose property it was, not willing it.

308. *Furtum non est ubi initium habet detentionis per dominum rei* (3 Inst. 107).—It is not theft where the commencement of the detention arises through the will of the owner of the thing detained.

309. *Generale dictum generaliter est interpretandum: generalia verba sunt generaliter intelligenda* (3 Inst. 76).—A general saying is to be interpreted generally: general words are to be understood generally.

310. *Generale nihil certi implicat* (2 Co. 33).—A general expression implies nothing certain.

311. *Generale tantum valet in generalibus quantum singulare in singulis* (11 Co. 59).—What is general prevails as much amongst things general as what is particular amongst things particular.

312. *Generalia specialibus non derogant* (Jenk. Cent. 120).
—General things do not derogate from special.

> Special Acts are not repealed by general Acts unless there be some express reference to the previous legislation, or a necessary inconsistency in the two Acts standing together, which prevents the maxim from being applied. (See Maxims 968, 988.)

313. *Generalia verba sunt generaliter intelligenda* (3 Inst. 76).—General words are to be understood generally.

Unless qualified by some special subsequent words, as they may be—*e.g.* the operative words of a bill of sale may be restricted by what follows.

314. *Generalibus specialia derogant* (Halk. 51).—Special things derogate from general. (See Maxim 312.)

315. *Generalis clausula non porrigitur ad ea quæ antea specialiter sunt comprehensa* (8 Co. 154).—A general clause does not extend to those things which are before specially provided for.

316. *Generalis regula generaliter est intelligenda* (6 Co. Rep. 65).—A general rule is to be understood generally. (See Maxim 426.)

317. *Habemus optimum testem confitentem reum* (Fost. Cr. L. 243).—We have the best witness in an accused who confesses the charge.

" What is taken *pro confesso* is taken as indubitable truth. The plea of guilty by the party accused shuts out all further inquiry. *Habemus confitentem reum* is demonstration, unless indirect motives can be assigned to it " (*Mortimer* v. *Mortimer*, 2 Hagg. 315).

318. *Hæreditas, alia corporalis, alia incorporalis: corporalis est, quæ tangi potest et videri; incorporalis quæ tangi non potest nec videri* (Co. Litt. 9).—Inheritance, some corporeal, others incorporeal: corporeal is that which can be touched and seen; incorporeal, that which can neither be touched nor seen.

319. *Hæreditas est successio in universum jus quod defunctus habuerat* (Co. Litt. 237).—Inheritance is the succession to every right which was possessed by the late possessor.

320. *Hæreditas nunquam ascendit* (Glanville, 1. 7, c. 1).—Inheritance never ascends.

This feudal maxim was altered by the Inheritance Act, 1833.

321. *Hæredum appellatione veniunt hæredes hæredum in infinitum* (Co. Litt. 9).—By the title of heirs come the heirs of heirs *in infinitum*.

322. *Hæres est aut jure proprietatis, aut jure repræsentationis* (3 Co. 40).—An heir is by right of property, or by right of representation.

323. *Hæres est eadem persona cum antecessore, pars antecessoris* (Co. Litt. 22).—The heir is the same person with his ancestor, a part of his ancestor.

324. *Hæres est nomen collectivum* (1 Vent. 215).—Heir is a collective name.

325. *Hæres est nomen juris, filius est nomen naturæ* (Bacon Max. Reg. 11).—Heir is a name of law, son is a name of nature. (See Maxims 190, 326.)

326. *Hæres legitimus est quem nuptiæ demonstrant* (Co. Litt. 7).—The lawful heir is he whom wedlock shows so to be.
By the common law no one can inherit any land who was not born after the lawful marriage of the parents. It excludes the rule of the civil and canon law (Maxim 792), which legitimises the children born out of wedlock by the subsequent marriage between the father and mother. (See Maxim 190.)

327. *Hæres minor uno et viginti annis non respondebit, nisi in casu dotis* (Moor, 348).—An heir minor under twenty-one years of age is not answerable, except in case of dower.

328. *Home ne serra puny pur suer des briefes en court le roy, soit il a droit ou a tort* (2 Inst. 228).—A man shall not be punished for suing out writs in the king's court, whether he has a right or a wrong.

329. *Homicidium vel hominis cædium, est hominis occisio ab homine facta* (3 Inst. 54).—Homicide or slaughter of a man, is the killing of a man by a man.

330. *Homo potest esse habilis et inhabilis diversis temporibus* (5 Co. 98).—A man may be capable and incapable at different times.

331. *Hostes sunt qui nobis vel quibus nos bellum decernimus; cæteri proditores vel prædones sunt* (7 Co. 24).—Enemies are those with whom we are at war; all others are traitors or robbers.

332. *Ibi semper debet fieri triatio, ubi juratores meliorem possunt habere notitiam* (7 Co. 1).—A trial should always be had where the jury can get the best information.

333. *Id certum est quod certum reddi potest; sed id magis certum est quod de semet ipso est certum* (9 Co. 47).—That is certain which can be made certain, but that is most certain which is certain on the face of it. (See Maxim 101.)

334. *Idem agens et patiens esse non potest* (Jenk. Cent. 40).—The same person cannot be both the agent and the patient.

335. *Idem est facere et non prohibere cum possis; et qui non prohibet cum prohibere possit in culpâ est* (3 Inst. 158).—To commit and not prohibit, when in your power, is the same thing; and he who does not, when he can prohibit, is in fault. (See Maxims 43, 161, 869.)

336. *Idem est nihil dicere et insufficienter dicere* (2 Inst. 178).—It is the same thing to say nothing and not to say sufficient. (See Maxims 295, 869.)

337. *Idem est non esse et non apparere* (Jenk. Cent. 207).—It is the same not to exist as not to appear.

    In general, land gained *per alluvionem* belongs to the Crown, as having been a part of the very *fundus maris*; but if such alluvion be formed so imperceptibly and insensibly that it cannot by any means be ascertained that the sea ever was there, the above maxim applies, and the land thus formed belongs as a perquisite to the owner of the land adjacent. (See Maxim 185.)

338. *Idem semper antecedenti proximo refertur* (Co. Litt. 20.)—The same is always referred to its next antecedent.

339. *Id perfectum est quod ex omnibus suis partibus constat; et nihil perfectum est dum aliquid restat, agendum*

(9 Co. 9).—That is perfect which is complete in all its parts; and nothing is perfect whilst anything remains to be done.

340. *Id possumus quod de jure possumus* (Lane, 116).—We may do what the law allows us to do.

341. *Id quod commune est, nostrum esse dicitur.*—That which is common is said to be ours.

> This maxim covers the contract of marine insurance by one partner, without a specification of the interest he means to cover, in which case Valin considers the insurance should extend to the whole cargo.

342. *Id quod est magis remotum non trahit ad se quod est magis junctum, sed è contrario in omni casu* (Co. Litt. 164).— That which is more remote does not draw to itself that which is nearer, but on the contrary in every case.

344. *Ignorantia eorum quæ quis scire tenetur non excusat* (Hale Pl. Cr. 42).—Ignorance of those things which everyone is bound to know, excuses not.

345. *Ignorantia facti excusat; ignorantia juris non excusat* (1 Co. 177).—Ignorance of the fact excuses; ignorance of the law does not excuse.

> Although ignorance of the law does not excuse persons so as to exempt them from the consequences of their acts—as, for example, from punishment for a criminal offence or from damages for breach of contract—yet the law takes notice that there may be a doubtful point of law, of the true solution of which a person may be ignorant. (See Maxim 534.)

346. *Ignorantia judicis est calamitas innocentis* (2 Inst. 591).—The ignorance of a judge is the misfortune of the innocent.

347. *Ignorantia juris quod quisque scire tenetur non excusat* (2 Co. Rep. 3*b*).—Ignorance of the law which everybody is supposed to know does not afford excuse.

348. *Ignorantia legis neminem excusat.*—Ignorance of the law does not afford excuse.

349. *Illud quod alias licitum non est necessitas facit licitum; et necessitas inducit privilegium quod jure privatur* (10 Co. 61).—That which is otherwise not permitted, necessity permits; and necessity makes a privilege which supersedes law. (See Maxims 219, 610-617.)

350. *Imperitia culpæ adnumeratur* (D. 50, 17, 132).— Inexperience is accounted a fault.

351. *Impossibilium nulla obligatio est* (D. 50, 17, 185).— There is no obligation to do impossible things.

> Where the consideration for a promise is such that its performance is naturally impossible, such consideration is insufficient, for no benefit can be conferred on the promissor.

352. *Impotentia excusat legem* (Co. Litt. 29).—Impotency excuses law.

> Where the law creates a duty or charge, and the party is disabled to perform it without any default in him, and has no remedy over, there the law will in general excuse him; and though impossibility of performance is in general no excuse for not performing an obligation which a party has expressly undertaken by contract, yet when the obligation is one implied by law impossibility of performance is a good excuse. (See Maxim 68.)

353. *Improbi rumores dissipati sunt rebellionis prodromi* (2 Inst. 226).—Wicked rumours spread abroad are the fore-runners of rebellion.

354. *Impunitas semper ad deteriora invitat* (5 Co. 69).— Impunity always invites to greater crimes. (See Maxims 581, 1040.)

355. *In æquali jure melior est conditio possidentis* (Plow. 296).—In equal rights the condition of the possessor is the better; or, where the rights of the parties are equal, the claim of the actual possessor shall prevail.

> The general rule is that possession constitutes a sufficient title against every person not having a better title. Hence, in ejectment the party controverting my title

must recover by his own strength, and not by my weakness. This maxim applies alike to equity and law, and embraces the case of fraudulent and illegal agreements, conveyances and transfers of property, and as well where the parties are *in pari delicto* as *in æquali jure*. (See Maxims 396, 574.)

356. *In altâ proditione nullus potest esse accessorius sed principalis solummodo* (3 Inst. 138).—In high treason there is no accessory, but principal alone.

357. *In ambiguâ voce legis ea potius accipienda est significatio quæ vitio caret, præsertim cum etiam voluntas legis ex hoc colligi possit* (Bac. Max. Reg. 3).—In an ambiguous expression of law, that signification is to be preferred which is consonant with equity, especially when the spirit of the law can be collected from that.

358. *In ambiguis orationibus maxime sententia spectanda est ejus qui eas protulisset* (D. 50, 17, 96).—In ambiguous expressions the intention of him who used them should especially be regarded. (See Maxim 164.)

359. *In Angliâ non est interregnum* (Jenk. Cent. 205).—In England there is no interregnum.
The sovereign always exists; the person only is changed. (See Maxim 952.)

360. *In atrocioribus delictis, punitur affectus licet non sequatur effectus* (2 Rol. Rep. 89).—In more atrocious crimes the intent is punished, though an effect does not follow.

361. *In casu extremæ necessitatis omnia sunt communia* (H. P. C. 54).—In cases of extreme necessity, everything is in common. (See Maxims 452, 958, 509, 615.)
There are many cases in which individuals sustain an injury for which the law gives no action; as where private houses are pulled down, or bulwarks raised on private property for the preservation and defence of the kingdom against the king's enemies or to arrest the progress of a fire. If a highway be out of repair a passenger may lawfully go over the adjoining land.

362. *Incerta pro nullis habentur* (Dav. 33).—What is not proved is reckoned as nothing. (See Maxim 896.)

363. *Incerta quantitas vitiat actum* (1 Rol. Rep. 465).—An uncertain quantity vitiates the act.

364. *Incivile est nisi totâ sententiâ perspectâ de aliquâ parte judicare* (Hob. 171).—It is unjust to judge of any part unless the whole sentence is examined.

365. *Inclusio unius est exclusio alterius* (Co. Litt. 210).— The inclusion of one is the exclusion of another.

366. *In consimili casu, consimile debet esse remedium* (Hard. 65).—In similar cases the remedy should be similar. (See Maxims 189, 497.)

367. *In consuetudinibus non diuturnitas temporis sed soliditas rationis est consideranda* (Co. Litt. 141).—In customs, not the length of time but the strength of the reason should be considered.

368. *In contractibus tacitè insunt quæ sunt moris et consuetudinis.*—In contracts, those things which are of manner and custom are considered as incorporated.

> For instance, an architect or builder may employ a surveyor to make out the quantities of the building proposed to be erected.

369. *In contractibus, benigna; in testamentis, benignior; in restitutionibus, benignissima interpretatio facienda est* (Co. Litt. 112).—In contracts, the interpretation is to be liberal; in wills, more liberal; in restitutions, most liberal.

370. *In conventionibus contrahentium voluntas potius quam verba spectari placuit.*—In agreements the intention of the parties, rather than the words actually used, should be considered.

371. *In criminalibus probationes debent esse luce clariores* (3 Inst. 210).—In criminal cases the proofs ought to be clearer than light.

372. *In criminalibus sufficit generalis malitia intentionis cum facto paris gradûs* (Bac. Max. Reg. 15).—In criminal actions a general malice of intention is sufficient with an act of corresponding degree.

> If the malefactor conceive a malicious intent in the execution of which he does harm to another person he is equally guilty, although he had no intention of doing that particular person an injury.

373. *In criminalibus voluntas reputabitur pro facto* (3 Inst. 106).—In criminal acts the will is taken for the deed.

> The will is not to be taken for the deed unless there be some external act which shows that progress has been made in the direction of it, or towards maturing or effecting it.

374. *Indefinitum equipollet universali* (1 Vent. 368).—The indefinite equals the universal.

375. *Indefinitum supplet locum universalis* (4 Co. 77).— The indefinite supplies the place of the universal.

376. *Index animi sermo est.*—Speech is the indication of thought.

377. *In disjunctivis sufficit alteram partem esse veram* (Wing. 13).—In disjunctives it suffices if either part be true.

> Where a condition inserted in a deed consists of two parts in the conjunctive, both must be performed, but otherwise where the condition is in the disjunctive.

378. *In eo, quod plus sit, semper inest et minus* (D. 50, 17, 110).—The greater always includes the less. (See Maxims 389, 423, 554, 746.)

379. *In favorem vitæ libertatis et innocentiæ omnia præsumuntur* (Lofft, 125).—In favour of life, liberty, and innocence all things are to be presumed.

380. *In fictione juris semper æquitas existit* (11 Co. 51).— In fiction of law equity always exists. (See Maxims 279, 280.)

381. *Infinitum in jure reprobatur* (9 Co. 45).—Want of finality in law is reprehensible. (See Maxims 448, 633.)

382. *In generalibus latet error.*—Error lurks in general expressions.

383. *In judicio non creditur nisi juratis* (Cro. Car. 64).—In judicial procedure there is no credit, save to things sworn.

384. *In jure non remota causa, sed proxima spectatur* (Bac. Max.: Reg. 1).—In law the proximate, and not the remote, cause is to be regarded.

> In order to entitle the assured to recover upon his policy of marine insurance, the loss must be a direct and not too remote a consequence of the peril insured against, and if the proximate cause of the loss be not reducible to some one of the perils mentioned in the policy the underwriter is not liable. In actions founded on negligence the plaintiff must generally prove that the defendant's negligence was the proximate and not merely a remote cause of the damage. (See Maxim 95.)

385. *In jure omnis definitio periculosa est.*—In law every definition is dangerous.

386. *Injuria illata judici, seu locum tenenti regis, videtur ipsi regi illata, maximè si fiat in exercente officium* (3 Inst. 1).— An injury offered to a judge, or person representing the king, is considered as offered to the king himself, especially if it be done in the exercise of his office.

387. *Injuria non excusat injuriam.*—One wrong does not justify another. (See Maxims 695, 732.)

388. *Injuria non præsumitur* (Co. Litt. 232).—Injury is not to be presumed.

389. *In majore summâ continetur minor* (5 Co. Rep. 115). —In the greater sum of money is contained the less. (See Maxims 378, 554, 746, 423.)

390. *In maleficiis voluntas, non exitus, spectatur* (D. 48, 8, 14).—In evil deeds regard must be had to the intention and not to the result.

391. *In novo casu, novum remedium apponendum est* (2 Inst. 3).—A new remedy is to be applied to a new case. (See Maxim 1028.)

392. *In odium spoliatoris omnia præsumuntur* (1 Vern. 19). —All things are presumed in odium of a despoiler. (See Maxim 754.)

393. *In omnibus quidem, maxime tamen in jure, æquitas spectanda sit* (D. 50, 17, 90).—In everything, but especially in law, equity is to be regarded.

394. *In omni re nascitur res quæ ipsam rem exterminat* (2 Inst. 15).—In everything is born that which destroys the thing itself.

395. *In pari causâ possessor potior haberi debet* (D. 50, 17, 128).—In an equal cause the possessor ought to have the stronger claim. (See Maxim 355.)

396. *In pari delicto, potior est conditio possidentis* (or *defendentis*) (4 T. R. 564).—In equal fault, the condition of the possessor (*or* defendant) is the best. (See Maxims 355, 574.)

397. *In pœnalibus causis benignius interpretandum est* (D. 50, 17, 155).—In penal causes the interpretation ought to be the more favourable. (See Maxim 1023.)

398. *In præparatoriis ad judicium favetur actori* (2 Inst. 57). —In things preceding judgment the plaintiff is favoured.

399. *In præsentiâ majoris cessat potentia minoris* (Jenk. Cent. 214).—In the presence of the greater, the power of the inferior ceases.

Usually cited with special reference to the transcendent nature of the powers vested in the King's Bench, which Court keeps all inferior jurisdictions within the bounds of their authority and corrects irregularities in their proceedings.

400. *In quo quis delinquit, in eo de jure est puniendus* (Co. Litt. 233).—In that in which anyone offends, in that according to law is he to be punished.

401. *In rebus quæ sunt favorabilia animæ, quamvis sunt damnosa rebus, fiat aliquando extensio statuti* (10 Co. 101).—In things that are favourable to the spirit, though injurious to the things, an extension of a statute should sometimes be made.

402. *In re dubiâ magis inficiatio quam affirmatio intelligenda* (Godb. 37).—In a doubtful case the negative is rather to be understood than the affirmative. (See Maxim 217.)

> This is because the burden of proof is upon him who affirms rather than upon him who denies, a negative being more difficult of proof than an affirmative.

403. *In republicâ maximè conservanda sunt jura belli* (2 Inst. 58).—The laws of war are especially to be preserved in the State.

404. *In restitutionem, non in pœnam hæres succedit* (2 Inst. 198).—The heir succeeds to the restitution, not to the penalty.

405. *Instans est finis unius temporis et principium alterius* (Co. Litt. 185).—An instant is the end of one time, and the beginning of another.

406. *In stipulationibus cum quæritur quid actum sit verba contra stipulatorem interpretanda sunt* (D. 45, 1, 38).—In the construction of contracts words are interpreted against the person using them.

> A maxim of the civil law. In case of doubt the construction of the *stipulatio* was against the *stipulator*, because the person stipulating should take care fully to express that which he proposes shall be done for his own benefit. (See Maxims 275, 1046.)

407. *Intentio cæca mala* (2 Bulst. 179).—A hidden intention is bad. (See *Wigram on Wills*, p. 98.)

408. *Intentio inservire debet legibus, non leges intentioni* (Co. Litt. 314).—Intention ought to be subservient to the laws; not the laws to intention. (See Maxim 421.)

409. *Inter arma leges silent.*—In war the laws remain inactive.

The law of military necessity supersedes all civil law, and in time of war administration of the municipal law may be suspended.

410. *Interest reipublicæ ne maleficia remaneant impunita* (Jenk. Cent. 31).—It concerns the State that evil deeds shall not remain unpunished.

411. *Interest reipublicæ quod homines conserventur* (12 Co. 62).—It concerns the State that men be preserved.

412. *Interest reipublicæ res judicatas non rescindi* (2 Inst. 359).—It concerns the State that judgments be not rescinded. (See Maxims 448, 633, 934.)

413. *Interest reipublicæ suprema hominum testamenta rata haberi* (Co. Litt. 236).—It concerns the State that men's last wills be confirmed. (See Maxims 421, 1012, 1034.)

414. *Interest reipublicæ ut quilibet re suâ bene utatur* (6 Co. 37).—It is to the advantage of the State that everyone uses his property properly. (See Maxims 32, 973.)

415. *Interest reipublicæ ut sit finis litium* (Co. Litt. 303).— It concerns the State that lawsuits be not protracted.

The doctrine of limitation of actions may be referred to this maxim. (See Maxims 412, 934.)

416. *Interpretare et concordare leges legibus est optimus interpretandi modus* (8 Co. 169).—To interpret and to reconcile the laws to laws is the best mode of interpretation. (See Maxim 418.)

417. *Interpretatio chartarum benigne facienda est ut res magis valeat quam pereat.*—The construction of a deed is to be made liberally, that the thing may rather avail than perish. (See Maxim 82.)

418. *Interpretatio fienda est ut res magis valeat quam pereat* (Jenk. Cent. 198).—That interpretation is to be made that the thing may rather stand than fall. (See Maxim 82.)

419. *Interpretatio talis in ambiguis semper fienda est, ut evitetur inconveniens et absurdum* (4 Inst. 328).—In ambiguous things such an interpretation is to be made, that what is inconvenient and absurd is to be avoided.

420. *Interruptio multiplex non tollit præscriptionem semel obtentam* (2 Inst. 654).—Frequent interruption does not take away a prescription once acquired.

421. *In testamentis plenius testatoris intentionem scrutamur* (3 Bulst. 103).—In wills we seek diligently the intention of the testator.
> The paramount principle in construing wills is the intention of the testator. (See Maxims 82, 413, 1012, 1034.)

423. *In toto et pars continetur* (D. 50, 17, 113).—In the whole a part is also contained. (See Maxims 378, 389, 554, 746.)

424. *In traditionibus scriptorum, non quod dictum est sed quod gestum est inspicitur* (9 Co. 137).—In the delivery of deeds, not what is said but what is done is regarded.
> A document under seal may be delivered to a third person, to be delivered by him to the grantee when the latter has performed certain specified conditions. The gist of the above maxim is that no words, however binding, will take the place of delivery which may be absolute or conditional. (See Maxim 1019b.)

425. *Inveniens libellum famosum et non corrumpens punitur* (Moor. 813).—He who meets with a notorious libel, and does not destroy it, is punished.

426. *In verbis non verba sed res et ratio quærenda est* (Jenk. Cent. 132).—In words, not the words but the thing and the meaning are to be inquired after. (See Maxim 316.)

427. *Invito beneficium non datur* (D. 50, 17, 69).—A benefit is not conferred upon anyone against his consent.
> Every man may renounce a benefit or waive a privilege which the law has conferred upon him.

428. *Ita semper fiat relatio ut valeat dispositio* (6 Co. Rep. 76).—Let the interpretation be always such that the disposition may prevail. (See Maxim 417.)

429. *Judex æquitatem semper spectare debet* (Jenk. Cent. 45).—A judge ought always to regard equity.

430. *Judex bonus nihil ex arbitrio suo faciat, nec propositione domesticæ voluntatis, sed juxta leges et jura pronunciet* (7 Co. 27).—A good judge does nothing from his own judgment, or from a dictate of private will; but he will pronounce according to law and justice.

431. *Judex est lex loquens* (7 Co. 4).—A judge is the law speaking. (See Maxim 502.)

432. *Judex habere debet duos sales: salem sapientiæ, ne sit insipidus, et salem conscientiæ, ne sit diabolus* (3 Inst. 147). —A judge should have two salts: the salt of wisdom, lest he be insipid; and the salt of conscience, lest he be devilish.

433. *Judex non potest esse testis in propriâ causâ* (4 Inst. 279).—A judge cannot be a witness in his own cause. (See Maxims 434, 635, 709.)

434. *Judex non potest injuriam sibi datam punire* (12 Co. 113).—A judge cannot punish an injury done to himself. (See Maxim 635.)

435. *Judex non reddit plus quam quod petens ipse requirit* (2 Inst. 286).—A judge does not give more than that which the plaintiff requires.

436. *Judices non tenentur exprimere causam sententiæ suæ* (Jenk. Cent. 75).—Judges are not bound to explain the reason of their sentence. (See Maxim 2.)

437. *Judici officium suum excedenti non paretur* (Jenk. Cent. 139).—To a judge exceeding his office there is no obedience.

438. *Judicia in deliberationibus crebro maturescunt, in accelerato processu nunquam* (3 Inst. 210).—Judgments become frequently matured by deliberations, never by hurried process.

439. *Judicia sunt tanquam juris dicta, et pro veritate accipiuntur* (2 Inst. 537).—Judgments are as it were the *dicta* of the law, and are received as truth.

440. *Judiciis posterioribus fides est adhibenda* (13 Co. 14).— Credit is to be given to the latest decisions. (See Maxim 934.)

441. *Judicis est judicare secundum allegata et probata* (Dyer, 12).—It is the duty of a judge to decide according to facts alleged and proved. (See Maxim 431.)

442. *Judicis est jus dicere, non dare* (Lofft, 42).—It is for the judge to administer, not to make law. (See Maxim 761.)

443. *Judicis officium est opus diei in die suo perficere* (2 Inst. 256).—It is the duty of a judge to finish the work of each day within that day.

444. *Judicis officium est ut res ita tempora rerum quærere, quæsito tempore tutus eris* (Co. Litt. 171).—It is the duty of a judge to inquire as well into the time of things as into things themselves; by inquiring into the time you will be safe.

445. *Judicium a non suo judice datum nullius est momenti* (10 Co. 76).—A judgment given by an improper judge is of no importance. (See Maxim 864.)

446. *Judicium non debet esse illusorium; suum effectum habere debet* (2 Inst. 341).—A judgment ought not to be illusory; it ought to have its consequence.

447. *Judicium redditur in invitum, in præsumptione legis* (Co. Litt. 248).—Judgment in presumption of law is given contrary to inclination.

448. *Judicium semper pro veritate accipitur* (2 Inst. 380).— A judgment (once given) is accepted as true. (See Maxim 412.)

449. *Jura ecclesiastica limitata sunt infra limites separatos* (3 Buls. 53).—Ecclesiastical laws are limited within separate bounds.

450. *Jura eodem modo destituuntur quo constituuntur* (2 Dwarr. Stat. 672).—Laws are abrogated by the same means by which they were made. (See Maxim 222.)

451. *Jura naturæ sunt immutabilia* (Jacob. 63).—The laws of nature are unchangeable. (See Maxim 533.)

452. *Jura publica anteferenda privatis* (Co. Litt. 130).—Public rights are to be preferred to private. (See Maxims 361, 958.)

453. *Jura publica ex privato promiscue decidi*non debent* (Co. Litt. 181b).—Public rights ought not to be promiscuously decided out of a private transaction.

454. *Jura regis specialia non conceduntur per generalia verba* (Jenk. Cent. 103).—The special rights of the king are not yielded by general words.

455. *Jura sanguinis nullo jure civili dirimi possunt* (Bac. Max. Reg. 11).—The rights of blood cannot be destroyed by any civil right. (See Maxim 800.)

456. *Juramentum est indivisibile, et non est admittendum in parte verum et in parte falsum* (4 Inst. 279).—An oath is indivisible, and is not to be received as partly true and partly false. (See Maxims 459, 748.)

457. *Jurato creditur in judicio* (3 Inst. 79).—In judgment credit is given to the swearer.

458. *Juratores debent esse vicini, sufficientes, et minus suspecti* (Jenk. Cent. 141).—Jurors ought to be neighbours, of sufficient estate, and free from suspicion.

459. *Jurare est Deum in testem vocare, et est actus divini cultus* (3 Inst. 165).—To swear is to call God to witness, and is an act of Divine worship. (See Maxim 689.)

460. *Juratores sunt judices facti* (Jenk. Cent. 61).—Juries are the judges of fact.

461. *Jure naturæ æquum est neminem cum alterius detrimento et injuriâ fieri locupletiorem* (D. 50, 17, 206).—By the law of nature it is not just that anyone should be enriched by the loss or injury of another.

462. *Juri non est consonum quod aliquis accessorius in curiâ regis convincatur antequam aliquis de facto fuerit attinctus* (2 Inst. 183).—It is not consonant to justice that any accessory should be convicted in the king's court before some one has been attainted of the fact.

463. *Juris effectus in executione consistit* (Co. Litt. 289).— The effect of law depends upon execution.

464. *Jus accrescendi inter mercatores, pro beneficio commercii locum non habet* (Co. Litt. 182).—For the benefit of commerce, there is not any right of survivorship among merchants.

> A rule of the law merchant, which evidently favours alienation, by rendering the capital invested by the partners in their trade applicable to the purposes of their partnership, and available to the creditors of the firm. (See Maxim 45.)

465. *Jus accrescendi præfertur oneribus* (Co. Litt. 185).— The right of survivorship is preferred to incumbrances.

466. *Jus accrescendi præfertur ultimæ voluntati* (Co. Litt. 185).—The right of survivorship is preferred to the last will.

467. *Jus constitui oportet in his quæ ut plurimum accidunt, non quæ ex inopinato* (D. 1, 3, 3).—Law ought to be made with a view to those cases which happen most frequently, and not to those which are unexpected. (See Maxim 27.)

468. *Jus descendit, et non terra* (Co. Litt. 345).—The right descends and not the land.

469. *Jus est norma recti; et quicquid est contra normam recti est injuria* (3 Buls. 313).—Law is a rule of right; and whatever is contrary to the rule of right is a wrong. (See Maxim 298.)

470. *Jus ex injuriâ non oritur* (4 Bing. 639).—A right does not arise out of a wrong. (See Maxims 237, 259.)

471. *Jusjurandi forma verbis differt, re convenit; hunc enim sensum habere debet, ut Deus invocetur* (Grotius l. 2. c. 13,

§ 10).—The form of taking an oath, though it differs in words, agrees in meaning; for it ought to have this sense, that the Deity be invoked.

472. *Jusjurandum inter alios factum nec nocere nec prodesse debet* (4 Inst. 279).—An oath made by others in another proceeding ought neither to hurt nor profit. (See Maxim 932.)

473. *Jus naturale est quod apud omnes homines eandem habet potentiam* (7 Co. 12).—Natural right is that which has the same force among all men. (See Maxim 488.)

474. *Jus non habenti tute non paretur* (Hob. 146).—It is not safe to obey him who has no right. (See Maxim 491.)

475. *Jus publicum et privatum est quod ex naturalibus præceptis, aut gentium, aut civilibus est collectum et quod in jure scripto jus appellatur, id in lege Angliæ rectum esse dicitur* (Co. Litt. 158).—Public and private law is that which is collected from natural principles, either of nations or in States; and what in written law is called " *jus* " by the law of England is said to be right.

476. *Jus respicit æquitatem* (Co. Litt. 24).—Law regards equity.

477. *Jus superveniens auctori accrescit successori* (Halk. 76).—A right growing to a possessor accrues to the successor. (See Maxim 861.)

478. *Justitia debet esse libera, quia nihil iniquius venali justitia; plena, quia justitia non debet claudicare; et celeris, quia dilatio est quædam negatio* (2 Inst. 56).—Justice ought to be unbought, because nothing is more hateful than venal justice; full, for justice ought not to be defective; and quick, for delay is a certain denial.

479. *Justitia est duplex; viz. severè puniens et verè præveniens* (3 Inst. Epil.).—Justice is double; punishing with severity, preventing with lenity.

480. *Justitia firmatur solium* (3 Inst. 140).—Justice strengthens the throne.

481. *Justitia nemini neganda est* (Jenk. Cent. 178).—Justice is to be denied to none.

That which is accorded to some and denied to others is not justice. (See Maxims 517, 520, 535.)

482. *Justitia non est neganda, non differenda* (Jenk. Cent. 93).—Justice is neither to be denied nor postponed.

483. *Justitia non novit patrem nec matrem, solam veritatem spectat justitia* (1 Buls. 199).—Justice knows neither father nor mother, but regards truth alone. (See Maxims 517, 535.)

484. *Justum non est aliquem antenatum mortuum facere bastardum qui pro totâ vitâ suâ pro legitimo habetur* (8 Co. 101).—It is not just to make an elder-born a bastard after his death, who all his life has been accounted legitimate. (See Maxim 691.)

485. *Legatus regis vice fungitur à quo destinatur et honorandus est sicut ille cujus vicem gerit* (12 Co. 17).—An ambassador fills the place of the king by whom he is sent, and is to be honoured as he is whose place he fills.

486. *Leges Angliæ sunt tripartitæ: jus commune, consuetudines, ac decreta comitiorum.*—The laws of England are threefold: common law, customs, and decrees of Parliament.

487. *Leges posteriores priores contrarias abrogant* (1 Co. 25).—Later laws abrogate prior contrary laws.

An earlier Act must give place to a later if the two cannot be reconciled, and one Act may repeal another by express words or by implication. Where the common law and the statute differ, the common law gives place to the statute so far as they are repugnant.

488. *Legibus sumptis desinentibus, lege naturæ utendum est* (2 Rol. Rep. 98).—Laws imposed by the State failing, we must act by the law of nature. (See Maxim 473.)

489. *Legis constructio non facit injuriam* (Co. Litt. 183).—The construction of the law does no injury.

490. *Legislatorum est viva vox rebus et non verbis legem imponere* (10 Co. 101).—The voice of legislators is a living voice to impose law on things and not on words.

491. *Legitimè imperanti parere necesse est* (Jenk. Cent. 120).—It is necessary to obey one legitimately commanding. (See Maxims 219, 474.)

492. *Lex aliquando sequitur æquitatem* (3 Wils. 119).— Law sometimes follows equity. (See Maxim 38.)

493. *Lex Angliæ est lex misericordiæ* (2 Inst. 315).—The law of England is a law of mercy.

494. *Lex Angliæ lex terræ est.*—The law of England is the law of the land.

495. *Lex Angliæ nunquam matris sed semper patris conditionem imitari partum judicat* (Co. Litt. 123).—The law of England rules that the offspring shall always follow the condition of the father; never that of the mother.

496. *Lex Angliæ sine Parliamento mutari non potest* (2 Inst. 619).—The law of England cannot be changed but by Parliament.

497. *Lex beneficialis rei consimili remedium præstat* (2 Inst. 689).—A beneficial law affords a remedy for a similar case. (See Maxim 366.)

498. *Lex citius tolerare vult privatum damnum quam publicum malum* (Co. Litt. 132).—The law should more readily tolerate a private loss than a public evil.

> No action lies against a member of Parliament for slanders uttered in Parliament, or against an advocate for slanders uttered in the course of a judicial enquiry, or against a witness in legal proceedings for defamation or perjury. A subordinate officer has no remedy by action against his superior officer who defames him in an official report upon his conduct. (See Maxims 361, 958.)

499. *Lex deficere non potest in justitiâ exhibendâ* (Co. Litt. 197).—The law cannot be wanting in dispensing justice.

500. *Lex dilationes semper exhorret* (2 Inst. 240).—The law always abhors delays.

501. *Lex est dictamen rationis* (Jenk. Cent. 117).—Law is the dictate of reason.

502. *Lex est exercitûs judicum tutissimus ductor* (2 Inst. 526).—The law is the safest leader of the army of judges. (See Maxim 431.)

504. *Lex est ratio summa, quæ jubet quæ sunt utilia et necessaria, et contraria prohibet* (Co. Litt. 319).—Law is the highest reason, which commands those things which are useful and necessary, and forbids what is contrary thereto. (See Maxim 35.)

505. *Lex est sanctio sancta, jubens honesta, et prohibens contraria* (2 Inst. 587).—Law is a sacred sanction, commanding what is proper and forbidding what is not.
>This definition of law is misleading, for laws enjoin and prohibit things for reasons of expediency only, the question of right and wrong not, in many instances, being at all applicable.

506. *Lex est tutissima cassis, sub clypeo legis nemo decipitur* (2 Inst. 56).—Law is the safest helmet; under the shield of the law none are deceived.

507. *Lex fingit ubi subsistit æquitas* (11 Co. 90).—The law feigns where equity pauses.

508. *Lex intendit vicinum vicini facta scire* (Co. Litt. 78).—The law presumes one neighbour to know the actions of another.

509. *Lex necessitatis est lex temporis, scilicet, instantis* (Hob. 159).—The law of necessity is the law of time—that is, present. (See Maxims 361, 958.)

510. *Lex neminem cogit ad vana seu inutilia peragenda* (5 Co. 21).—The law does not require anyone to do vain or useless things.
>When the condition of an obligation is possible at the time of its making, but before it can be performed becomes

impossible by an act of God, the law, or the obligee, the obligation is saved. (See Maxims 352, 512.)

511. *Lex neminem cogit ostendere quod nescire præsumitur* (Lofft, 569).—The law compels no one to declare that which he is presumed not to know.

512. *Lex nil frustra facit* (Jenk. Cent. 17).—The law does nothing in vain.
The law will not attempt to do, or compel one to do, an act which would be vain. (See Maxims 352, 510.)

513. *Lex non a rege est violanda* (Jenk. Cent. 7).—The law is not to be violated by the king. (See Maxim 951.)

514. *Lex non curat de minimis* (Hob. 88).—The law cares not about trifles. (See Maxim 183.)

515. *Lex non cogit ad impossibilia* (Hob. 96).—The law does not compel the impossible. (See Maxim 352.)

516. *Lex non debet deficere conquerentibus in justitiâ exhibendâ* (Co. Litt. 197b).—The law wills that in every case where a man is wronged and endamaged he shall have remedy.

517. *Lex non deficit in justitiâ exhibendâ* (Jenk. Cent. 31.) —The law is not defective in dispensing justice. (See Maxim 481.)

518. *Lex non favet delicatorum votis* (9 Co. 58).—The law favours not the wishes of the dainty. (See Maxims 183, 514.)

519. *Lex non intendit aliquid impossibile* (12 Co. 89).—The law intends not anything impossible. (See Maxim 352.)

520. *Lex non novit patrem, nec matrem; solam veritatem.* —The law knows neither father nor mother; only the truth. (See Maxims 517, 535.)

521. *Lex non oritur ex injuriâ.*—The law does not arise from an injury. (See Maxims 13, 170.)

522. *Lex non patitur fractiones et divisiones statutorum* (1 Co. 87).—The law suffers no fractions and divisions of statutes.

523. *Lex non requirit verificari quod apparet curiæ* (9 Co. 54).—The law does not require that which is apparent to the Court to be verified. (See Maxim 709.)

524. *Lex plus laudatur quando ratione probatur* (Litt. Epil.).—The law is most worthy of approval when it is consonant to reason. (See Maxims 103, 917, 1027.)

525. *Lex posterior derogat priori* (Mackeld. Civ. L. 5.)— A later Act takes away the effect of an earlier one. (See Maxims 487, 132.)

526. *Lex prospicit non respicit* (Jenk. Cent. 284).—The law looks forward, not backward. (See Maxim 717.)

527. *Lex punit mendacium* (Jenk. Cent. 15).—The law punishes a lie. (See Maxim 579.)

528. *Lex rejicit superflua, pugnantia, incongrua* (Jenk. Cent. 133).—The law rejects superfluous, contradictory, and incongruous things. (See Maxim 418.)
This is a rule applied to the interpretation of instruments, which holds what is superfluous to be disregarded, and also what is contradictory or incongruous.

529. *Lex reprobat moram* (Jenk. Cent. 35.)—The law dislikes delay.

530. *Lex scripta si cesset id custodiri oportet quod moribus et consuetudine inductum est, et si qua in re hoc defecerit tunc id quod proximum et consequens ei est* (7 Co. 19).—If the written law be silent, that which is drawn from manners and custom ought to be observed, and if in that anything is defective, then that which is next and analogous to it.

531. *Lex semper dabit remedium* (Jacob, 69).—The law will always give a remedy. (See Maxim 1028.)

532. *Lex semper intendit quod convenit rationi* (Co. Litt. 78).—The law always intends what coincides with reason.

533. *Lex spectat naturæ ordinem* (Co. Litt. 197).—The law regards the order of nature.
Thus, the law will not permit a man to demand that which he cannot recover, and where the thing sued for by

tenants in common is in its nature entire, as in detinue for a chattel, they must of necessity join in the action, contrary to the rule which in other cases obtains, and according to which they must sue separately. (See Maxims 451, 524.)

534. *Lex succurrit ignoranti* (Jenk. Cent. 15).—The law assists the ignorant. (See Maxim 345.)

535. *Lex uno ore omnes alloquitur* (2 Inst. 184).—The law speaks to all with the same mouth. (See Maxims 481, 517, 520.)

536. *Liberata pecunia non liberat offerentem* (Co. Litt. 207).—Money being restored does not set free the party offering.

537. *Libertas est naturalis facultas ejus quod cuique facere libet, nisi quod de jure aut vi prohibetur* (Co. Litt. 116).—Liberty is that rational faculty which permits everyone to do anything but that which is restrained by law or force.

538. *Libertas est res inestimabilis* (Jenk. Cent. 52).—Liberty is an inestimable thing.

539. *Libertates regales ad coronam spectantes ex concessione regum a corona exierunt* (2 Inst. 496).—Royal prerogatives pertaining to the Crown depart from the Crown by the consent of the kings.

540. *Libertinum ingratum leges civiles in pristinam servitutem redigunt; sed leges Angliæ semel manumissum semper liberum judicant* (Co. Litt. 137).—The civil laws reduce an ungrateful freedman to his original slavery, but the laws of England regard a man once manumitted as ever after free.

541. *Licet dispositio de interesse futuro sit inutilis, tamen fieri potest declaratio præcedens quæ sortiatur effectum, interveniente novo actu* (Bac. Max. Reg. 14).—Although the grant of a future interest is inoperative, yet it may become a declaration precedent, which will take effect on the intervention of some new act.

" The law," said Lord Bacon, " doth not allow of grants except there be a foundation of an interest in the grantor;

for the law will not accept of grants of titles, or of things in action which are imperfect interests, much less will it allow a man to grant or encumber that which is no interest at all, but merely future. But of declarations precedent, before any interest vested, the law doth allow, but with this difference, so that there be some new act or conveyance to give life and vigour to the declaration precedent."

542. *Licita bene miscentur, formula nisi juris obstet* (Bac. Max. Reg. 24).—Things permitted are properly united unless the form of law oppose.

" The law," says Lord Bacon, " giveth that favour to lawful acts, that, though they be executed by several authorities, yet the whole act is good "; if, therefore, tenant for life and remainderman join in granting a rent, " this is one solid rent out of both their estates, and no double rent, or rent by confirmation."

543. *Ligeantia est quasi legis essentia; est vinculum fidei* (Co. Litt. 129).—Allegiance is, as it were, the essence of law; it is the chain of faith.

544. *Ligeantia naturalis nullis claustris coercetur, nullis metis refrænatur, nullis finibus premitur* (7 Co. 10).—Natural allegiance is restrained by no barriers, reined by no bounds, stopped by no limits.

545. *Linea recta semper præfertur transversali* (Co. Litt. 10).—The right line is always preferred to the collateral.

It is a rule of descent that the lineal descendants *ad infinitum* of any person deceased shall represent their ancestor—that is, shall stand in the same place as the person himself would have done had he been living.

546. *Litis nomen omnem actionem significat, sive in rem, sive in personam sit* (Co. Litt. 292).—" Lawsuit " signifies every action, whether it be for the thing or against the person.

547. *Locus pro solutione reditûs aut pecuniæ secundum conditionem dimissionis aut obligationis est strictè observandus* (4 Co. 73).—A place, according to the condition of a lease or

bond, for the payment of rent or money, is to be strictly observed.

548. *Locus regit actum.*—The act is governed by the law of the place where it is done.

549. *Longa possessio est pacis jus* (Co. Litt. 6).—Long possession is the law of peace.

550. *Longa possessio parit jus possidendi et tollit actionem vero domino* (Co. Litt. 110).—Long possession produces the right of possession, and takes away an action from the true owner.

551. *Longum tempus et longus usus, qui excedit memoriam hominum, sufficit pro jure* (Co. Litt. 115).—Long time and long use, which exceeds the memory of man, suffices in law.

552. *Magister rerum usus; magistra rerum experientia* (Co. Litt. 229).—Use is the master of things; experience the mistress of things. (See Maxim 599.)

553. *Major hæreditas venit unicuique nostrum à jure et legibus quam à parentibus* (2 Inst. 56).—A greater inheritance comes to every one of us from right and the laws than from parents.

554. *Majus continet minus* (Jenk. Cent. 208).—The greater contains the less. (See Maxim 746.)

555. *Majus dignum trahit ad se minus dignum* (1 Inst. 43). —The more worthy draws with it the less worthy. (See Maxims 155, 746.)

556. *Majus est delictum seipsum occidere quam alium* (3 Inst. 54).—It is a greater crime to kill one's self than another.

557. *Mala grammatica non vitiat chartam. Sed in expositione instrumentorum mala grammatica quoad fieri possit evitanda est* (6 Co. 39).—Bad grammar does not vitiate a charter. But in the exposition of instruments, bad grammar, so far as it can be done, is to be avoided.

False English does not make a deed void when its meaning is apparent. Where, however, a proviso in a lease was altogether ungrammatical and insensible, the Court declared that they did not consider themselves bound to find out a meaning for it. (See Maxims 263, 578, 633.)

558. *Maledicta expositio quæ corrumpit textum* (4 Co. 35).— It is a bad exposition which corrupts the text.

A Court of law will not make any interpretation contrary to the express letter of a statute, for nothing can so well explain the meaning of the makers of the Act as their own direct words. (See Maxim 376.)

559. *Maleficia non debent remanere impunita; et impunitas continuum affectum tribuit delinquenti* (4 Co. 45).—Evil deeds ought not to remain unpunished; and impunity affords continual incitement to the delinquent.

560. *Maleficia propositis distinguuntur* (Jenk. Cent. 290).— Evil deeds are distinguished from evil purposes.

561. *Malitia supplet ætatem* (Dyer, 104b).—Malice makes up for the want of years.

This maxim does not apply to an infant under seven, who is incapable of crime. Between seven and fourteen years an infant is *primâ facie* incapable of criminal intention, though strong evidence of mischievous discretion will rebut this assumption.

562. *Malum non præsumitur* (4 Co. 72).—Evil is not presumed.

563. *Malus usus est abolendus, quia in consuetudinibus, non diuturnitas temporis, sed soliditas rationis est consideranda* (Co. Litt. 141).—An evil custom is to be abolished, because, in customs, not length of time, but solidity of reason, is to be considered.

564. *Mandata licita strictam recipiunt interpretationem, sed illicita latam et extensam* (Bac. Max. Reg. 16).—Lawful authority should receive a strict interpretation, unlawful authority a wide and extended one.

A principal is civilly liable for those acts only which are within the scope of the agent's employment. But if a

man incite another to do an unlawful act, he shall not
" excuse himself by circumstances not pursued "; as
if he command his servant to rob I. D. on Shooter's Hill,
and he does it on Gad's Hill; or to kill him by poison,
and he doth it by violence.

565. *Mandatarius terminos sibi positos transgredi non
potest* (Jenk. Cent. 53).—A mandatory cannot exceed the
bounds placed upon himself.

566. *Manerium dicitur à manendo, secundum excellentiam,
sedes magna, fixa et stabilis* (Co. Litt. 58).—A manor is called
from " *manendo*," according to its excellence, a seat, great,
fixed, and firm.

567. *Manus mortua, quia possessio est immortalis, manus
pro possessione et mortua pro immortali* (Co. Litt. 2).—Mortmain (dead hand) because it is an immortal possession;
" *manus* " stands for possession, and " *mortua* " for immortal.

568. *Matrimonia debent esse libera* (Halk. 86).—Marriages
ought to be free.

569. *Matrimonium subsequens legitimos facit quoad sacer-
dotium non quoad successionem propter consuetudinem regni
quæ se habet in contrarium* (Co. Litt. 345).—A subsequent
marriage makes the children legitimate so far as relates to the
priesthood, not as to the succession, on account of the custom
of the kingdom, which is contrary thereto.

570. *Maturiora sunt vota mulierum quam virorum* (6 Co.
71).—The promises of women are prompter than those of men.

571. *Maxime,* so called *quia maxima est ejus dignitas et
certissima auctoritas, atque quod maximè omnibus probetur*
(Co. Litt. 11).—" *Maxime,*" so called because its dignity is
chiefest, and its authority the most certain, and because
universally approved by all.

572. *Maximus erroris populus magister* (Bac. Max.).—The
people is the greatest master of error.   (See Maxim 118.)

573. *Melior est justitia verè præveniens, quam severè puniens* (3 Inst. Epil.).—Justice truly preventing is better than severely punishing. (See Maxim 581.)

574. *Melior est conditio possidentis et rei quam actoris* (4 Inst. 180).—The condition of the possessor is the best; and that of the defendant than that of the plaintiff. (See Maxims 355, 395.)

575. *Melior est conditio possidentis, ubi neuter jus habet* (Jenk. Cent. 118).—The condition of the possessor is the better, where neither of the two has a right.

576. *Meliorem conditionem ecclesiæ suæ facere potest prælatus, deteriorem nequaquam* (Co. Litt. 101).—A bishop can make the condition of his own church better, by no means worse.

577a. *Meliorem conditionem suam facere potest minor, deteriorem nequaquam* (Co. Litt. 337).—A minor can make his own condition better, but by no means worse.

> The Courts will see to it generally that the condition of a minor is not made worse by his own acts of improvidence. He may, if imposed upon, avoid any contract not for necessaries, after he comes of age. (See Maxims 584-587, 997.)

577b. *Melius est petere fontem quam sectari rivulos.*—It is better to go to the fountain-head than to follow the streams.

578. *Mens testatoris in testamentis spectanda est* (Jenk. Cent. 277).—The testator's intention is to be regarded in wills. (See Maxims 263, 557, 633, 1050.)

579. *Mentiri est contra mentem ire* (3 Buls. 260).—To lie is to go against the mind. (See Maxim 527.)

580. *Meritò beneficium legis amittit, qui legem ipsam subvertere intendit* (2 Inst. 53).—He justly loses the benefit of law who purposes to overturn the law itself.

> This maxim finds application in cases of fraud, where the party committing it seeks a benefit thereby in the Courts.

581. *Minatur innocentibus, qui parcit nocentibus* (4 Co. 45). —He threatens the innocent who spares the guilty. (See Maxims 354, 410, 573.)

582. *Minima pœna corporalis est major qualibet pecuniariâ* (2 Inst. 220).—The smallest bodily punishment is greater than any pecuniary one.

583. *Minimè mutanda sunt quæ certam habent interpretationem* (Co. Litt. 365).—Things which have a certain interpretation are to be altered as little as possible.

584. *Minor ante tempus agere non potest in casu proprietatis, nec etiam convenire; differetur usque ætatem; sed non cadit breve* (2 Inst. 291).—A minor before majority cannot act in a case of property, not even to agree; it should be deferred until majority; but a writ does not fail.

585. *Minor jurare non potest* (Co. Litt. 172).—A minor cannot swear.
> This maxim has reference to the swearing of a jury; an infant not being allowed to sit as a juror.

586. *Minor minorem custodire non debet; alios enim præsumitur male regere qui seipsum regere nescit* (Co. Litt. 88).— A minor cannot be guardian to a minor, for he is presumed to direct others badly who knows not how to direct himself.

587. *Minor, qui infra ætatem* 12 *annorum fuerit, utlagari non potest, nec extra legem poni, quia ante talem ætatem non est sub lege aliqua* (Co. Litt. 128).—A minor who is under twelve years of age cannot be outlawed, nor placed without the law, because, before such age, he is not under any law. (See Maxim 561, *note*.)

588. *Misera est servitus, ubi jus est vagum aut incertum* (4 Inst. 246).—Obedience is miserable, where the law is vague and uncertain.
> Obedience to law becomes a hardship when that law is unsettled or doubtful. This maxim applies with peculiar force to questions respecting real property; as, for instance, to family settlements, by which provision is

made for unborn generations. (See Maxims 412, 415, 934.)

589. *Mobilia sequuntur personam.*—Movables follow the person.

    The personal estate of a testator accompanies him wherever he may reside and become domiciled, so that he acquires the right of disposing of and dealing with it, according to the law of his domicil.

590. *Modus et conventio vincunt legem* (2 Co. 73).—Custom and agreement overrule law.

    The conditions annexed to a grant or devise, the covenants inserted in a conveyance or lease, and the agreements entered into between parties, have, subject to certain restrictions, the force of law over those who are parties to such agreements or instruments.

    The rule, however, is subject to limitation, and does not apply where the express provisions of any law are violated by the contract, nor, in general, where the interests of the public, or of third parties, would be injuriously affected by its fulfilment. (See Maxims 149, 779, 780, 820.)

591. *Modus legem dat donationi* (Plow. Com. 251).—Agreement gives law to the gift. (See Maxim 158.)

592. *Monetandi jus comprehenditur in regalibus quæ nunquam à regio sceptro abdicantur* (Dav. 18).—The right of coining money is comprehended amongst those rights of royalty which are never separated from the kingly sceptre.

593. *Monumenta quæ nos recorda vocamus sunt veritatis et vetustatis vestigia* (Co. Litt. 118).—Monuments which we call records are the vestiges of truth and antiquity.

594. *Mora debitoris non debet esse creditori damnosa* (Pothier).—Delay on the part of a debtor ought not to be injurious to a creditor.

    Where delivery of the goods has been delayed through the fault of either buyer or seller, the goods are at the risk of the party in fault as regards any loss which might not have occurred but for such fault.

595. *Mors dicitur ultimum supplicium* (3 Inst. 212).—Death is denominated the extreme penalty.

596. *Mors omnia solvit* (Jenk. Cent. 160).—Death dissolves all things.

597. *Mulieres ad probationem status hominis admitti non debent* (Co. Litt. 6).—Women ought not to be admitted to proof of the estate of a man.

598. *Multa conceduntur per obliquum, quæ non conceduntur de directo* (6 Co. 47).—Many things are obliquely conceded which are not conceded directly.

599. *Multa exercitatione facilius quam regulis percipies* (4 Inst. 50).—You will perceive many things more easily by experience than by rules.   (See Maxim 552.)

600. *Multa in jure communi, contra rationem disputandi, pro communi utilitate introducta sunt* (Co. Litt. 70).—Many things contrary to the rule of argument are introduced into the common law for common utility.

601. *Multa multo exercitatione facilius quam regulis percipies* (4 Inst. 50).—You will perceive many things more easily by practice than by rules.

602. *Multitudinem decem faciunt* (Co. Litt. 257).—Ten make a multitude.

603. *Multitudo errantium non parit errori patrocinium* (11 Co. 75).—The multitude of those who err gives no excuse to error.

604. *Multitudo imperitorum perdit curiam* (2 Inst. 219).—A multitude of ignorant persons destroys a Court.

605. *Natura appetit perfectum; ita et lex* (Hob. 144).—Nature desires perfection; so does law.

606. *Natura non facit saltum; ita nec lex* (Co. Litt. 238).—Nature takes no leap; neither does law.

607. *Natura non facit vacuum, nec lex supervacuum* (Co. Litt. 79).—Nature makes no vacuum; law nothing purposeless.

608. *Naturæ vis maxima* (Noy Max. 26).—The highest force is that of nature.

609. *Naturale est quidlibet dissolvi eo modo quo ligatur* (Jenk. Cent. 70).—It is natural for a thing to be unbound in the same way in which it was bound.

 " An obligation is not made void but by a release; a record by a record; a deed by a deed; and a parol promise or agreement is dissolved by parol, and an Act of Parliament by an Act of Parliament. This reason and this rule of law are always of force in the common law." (See Maxims 221, 671.)

610. *Necessitas est lex temporis et loci* (Hale P.C. 54).—Necessity is the law of time and place.

611. *Necessitas excusat aut extenuat delictum in capitalibus, quod non operatur idem in civilibus* (Bacon Max. Reg. 25).—Necessity excuses or extenuates delinquency in capital, which would not operate the same in civil cases.

612. *Necessitas facit licitum quod alias non est licitum* (10 Co. 61).—Necessity makes that lawful which otherwise is not lawful. (See Maxim 349.)

613. *Necessitas inducit privilegium quoad jura privata* (Bac. Max. 25).—Necessity induces, or gives, a privilege as to private rights.

 The law excuses the commission of an act *primâ facie* criminal, if such act be done involuntarily, and under circumstances which show that the individual doing it was not really a free agent. (See Maxims 614, 895.)

614. *Necessitas non habet legem* (Plowd. 18).—Necessity has no law. (See Maxim 895.)

615. *Necessitas publica major est quam privata* (Noy Max. 34).—Public necessity is greater than private. (See Maxims 361, 509, 958.)

616. *Necessitas, quod cogit, defendit* (Hale P.C. 54).—Necessity defends what it compels. (See Maxim 895.)

617. *Necessitas vincit legem; legum vincula irridet* (Hob. 144).—Necessity overcomes law; it laughs at the chains of law.

618. *Nec tempus nec locus occurrit regi* (Jenk. Cent. 190).—Neither time nor place affects the king.

619. *Nec veniam, effuso sanguine, casus habet* (3 Inst. 57).—Where blood is spilled the case is unpardonable.

620. *Nec veniam, læso numine, casus habet* (Jenk. Cent. 167).—Where the Divinity is insulted, the case is unpardonable.

621. *Negatio conclusionis est error in lege* (Wing. 268).—The negation of a conclusion is error in law.

622. *Negatio destruit negationem, et ambo faciunt affirmativum* (Co. Litt. 146).—A negative destroys a negative, and both make an affirmative.

623. *Negligentia semper habet infortuniam comitem* (Co. Litt. 246).—Negligence always has misfortune for a companion.

624. *Neminem oportet esse sapientiorem legibus* (Co. Litt. 97).—Nobody need be wiser than the laws.

625. *Nemo admittendus est inhabilitare seipsum* (Jenk. Cent. 40).—Nobody is to be admitted to incapacitate himself. (See Maxim 659.)

626. *Nemo agit in seipsum* (Jenk. Cent. 40).—No one impleads himself.

> Where a creditor is made executor or administrator to his debtor he cannot, without an evident absurdity, commence a suit against himself as representative of the deceased to recover that which is due to him in his own private capacity; but, having the whole personal estate in his hands, so much as is sufficient to answer his own demand is, by operation of law, applied to that particular purpose. (See Maxim 904.)

627. *Nemo aliquam partem recte intelligere potest ante-quam totum perlegit* (3 Co. Rep. 59).—No one can properly understand a part until he has read the whole.

> " The sages of the law have been used to collect the sense and meaning of the law by comparing one part with another and by viewing all the parts together as one whole, and not one part only by itself."

628. *Nemo allegans turpitudinem suam est audiendus* (4 Inst. 279).—No one alleging his own baseness is to be heard. (See Maxims 51, 247.)

629. *Nemo cogitur rem suam vendere, etiam justo pretio* (4 Inst. 275).—No one is obliged to sell his own property, even for the full value.

> This is true as between individuals, but where individual rights clash with the public interests Maxim 958 applies, and private property may be compulsorily acquired under the Lands Clauses Consolidation Act. (See Maxim 958.)

630. *Nemo contra factum suum venire potest* (2 Inst. 66). —No one can come against his own deed.

> This is the doctrine of estoppel as applied to matter contained in a valid sealed instrument. Thus, in the case of a bond reciting a certain fact, the party executing that bond will be precluded from afterwards denying, in an action brought upon that instrument, the fact so recited. (See Maxims 50, 644.)

631. *Nemo dat qui non habet* (Jenk. Cent. 250).—No one gives who possesses not. (See Maxim 662.)

> The owner of a base or determinable fee can do no more than transfer to another his own estate, or some interest of inferior degree created out of it. The rule also holds generally in mercantile transactions, and applies to *choses in action* as well as to goods, but with certain exceptions, two of the more important relating to sales in market overt and to the transfer of negotiable instruments.

632. *Nemo debet bis puniri pro uno delicto; et Deus non agit bis in ipsum* (4 Co. 43).—No one should be punished twice for one fault; and God punishes not twice against Himself.

> When a criminal charge has once been adjudicated upon by a Court of competent jurisdiction, that adjudication is final, whether it takes the form of an acquittal or a conviction, and it may be pleaded in bar of a subsequent prosecution for the same offence, whether charged with or without matters of mere aggravation, and whether such matters relate to the intent with which the offence was committed or to the consequences of the offence.

633. *Nemo debet bis vexari, si constat curiæ quod sit pro unâ et eâdem causâ* (5 Co. 61).—No man ought to be twice vexed, if it be proved to the Court that it be for one and the same cause.

> If an action be brought, and the merits of the question be discussed between the parties, and a final judgment obtained by either, the parties are concluded, and cannot canvass the same question again in another action, although, perhaps, some objection or argument might have been urged upon the first trial which would have led to a different judgment. (See Maxims 263, 381, 557, 578.)

634. *Nemo debet ex alienâ jacturâ lucrari* (Jenk. Cent. 4).—No person ought to gain by another person's loss.

635. *Nemo debet esse judex in propriâ causâ* (12 Co. 113).—No one should be judge in his own cause.

636. *Nemo de domo suâ extrahi debet* (D. 50, 17, 103).—No one can be dragged out of his own house.   (See Maxim 200.)

637. *Nemo est hæres viventis* (Co. Litt. 8).—No one is heir of the living.

> By law, no inheritance can vest, nor can any person be the actual complete heir of another, till the ancestor is dead; before the happening of this event he is called the heir-apparent, or heir-presumptive, and his claim, which can only be to an estate remaining in the ancestor

at the time of his death and of which he has made
no testamentary disposition, may be defeated by the
superior title of an alienee in the ancestor's lifetime, or
of a devisee under his will.

638. *Nemo ex alterius incommodo debet locupletari* (Jenk.
Cent. 8).—No man ought to be made rich out of another's
injury.

639. *Nemo ex dolo suo proprio relevetur, aut auxilium
capiat* (Jur. Civ.).—No one is relieved or gains an advantage
from his own proper deceit.

640. *Nemo inauditus nec insummonitus condemnari debet,
si non sit contumax* (Jenk. Cent. 8).—No man should be condemned unheard and unsummoned, unless for contumacy.

641. *Nemo militans Deo implicetur secularibus negotiis*
(Co. Litt. 70).—No man warring for God should be associated
with secular business.

642. *Nemo nascitur artifex* (Co. Litt. 97).—No one is born
an artificer.

643. *Nemo patriam in quâ natus est exuere nec ligeantiæ
debitum ejurare possit* (Co. Litt. 129).—A man cannot abjure
his native country, nor the allegiance he owes his sovereign.
> Natural allegiance is such as is due from all men born
> within the dominions of the Crown, immediately upon
> their birth. It cannot be forfeited, cancelled, or altered
> by any change of time, place, or circumstance, nor by
> anything but the united concurrence of the Legislature.
> The Naturalisation Act, 1870, provides means whereby
> persons who were born British subjects may declare
> themselves aliens, and cease to be British subjects.

644. *Nemo potest contra recordum verificare per patriam*
(2 Inst. 380).—No one can verify by jury against a record.
(See Maxim 630.)

645. *Nemo potest esse simul actor et judex.*—No one can
be at once suitor and judge. (See Maxim 635.)

646. *Nemo potest esse tenens et dominus* (Gilb. Ten. 142).
—No man can be tenant and lord.

647. *Nemo potest facere per alium, quod per se non potest* (Jenk. 237).—No one can do through another what he cannot do himself.   (See Maxims 4, 77.)

648. *Nemo potest mutare consilium suum in alterius injuriam* (D. 50, 17, 75).—No one can change his purpose to the injury of another.   (See Maxims 630, 644.)

649. *Nemo potest plus juris ad alium transferre quam ipse habet* (Co. Litt. 309).—No one can transfer a greater right to another than he himself has.   (See Maxims 77, 631.)

650. *Nemo præsumitur alienam posteritatem suæ prætulisse* (Wing. 285).—No one is presumed to have preferred another's posterity to his own.

651. *Nemo præsumitur esse immemor suæ æternæ salutis, et maxime in articulo mortis* (6 Co. 76).—No one is presumed to be forgetful of his own eternal welfare, and more particularly in the moment of death.

652. *Nemo prohibetur pluribus defensionibus uti* (Co. Litt. 304).—No one is restrained from using several defences.   (See Maxim 262.)

653. *Nemo punitur pro alieno delicto* (Wing. 336).—No one is punished for the crime of another.

654. *Nemo punitur sine injuriâ, facto, seu defaltâ* (2 Inst. 287).—No one is punished unless for some injury, deed, or default.

655. *Nemo sibi esse judex vel suis jus dicere debet.*—No one ought to be his own judge, or the tribunal in his own affairs. (See Maxim 635.)

656. *Nemo tenetur ad impossibile* (Jenk. Cent. 7).—No one is bound to an impossibility.   (See Maxims 352, 515.)

657. *Nemo tenetur armare adversarium contra se* (Wing. 665).—No one is bound to arm his adversary against himself.

658. *Nemo tenetur divinare* (4 Co. 28).—No one is bound to foretell.

659. *Nemo tenetur seipsum accusare* (Wing. Max. 486).—No one is bound to criminate himself.

Hence, although an accused person may of his own accord make a voluntary statement as to the charge against him, a Justice, before receiving his statement, is required to caution him that he is not obliged to say anything, and that what he does say may be given in evidence against him. Hence also arises the rule that evidence of a confession by the accused is not admissible, unless it be proved that such confession was free and voluntary. It may be stated as a general rule that a witness is privileged from answering, not merely where his answer will criminate him directly, but also where it may have a tendency to criminate him. (See Maxim 625.)

660. *Nihil aliud potest rex quam quod de jure potest* (11 Co. Rep. 74).—The king can do nothing other than what he can do by law. (See Maxim 947.)

661. *Nihil consensui tam contrarium est quam vis et metus* (D. 50, 17, 116).—Nothing is so opposed to consent as force and fear.

Money is recoverable which was paid, and an instrument may be avoided which was executed, under threats of personal violence, duress, or illegal restraint of liberty.

662. *Nihil dat qui non habet* (Jur. Civ.).—He gives nothing who has nothing. (See Maxim 631.)

663. *Nihil facit error nominis cum de corpore constat* (11 Co. 21).—An error of name is nothing when there is certainty as to the person. (See Maxim 263.)

664. *Nihil infra regnum subditos magis conservat in tranquillitate et concordiâ quam debita legum administratio* (2 Inst. 158).—Nothing more preserves in tranquillity and concord those subjected to the Government than a due administration of the laws.

665. *Nihil in lege intolerabilius est, eandem rem diverso jure censeri* (4 Co. 93).—Nothing in law is more intolerable than to rule a similar case by a diverse law.

666. *Nihil perfectum est dum aliquid restat agendum* (9 Co. Rep. 9b).—Nothing is perfect while something remains to be done.

667. *Nihil præscribitur nisi quod possidetur* (5 B. & A. 277). —Nothing is prescribed except what is possessed.

668. *Nihil quod est contra rationem est licitum* (Co. Litt 97).—Nothing is permitted which is contrary to reason.

669. *Nihil quod inconveniens est licitum est* (Co. Litt. 97) —Nothing which is inconvenient is lawful. (See Maxims 973 958.)

    This maxim should be received with some qualification, and must be understood to mean that, against the introduction or establishing of a particular rule or precedent, inconvenience is a forcible argument. It also finds application in the principle that the law will sooner suffer a private mischief than a public inconvenience, for it is better to suffer a mischief which is peculiar to one than an inconvenience which may prejudice many. (See Maxims 79, 958.)

670. *Nihil simul inventum est et perfectum* (Co. Litt. 230). —Nothing is invented and perfected at the same moment.

671. *Nihil tam conveniens est naturali æquitati, quam unumquodque dissolvi eo ligamine quo ligatum est* (2 Inst. 359). —Nothing is so agreeable to natural equity as that, by the like means by which anything is bound, it may be loosed. (See Maxims 221, 609.)

672. *Nihil tam conveniens est naturali æquitati, quam voluntatem domini rem suam in alium transferre, ratam habere* (1 Co. 100).—Nothing is so consonant to natural equity as to regard the intention of the owner in transferring his own property to another.

673. *Nihil tam proprium est imperii quam legibus vivere* (2 Inst. 63).—Nothing is so becoming to authority as to live according to the laws.

674. *Nihil habet forum ex scenâ* (Bac. Max.).—The Court has nothing to do with what is not before it.

675. *Nimia subtilitas in jure reprobatur, et talis certitudo certitudinem confundit* (4 Co. 5).—Nice and subtle distinctions are not sanctioned by the law; for so, apparent certainty would be made to confound true and legal certainty.

676. *Nimium altercando veritas amittitur* (Hob. 344).—By too much altercation truth is lost.

677. *Nobiliores et benigniores presumptiones in dubiis sunt præferendæ* (Reg. Jur. Civ.).—In cases of doubt, the more generous and more favourable presumptions are to be preferred.

678. *Nobilitas est duplex, superior et inferior* (2 Inst. 583).—There are two sorts of nobility, the higher and the lower.

679. *Nomen dicitur à noscendo, quia notitiam facit* (6 Co. 65).—A name is called from the word " to know," because it makes recognition.

680. *Nomina sunt mutabilia, res autem immobiles* (6 Co. 66).—Names are mutable, but things immutable.

681*a*. *Non accipi debent verba in demonstrationem falsam quæ competunt in limitationem veram* (Bac. Max. Reg. 3).—Words which agree in a true meaning ought not to be received in a false sense.

> This embodies a rule which sets an important limit to the application of Maxim 263; and the rule means that if it stand doubtful upon the words, whether they import a false reference or demonstration, or whether they be words of restraint that limit the generality of the former words, the law will never intend error or falsehood.

681*b*. *Non alio modo puniatur aliquis, quam secundum quod se habet condemnatio* (3 Inst. 217).—A person may not be punished otherwise than according to what the sentence enjoins.

682. *Non aliter a significatione verborum recedi oportet quam cum manifestum est aliud sensisse testatorem* (D. 32, 69).—It behoves us not to depart from the literal meaning of words, unless it is evident that the testator intended some other meaning. (See Maxim 82.)

683a. *Non debeo melioris conditionis esse, quam auctor meus, a quo jus in me transit* (D. 50, 17, 175).—I ought not to be in a better position than my assignor, from whom the right passes to me.

683b. *Non debet alteri per alterum iniqua conditio inferri* (D. 50, 17, 74).—An unjust condition ought not to be imposed upon one by another.

684. *Non debet, cui plus licet, quod minus est non licere* (D. 50, 17, 21).—A man having a power may do less than such power enables him to do.

> He may, for instance, lease for fourteen years under a power to lease for twenty-one; or if he have a licence or authority to do any number of acts for his own benefit he may do some of them and need not do all. (See Maxim 155.)

685. *Non decipitur qui scit se decipi* (5 Co. 60).—He is not deceived who knows himself to be deceived. (See Maxims 130, 1068.)

686. *Non definitur in jure quid sit conatus* (6 Co. 42).— What an attempt is, is not defined in law.

687. *Non differunt quæ concordant re, tametsi non in verbis iisdem* (Jenk. Cent. 70).—Those things that agree in substance, though not in the same words, do not differ.

688. *Non officit affectus nisi sequatur effectus. Sed in atrocioribus delictis punitur affectus, licet non sequatur effectus* (1 Rol. Rep. 226; 2 ib. 89).—The intention is not hurtful unless an effect follow. But in the deeper delinquencies the intention is punished, although an effect do not follow.

689. *Non est arctius vinculum inter homines quam jusjurandum* (Jenk. Cent. 126).—There is no tighter link than an oath, among mankind. (See Maxim 459.)

690. *Non est disputandum contra principia negantem* (Co. Litt. 343).—We cannot dispute against a man denying first principles.

691. *Non est justum aliquem antenatum post mortem facere bastardum qui toto tempore vitæ suæ pro legitimo habebatur* (Co. Litt. 244).—It is not just to make an elder born a bastard after his death, who during his lifetime was accounted legitimate. (See Maxim 484.)

692. *Non est recedendum a communi observantiâ* (2 Co. 74).—There is no departing from common observance.

693. *Non est regula quin fallit* (Plow. Com. 162).—There is no rule but what may fail.

694. *Non ex opinionibus singulorum sed ex communi usu nomina exaudiri debent* (D. 3, 10, 7).—Names ought to be regarded not by the opinions of individuals, but by common use.

695. *Non facias malum ut inde veniat bonum* (11 Co. 74).—You are not to do evil that good may thence arise. (See Maxim 387.)

696. *Non impedit clausula derogatoria quo minus ab eadem potestate res dissolvantur a quâ constituuntur* (Bac. Max. Reg. 19).—A derogatory clause does not prevent things from being dissolved by the same power which created them.

> If an Act of Parliament contain a clause, " that it shall not be lawful for the king, by authority of Parliament during a space of seven years, to repeal this Act," such a clause, which is technically termed " *clausula derogatoria,*" is void; for one Parliament cannot by its ordinances bind another. (See Maxims 487, 799.)

697. *Non in legendo sed in intelligendo leges consistunt* (8 Co. 167).—The laws consist not in being read, but in being understood.

698. *Non jus, sed seisina, facit stipitem* (Fleta, 6, c. 14).—Not right, but seisin, makes the stock. (But see now 3 & 4 Will. IV. c. 106.)

699. *Non observatâ formâ infertur adnullatio actûs* (5 Co. Eccl. 1. 98).—When form is not observed, a failure of the action ensues. (See Maxims 167, 289, 891.)

700. *Non omnium quæ a majoribus nostris constituta sunt ratio reddi potest* (D. 1, 3, 20).—A reason cannot be given for all the laws that have been established by our ancestors. (See Maxim 874.)

701. *Non pertinet ad judicem secularem cognoscere de iis quæ sunt merè spiritualia annexa* (2 Inst. 488).—It belongs not to the secular Judge to take cognisance of things which are merely spiritual.

702. *Non possessori incumbit necessitas probandi possessiones ad se pertinere* (C. 4, 19, 2).—A person in possession is not bound to prove that the possessions belong to him. (See Maxim 355.)

703. *Non potest adduci exceptio ejusdem rei cujus petitur dissolutio* (Bac. Max. 22).—It is not permitted to adduce a plea of the matter in issue as a bar thereto.

Where the legality of some proceeding is the matter in dispute between two parties, he who maintains its legality, and seeks to take advantage of it, cannot rely upon the proceeding itself as a bar to the adverse party. To do so would involve the logical fallacy of *petitio principii*, and would in many cases preclude all redress to the aggrieved party.

704. *Non potest probari quod probatum non relevat* (1 Exch. 91, 92).—That cannot be proved, which, if proved, is immaterial.

705. *Non potest rex gratiam facere cum injuriâ et damno aliorum* (3 Inst. 236).—The king cannot confer a favour on one subject to the injury and damage of others.

For example, the Crown cannot enable a subject to erect a market so near to the legally established market of another as to be a disturbance thereof. Nor can the king grant the same thing in possession to one, which he or his progenitors have granted to another.

706. *Non quod dictum est, sed quod factum est, in jure inspicitur* (Co. Litt. 36a).—Not what is said, but what is done, is regarded in law.

707. *Non quod voluit testator, sed quod dixit in testamento inspicitur.*—Not what the testator wished, but what he said, is considered in construing a will.

> In *Doe* v. *Garlick*, 14 M. & W. 701, Parke, B., observed that difficulties have arisen from confounding the testator's *intention* with his *meaning*. "*Intention* may mean what the testator intended to have done, whereas the only question in the construction of wills is on the *meaning of the words*."

708. *Non refert an quis assensum suum præfert verbis, an rebus ipsis et factis* (10 Co. 52).—It matters not whether a man gives his assent by his words, or by his acts and deeds.

709. *Non refert quid notum sit judici, si notum non sit in formâ judicii* (3 Buls. 115).—It matters not what is known to the Judge, if it be not known judicially.

> A Judge must rely upon other witnesses or upon other sources of information, otherwise he would be passing upon the admissibility and weight of his own testimony. (See Maxims 433, 523.)

710. *Non refert verbis an factis fit revocatio* (Cro. Car. 49).—It matters not whether a revocation is made by words or by deeds.

711. *Non solent quæ abundant vitiare scripturas* (D. 50, 17, 94).—Surplusage is not wont to vitiate writings. (See Maxims 1002, 1038.)

712. *Non valet confirmatio, nisi ille, qui confirmat, sit in possessione rei vel juris unde fieri debet confirmatio; et eodem modo, nisi ille cui confirmatio fit, sit in possessione* (Co. Litt. 295).—Confirmation is not valid unless he who confirms is either in possession of the thing itself or of the right of which

confirmation is to be made, and, in like manner, unless he to whom confirmation is made is in possession.

713. *Non videntur qui errant consentire* (D. 50, 17, 116).— They do not appear to consent who make a mistake.

Equity will relieve where an act has been done, or contract made, under a mistake, or ignorance of a material fact.

714. *Non videtur consensum retinuisse si quis ex præscripto minantis aliquid immutavit* (Bac. Max. reg. 22).—He does not appear to have retained consent who has changed anything through menaces. (See Maxim 661.)

715. *Non videtur quisquam id capere, quod ei necesse est alii restituere* (D. 50, 17, 51).—No one is considered entitled to recover that which he must give up to another.

716. *Noscitur à sociis* (3 T. R. 87).—The meaning of a word may be ascertained by reference to those associated with it.

It is a rule laid down by Lord Bacon that the coupling of words together shows that they are to be understood in the same sense (Maxim 150). And where the meaning of a particular word is doubtful or obscure, or where a particular expression when taken singly is inoperative, the intention of a party who used it may frequently be ascertained by looking at adjoining words, or at expressions occurring in other parts of the same instrument (Maxim 836). One provision of an instrument must be construed by the bearing it will have upon another.

717. *Nova constitutio futuris formam imponere debet, non præteritis* (2 Inst. 292).—A new law ought to impose form on what is to follow, not on the past.

It is a general principle that no statute shall be construed so as to have a retrospective operation, unless its language is such as plainly to require that construction; and this involves the subordinate rule that a statute is not to be construed so as to have a greater retrospective operation than its language renders necessary. Except in special cases, a new Act ought to be construed so as to interfere as little as possible with vested rights; and where the words admit of another construction, they should not be so construed as to impose disabilities not existing at the passing of the Act. (See Maxim 648.)

718. *Novatio non præsumitur* (Halk. 109).—A novation is. not presumed.

719. *Novitas non tam utilitate prodest quam novitate perturbat* (Jenk. Cent. 167).—Novelty benefits not so much by its utility as it disturbs by its novelty. (See Maxim 761.)

720. *Novum judicium non dat jus novum, sed declarat antiquum, judicium est juris dictum et per judicium jus est noviter revelatum quod diu fuit velatum* (10 Co. 42).—A new adjudication does not make a new law, but explains the old; because adjudication is the *dictum* of law, and by adjudication the law is newly revealed which was previously hidden.

721. *Nudum pactum est ubi nulla subest causa præter conventionem; sed ubi subest causa, fit obligatio, et parit actionem* (Plow. 309).—A naked contract is where there is no consideration to support the agreement; but where there is a consideration, an obligation exists, and produces an action.

722. *Nulla curia quæ recordum non habet potest imponere finem, neque aliquem mandare carceri; quia ista spectant tantummodo ad curias de recordo* (8 Co. 60).—No Court which has not a record can impose a fine, or commit any person to prison; because those powers belong only to Courts of record.

723. *Nulla impossibilia aut inhonesta sunt præsumenda; vera autem et honesta et possibilia* (Co. Litt. 78).—Impossibilities or dishonesty are not to be presumed; but honesty, and truth, and possibility.

724. *Nullâ pactione effici potest ut dolus præstetur* (D. 2, 14, 27).—A man cannot validly contract that he shall be irresponsible for his own fraud.

725. *Nullius hominis auctoritas apud nos valere debet, ut meliora non sequeremur si quis attulerit* (Co. Litt. 383).—The authority of no man ought to prevail with us, so that we should not adopt better things, if another bring them.

14

726. *Nullum crimen majus est inobedientiâ* (Jenk. Cent. 77).—No crime is greater than disobedience.

727. *Nullum exemplum est idem omnibus* (Co. Litt. 212).— No example is the same to all.

728. *Nullum iniquum est præsumendum in jure* (7 Co. 71). —No iniquity is to be presumed in law.

729. *Nullum simile quatuor pedibus currit* (Co. Litt. 3).— No simile runs on four feet.

730. *Nullum tempus aut locus occurrit regi* (2 Inst. 273).— No time runs against, or place affects, the king.
>   This maxim implies that there can be no *laches* on the part of the king, and that therefore no delay will bar his right. Several statutes have, however, made inroads, for the public welfare, into this royal prerogative. (See 21 Jac. 1, cc. 14 and 16, and 9 Geo. 3, c. 16.)

731. *Nullus alius quam rex possit episcopo demandare inquisitionem faciendam* (Co. Litt. 134).—No other than the king can command the bishop to make an inquisition.

732. *Nullus commodum capere potest de injuriâ suâ propriâ* (Co. Litt. 148).—No one can take advantage of his own wrong.
>   Thus, A shall not have an action of trespass against B, who lawfully enters to abate a nuisance caused by A's wrongful act; nor shall an executor *de son tort* obtain that assistance which the law affords to a rightful executor. So if A, on whose goods a distress has been levied, by his own misconduct prevent the distress from being realised, A cannot complain of a second distress as unlawful. So if a man be bound to appear on a certain day, and before that day the obligee put him in prison, the bond is void. The maxim applies also to that extensive class of cases where fraud has been committed by one party to a transaction, and is relied upon as a defence by the other. (See Maxim 387.)

733. *Nullus dicitur accessorius post feloniam, sed ille qui novit principalem feloniam fecisse et illum receptavit et com-*

fortavit (3 Inst. 138).—No one is called an accessory after the fact but he who knew the principal to have committed a felony and received and comforted him.

734. *Nullus dicitur felo principalis nisi actor, aut qui præsens est abettans aut auxilians ad feloniam faciendam* (3 Inst. 138).—No one shall be called a principal felon except the party actually committing the felony, or the party present aiding and abetting in its commission.

735. *Nullus recedat e curiâ cancellariâ sine remedio* (4 H. 7, 4).—Let no one depart from the Court of Chancery without a remedy. (See Maxims 481, 517.)

736. *Nullus videtur dolo facere qui suo jure utitur* (D. 50, 17, 55).—No one is to be esteemed a wrongdoer who merely avails himself of his legal rights.

737. *Nunquam crescit ex post facto præteriti delicti æstimatio* (Bac. Max. Reg. 8).—The estimation of a past offence is never increased by a later fact.

It is contrary to justice that an act legal at the time when it was done should be made unlawful by a new enactment; and the injustice of *ex post facto* legislation is most apparent in the case of new criminal laws.

738. *Nunquam res humanæ prosperè succedunt ubi negliguntur divinæ* (Co. Litt. 95).—Human things never prosper where divine things are neglected.

739. *Nuptias non concubitus sed consensus facit* (Co. Litt. 33).—Not cohabitation but consent makes marriage. (See Maxim 129.)

740. *Obtemperandum est consuetudini rationabili tanquam legi* (4 Co. 38).—A reasonable custom is to be obeyed like law.

741. *Occultatio thesauri inventi fraudulosa* (3 Inst. 133).—The concealment of discovered treasure is fraudulent. (See Maxims 873b, 1017, 1018, 1019.)

742. *Officia magistratus non debent esse venalia* (Co. Litt. 234).—The offices of magistrates ought not to be sold.

743. *Officit conatus si effectus sequatur* (Jenk. Cent. 55).— The attempt becomes of consequence if the effect follows.

744. *Omne crimen ebrietas et incendit et detegit* (Co. Litt. 247).—Drunkenness both illuminates and reveals every crime.

745. *Omne jus aut consensus fecit aut necessitas constituit aut firmavit consuetudo* (D. 1, 3, 40).—Every right is either made by consent, or is constituted by necessity, or is established by custom. (See Maxim 590.)

746. *Omne majus continet in se minus* (5 Co. 115).—The greater contains the less.

 When a less estate and a greater estate, limited subsequent to it, coincide and meet in one and the same person without any intermediate estate, the less is immediately annihilated; or in the law phraseology is said to be merged. In criminal law, whenever a person is indicted for an offence which includes in it an offence of minor extent and gravity of the same class, he may be convicted of such minor offence. (See Maxims 4, 155, 684, 847, 892.)

747. *Omne quod solo inædificatur solo cedit* (I. 2, 1, 29).— Everything which is built upon the soil passes with the soil. (See Maxim 854.)

748. *Omne sacramentum debet esse de certâ scientiâ* (4 Inst. 279).—Every oath ought to be of certain knowledge. (See Maxims 456, 689.)

749. *Omnes licentiam habent his, quæ pro se indulta sunt, renunciare* (C. 1, 3, 51).—Every one has liberty to renounce those things which are granted for his own benefit.

 A man may not merely relinquish a particular line of defence, but he may also renounce a claim which might have been substantiated, or release a debt which might have been recovered by ordinary legal process. (See Maxim 863.)

750. *Omnes sorores sunt quasi unus hæres de unâ hæreditate* (Co. Litt. 67).—All sisters are as it were one heir to one inheritance.

751. *Omnes subditi sunt regis servi* (Jenk. Cent. 126).—
All subjects are the king's servants.

752. *Omne testamentum morte consummatum est* (3 Co.
29).—Every will is completed by death.

753. *Omnia delicta in aperto leviora sunt* (8 Co. 127).—
All crimes done openly are lighter.

754. *Omnia præsumuntur contra spoliatorem* (Branch, Max.
80).—All things are presumed against a robber.

> The following case will illustrate this maxim: An account
> of personal estate having been decreed in equity, the
> defendant charged the plaintiff with a debt as due to the
> estate. It was proved that the defendant had wrong-
> fully opened a bundle of papers relating to the account
> which had been sealed up and left in his hands; that he
> had altered and displaced the papers; and that it could
> not be known what papers might have been abstracted.
> The Court, upon these facts, disallowed defendant's
> whole demand, although the Lord Chancellor declared
> himself satisfied, as indeed the defendant swore, that all
> the papers entrusted to the defendant had been produced;
> the ground of this decision being that *in odium spoliatoris
> omnia præsumuntur* (1 Vern. 452).

755. *Omnia præsumuntur legitimè facta donec probetur in
contrarium* (Co. Litt. 232).—All things are presumed legitimately done, until the contrary be proved.

756. *Omnia præsumuntur ritè et solemniter esse acta*
(Co. Litt. 6).—All things are presumed to be correctly and
solemnly done. (See Maxim 236.)

757. *Omnia quæ jure contrahuntur, contrario jure pereunt*
(D. 50, 17, 100).—All things which are contracted by law
perish by a contrary law.

758. *Omnia quæ sunt uxoris sunt ipsius viri; non habet uxor
potestatem sui, sed vir* (Co. Litt. 112).—All things which
belong to the wife belong to the husband; the wife has no power
of her own, the husband has it all. (See Maxim 1042.)

759. *Omnis actio est loquela* (Co. Litt. 292).—Every action is a complaint.

760. *Omnis conclusio boni et veri judicii sequitur ex bonis et veris præmissis et dictis juratorum* (Co. Litt. 226).—Every conclusion of a good and true judgment arises from good and true premises, and sayings of juries.

761. *Omnis innovatio plus novitate perturbat quam utilitate prodest* (2 Buls. 338).—Every innovation disturbs more by its novelty than benefits by its utility.

> It has been a matter of common observation that whenever a standing rule of the law has been broken down, although the reason of the rule may not have been apparent, its wisdom has in the end appeared from the inconveniences that have followed the innovation.
>
> It is an established rule to abide by former precedents, *stare decisis*, where the same points come up again in litigation, for it should not be within the power of any judge to alter a permanent rule of the law, he being sworn to determine, not according to his private judgment, but according to the known laws of the land: not delegated to pronounce a new law, but to maintain and expound the old one. (See Maxims 442, 1060, 719.)

762. *Omnis interpretatio si fieri potest ita fienda est in instrumentis, ut omnes contrarietates amoveantur* (Jenk. Cent. 96).—Every interpretation, if it can be done, is to be so made in instruments as that all contradictions may be removed.

763. *Omnis nova constitutio futuris temporibus formam imponere debet, non præteritis* (2 Inst. 95).—Every new law should give a form to future times, not to past.

764. *Omnis privatio præsupponit habitum* (Co. Litt. 339).—Every privation presupposes former enjoyment.

765. *Omnis querela et omnis actio injuriarum limitata est infra certa tempora* (Co. Litt. 114).—Every plaint and every action for injuries is limited within certain times.

766. *Omnis ratihabitio retrotrahitur et mandato priori æqui-paratur* (Co. Litt. 207).—Every ratification of an act already done has a retrospective effect, and is equal to a previous request to do it.

If an action is brought in a person's name and for his benefit, but without his knowledge, his subsequent ratification of the proceedings in the action renders them as much his own as if he had originally authorised them. As a general proposition, the subsequent assent by the principal to his agent's conduct not only exonerates the agent from the consequences of a departure from his orders, but likewise renders the principal liable on contracts made in violation of such orders, or even where there has been no previous retainer or employment.

767. *Omnium contributione sarciatur quod pro omnibus datum est* (4 Bing. 121).—That which is given for all is restored by the contribution of all.

A maxim embodying a principle of general average.

768. *Omnium rerum quarum usus est, potest esse abusus, virtute solo excepta* (Dav. 79).—There may be an abuse of everything of which there is an use, virtue alone excepted.

769. *Oportet quod certa res deducatur in judicium* (Jenk. Cent. 84).—A thing certain must be brought to judgment.

770. *Optima est lex quæ minimum relinquit arbitrio judicis; optimus judex qui minimum sibi* (Bac. Aphor. 46).—That system of law is best which confides as little as possible to the discretion of a judge; that judge the best who trusts as little as possible his own judgment. (See Maxims 192, 86.)

771. *Optima statuti interpretatrix est (omnibus particulis ejusdem inspectis) ipsum statutum* (8 Co. 117).—The best interpreter of a statute is (all the separate parts being considered) the statute itself.

772. *Optima legum interpres est consuetudo* (Plow. Com. 336).—Custom is the best interpreter of the law.

Thus, the Court was influenced in its construction of a statute of Anne by the fact that it was that which had been generally considered the true one for one hundred and sixty years (*Cox* v. *Leigh*, 43 L. J. Q.B. 123). (See Maxims 139, 773.)

773. *Optimus interpres rerum usus* (2 Inst. 282).—The best interpreter of things is usage.

> The office of a custom is to interpret the otherwise indeterminate intentions of parties, and to ascertain the nature and extent of their contracts. A custom may also be admitted to ascertain the true meaning of particular words in an instrument, when they have various meanings, some common, some qualified, and some technical, according to the subject-matter to which they are applied. An express contract is always admissible to supersede, vary, or control a usage or custom, but such a contract cannot be controlled, varied, or contradicted by a usage or custom. (See Maxims 137, 139, 245, 563.)

774. *Optimus interpretandi modus est et sic interpretare et concordare leges legibus* (8 Co. 169).—The best mode of interpretation is so to interpret that the laws may accord with the laws.

775. *Origine propriâ neminem posse voluntate suâ eximi manifestum est* (Cod. 10, 38, 4).—It is manifest that no one is able, of his own will, to get rid of his proper origin. (See Maxim 643.)

776. *Origo rei inspici debet* (1 Co. 99).—The origin of a thing ought to be inquired into.

777. *Pacta conventa quæ neque contra leges neque dolo malo inita sunt omnimodo observanda sunt* (C. 2, 3, 29).— Compacts which are not illegal, and do not originate in fraud, must in all respects be observed. (See Maxims 285, 590.)

778. *Pacta dant legem contractui* (Halk. 118).—Agreements constitute the law of the contract.

779. *Pacta privata juri publico derogare non possunt* (7 Co. 23).—Private compacts cannot derogate from public right. (See Maxims 148, 149, 590.)

780. *Pacta quæ contra leges constitutionesque vel contra bonos mores fiunt, nullam vim habere, indubitati juris est* (C. 2, 3, 6).—It is undoubted law that agreements which are contrary to the laws and constitutions, or contrary to good morals, have no force. (See Maxim 590.)

781. *Pacta quæ turpem causam continent non sunt observanda* (D. 2, 14, 27).—Agreements founded upon a base consideration are not to be observed.

> "Wherever the consideration, which is the ground of the promise, or the promise which is the consequence or effect of the consideration, is unlawful, the whole contract is void." (See Maxims 237, 247.)

782. *Parens est nomen generale ad omne genus cognationis* (Co. Litt. 80).—Parent is a name general to every kind of blood-relationship.

783. *Paribus sententiis reus absolvitur* (4 Inst. 64).—Where opinions are equal, a defendant is acquitted.

784. *Par in parem imperium non habet* (Jenk. Cent. 174).—An equal has no authority over an equal.

785. *Parochia est locus quo degit populus alicujus ecclesiæ* (5 Co. 67).—A parish is a place in which the population of a certain church resides.

786. *Partem aliquam rectè intelligere nemo potest, antequam totum iterum atque iterum perlegerit* (3 Co. 59).—No one can rightly understand any part until he has read the whole again and again.

787. *Participes plures sunt quasi unum corpus, in eo quod unum jus habent, et oportet quod corpus sit integrum et quod in nullâ parte sit defectus* (Co. Litt. 164).—Many partners are as one body, inasmuch as they have one right, and it is necessary that the body be perfect, and that there be defect in no part.

788. *Participes, quasi partis capaces, sive partem capientes, quia res inter eas est communis, ratione plurium personarum* (Co. Litt. 146).—Partners are as it were "*partis capaces*," or

" *partem capientes,*" because the thing is common to them, by reason of their being many persons.

789. *Partus sequitur ventrem* (I. 2, 1, 19).—The offspring follows the dam.

    The rule respecting property in the young of animals is in accordance with this maxim.

790. *Parum est latam esse sententiam nisi mandetur executioni* (Co. Litt. 289).—It is not enough that sentence be given unless it be carried to execution.

791. *Parum proficit scire quid fieri debet si non cognoscas quomodo sit facturum* (2 Inst. 503).—It avails little to know what ought to be done if you do not know how it is to be done.

792. *Pater est quem nuptiæ demonstrant* (Co. Litt. 123).— He is the father whom the nuptials indicate. (See Maxims 190, 326, 966.)

793. *Patria laboribus et expensis non debet fatigari* (Jenk. Cent. 6).—A jury ought not to be fatigued by labours and expenses.

794. *Peccata contra naturam sunt gravissima* (3 Inst. 20). —Crimes against nature are the most heinous.

795. *Peccatum peccato addit qui culpæ quam facit patrocinium defensionis adjungit* (5 Co. 49).—He adds one offence to another who, when he commits an offence, joins the protection of a defence.

796. *Pecunia dicitur à pecus, omnes enim veterum divitiæ in animalibus consistebant* (Co. Litt. 207).—Money (*pecunia*) is so called from cattle (*pecus*), because the wealth of our ancestors consisted in cattle.

797. *Pendente lite nihil innovetur* (Co. Litt. 344).—During a litigation nothing new should be introduced.

798. *Periculum rei venditæ, nondum traditæ, est emptoris.* —The risk of a thing sold, and not yet delivered, is the purchaser's. (See Maxims 169, 937, 594.)

799. *Perpetua lex est, nullam legem humanam ac positivam perpetuam esse, et clausula quæ abrogationem excludit, ab initio non valet* (Bac. Max. Reg. 19).—It is an everlasting law, that no positive and human law shall be perpetual, and a clause which excludes abrogation is not good from its commencement. (See Maxim 696.)

800. *Persona conjuncta æquiparatur interesse proprio* (Bac. Max. 18).—A personal connection equals, in law, a man's own proper interest.

> This rule applies in the following and similar cases: Where the rights and liabilities of man and woman are changed by marriage; where a parent is permitted to defend his child against injury; where the parent, though an infant, is liable upon his contract for the nursing of his child; where an infant widow is liable upon her contract for the funeral expenses of her dead husband; where relationship is a good consideration in a deed.

801. *Plures cohæredes sunt quasi unum corpus, propter unitatem juris quod habent* (Co. Litt. 163).—Several co-heirs are, as it were, one body, by reason of the unity of right which they possess.

802. *Plures participes sunt quasi unum corpus, in eo quod unum jus habent* (Co. Litt. 164).—Several partners are as one body, in that they have one right. (See Maxim 788.)

803. *Plus valet unus oculatus testis quam auriti decem* (4 Inst. 279).—One eye-witness is better than ten ear-witnesses.

804. *Plus valet vulgaris consuetudo quam regalis concessio* (Co. Cop. § 31).—Common custom is better than royal grant.

805. *Pœnâ ex delicto defuncti, hæres teneri non debet* (2 Inst. 198).—The heir ought not to be bound in a penalty for the crime of the defunct.

806. *Politiæ legibus non leges politiis adaptandæ* (Hob. 154).—Politics are to be adapted to the laws, and not the laws to politics.

807. *Polygamia est plurium simul virorum uxorumve connubium* (3 Inst. 88).—Polygamy is the marriage of many husbands or wives at one time.

808. *Possessio est quasi pedis positio* (3 Co. 42).—Possession is, as it were, the position of the foot.

809. *Potestas suprema seipsam dissolvere potest, ligare non potest* (Bac. Max. Reg. 19).—The supreme power may loose, but cannot bind, itself.

810. *Potior est conditio defendentis.*—The condition of a defendant is better.

> If the cause of action appear to arise *ex turpi causâ* or from the transgression of a positive law, the Court says the plaintiff has no right to be assisted. (See Maxim 237.)

811. *Potior est conditio possidentis.*—The condition of one in possession is the better.

> Every claimant must succeed by the strength of his own title, and not by the weakness of his antagonist's. The principle of retainer is by some writers referred to this maxim and not to Maxim 626.

812. *Præscriptio est titulus ex usu et tempore substantiam capiens ab auctoritate legis* (Co. Litt. 113).—Prescription is a title by authority of law, deriving its force from use and time.

813. *Præsentia corporis tollit errorem nominis: et veritas nominis tollit errorem demonstrationis* (Bac. Max. Reg. 25).— The presence of the body cures error in the name: the truth of the name cures error of description.

> This rule is included in Maxim 263.

814. *Præsumptio violenta valet in lege* (Jenk. Cent. 56).— Strong presumption avails in law.

815. *Praxis judicum est interpres legum* (Hob. 96).—The practice of the judges is the interpreter of the laws.

816. *Primo excutienda est verbi vis, ne sermonis vitio obstruetur oratio, sive lex sine argumentis* (Co. Litt. 68).—The force of a word is to be especially examined, lest by the fault

of the words the sentence is destroyed, or the law be without argument.

> " The golden rule of construction is that words are to be construed according to their natural meaning, unless such a construction would either render them senseless or would be opposed to the general scope and intent of the instrument, or unless there be some very cogent reason of convenience in favour of a different interpretation "—*per* Bramwell, B. (3 H. & C. 461).

817. *Principiorum non est ratio* (2 Buls. 239).—Of principles there is no rule.

818. *Prior tempore potior jure.*—See Maxim 873.

819. *Privatis pactionibus non dubium est non lædi jus cæterorum* (D. 2, 15, 3).—There is no doubt that the rights of others are not prejudiced by private agreements. (See Maxim 175.)

820. *Privatorum conventio juri publico non derogat* (9 Co. Rep. 141).—The agreement of private persons does not derogate from the public right. (See Maxim 590.)

821. *Privatum commodum publico cedit* (Jenk. Cent. 223). —Private good yields to public. (See Maxim 958.)

822. *Privatum incommodum publico bono pensatur* (Jenk. Cent. 85).—Private loss is compensated by public good.

> " Where authority is given by the Legislature to do an act, parties damaged by the doing of it have no legal remedy, but should appeal to the Legislature " (7 C. B. 266). (See Maxim 958.)

823. *Privilegium non valet contra rempublicam* (Bac. Max. 25).—A privilege avails not against public good.

> For this reason the husband's coercion does not excuse the wife if she join him in committing treason.

824. *Probandi necessitas incumbit illi qui agit* (I. 2, 20, 4). —The necessity of proving lies upon him who commences proceedings.

825. *Protectio trahit subjectionem, et subjectio protectionem* (Co. Litt. 65).—Protection begets subjection, subjection protection. (See Maxim 258.)

As the prince affords his protection to an alien only during his residence in this realm, the allegiance of an alien is confined, in point of time, to the duration of such his residence, and, in point of locality, to the dominions of the British Empire. The maxim extends not only to those who are born within the king's dominions, but also to foreigners who live within them, even though their sovereign is at war with this country, for they equally enjoy the protection of the Crown.

826. *Quæ ab initio inutilis fuit institutio, ex post facto convalescere non potest* (D. 50, 17, 210).—That which was a useless institution at the commencement cannot gain strength from an after-fact.

827. *Quæ accessionum locum obtinent extinguuntur cum principales res peremptæ fuerint* (2 Pothier Ob. 202).—Things which are incidents are extinguished when the principals are extinguished. (See Maxim 4.)

828. *Quæ ad unum finem loquuta sunt, non debent ad alium detorqueri* (4 Co. 14).—Those things which are spoken to one end, ought not to be perverted to another.

829. *Quæ communi legi derogant strictè interpretantur* (Jenk. Cent. 221).—Things derogating from the common law are to be strictly interpreted. (See Maxim 993.)

830. *Quæ contra rationem juris introducta sunt, non debent trahi in consequentiam* (12 Co. 75).—Things introduced contrary to the reason of law ought not to be drawn into a precedent.

831. *Quæ dubitationis tollendæ causâ inseruntur, communem legem non lædunt* (Co. Litt. 205).—Things which are inserted for the purpose of removing doubt do not injure the common law.

832. *Quæ in curiâ regis acta sunt rité agi præsumuntur* (3 Bulst. 43).—Things which are done in the king's court are presumed to be rightly done.

833. *Quæ in testamento ita sunt scripta, ut intelligi non possint, perinde sunt ac si scripta non essent* (D. 50, 17, 73).—Those things which in a testament are so written that they are not able to be understood are as if they had not been written.

834. *Quælibet concessio fortissimè contra donatorem interpretanda est* (Co. Litt. 183).—Every grant is to be most strongly taken against the grantor.

835. *Quæ mala sunt inchoata in principio vix est ut bono peragantur exitu* (4 Co. 2).—Things bad in the commencement seldom achieve a good end.

836. *Quæ non valeant singula, juncta juvant* (3 Buls. 132). —Things which do not avail separate avail joined. (See Maxim 716.)

837. *Quam longum debet esse rationabile tempus, non definitur in lege, sed pendet ex discretione justiciariorum* (Co. Litt. 56).—How long reasonable time ought to be is not defined by law, but depends upon the discretion of the judges.

838. *Quando abest provisio partis, adest provisio legis* (cited 13 C. B. 960).—When provision of party is wanting, provision of law is present.

839. *Quando aliquid mandatur, mandatur et omne per quod pervenitur ad illud* (5 Co. 116).—When anything is commanded, everything by which it can be accomplished is also commanded.

> Upon this maxim rests the authority of the master of a ship to bind the owner for all that is necessary for the purpose of conducting the navigation of the ship to a favourable termination; and the maxim applies to the authority of agents generally.

840. *Quando aliquid prohibetur ex directo prohibetur et per obliquum* (Co. Litt. 223).—When anything is prohibited directly, it is also prohibited indirectly.

> So, a transaction will not be upheld which is a mere device for carrying into effect that which the Legislature has

said shall not be done. Wherever Courts of law see
attempts made to conceal illegal or void transactions by
fictitious documents, they "brush away the cobweb
varnish, and show the transactions in their true light."

841. *Quando aliquid prohibetur, prohibetur et omne per
quod devenitur ad illud* (2 Inst. 48).—When anything is
prohibited, everything relating to it is prohibited.

842. *Quando duo jura in una persona concurrunt, æquum
est ac si essent diversis* (2 Preston Abs. 430).—When two
rights concur in one person it is the same as if they were in
different persons.

843. *Quando jus domini regis et subditi concurrunt jus regis
præferri debet* (9 Co. 129).—When the rights of the king and of
the subject concur, those of the king are to be preferred.

> The king cannot have a joint property with any person in
> one entire chattel; where the titles of the king and of
> a subject concur, the king takes the whole. The king's
> debts, in suing out execution, shall be preferred to that
> of every other creditor who had not obtained judgment
> before the king commenced his suit. So, too, Crown
> debts have priority in administering the assets of a
> company in liquidation. The chattels of the Crown on
> land occupied by a subject are privileged from distress
> for rent.

844. *Quando lex aliquid alicui concedit, concedere videtur
id sine quo res ipsa esse non potest* (5 Co. 47).—When the law
gives anything to anyone, it gives also all those things without
which the thing itself would be unavailable.

> A person who is entitled to expose goods for sale in a
> public market has a right to occupy the soil with baskets
> necessary and proper for containing the goods; and that
> as against one to whom the owner of the fee-simple of
> the soil has made a devise. (See Maxim 156.)

845. *Quando lex est specialis, ratio autem generalis,
generaliter lex est intelligenda* (2 Inst. 83).—Where a law is
special, but its reason general, the law is to be understood
generally. (See Maxim 849.)

846. *Quando mulier nobilis nupserit ignobili desinit esse nobilis nisi nobilitas nata fuit* (4 Co. 118).—When a noble woman marries a man not noble, she ceases to be noble, unless her nobility was born with her.

847. *Quando plus fit quam fieri debet, videtur etiam illud fieri quod faciendum est* (8 Co. 85).—When more is done than ought to be done, then that is considered to have been done which ought to have been done.

> The act shall be void *quoad* the excess only. Thus, if a man have power to lease for ten years, and he lease for twenty, the lease for the twenty years shall in equity be good for ten years of the twenty. (See Maxim 746.)

848. *Quando res non valet ut ago, valeat quantum valere potest* (Cowp. 600).—When anything does not operate in the way I intend, let it operate as far as it can.

> Deeds shall be so construed as to operate according to the intention of the parties, if by law they may; and if they cannot in one form, they shall operate in that which by law will effectuate the intention. (See Maxim 82.)

849. *Quando verba statuti sunt specialia, ratio autem generalis, generaliter statutum est intelligendum* (10 Co. 101). —When the words of a statute are special, but the reason general, the statute is to be understood generally.

850. *Qui accusat integræ famæ sit et non criminosus* (3 Inst. 26).—Let him who accuses be of clear fame, and not criminal.

851. *Qui aliquid statuerit parte inaudita altera, æquum licet statuerit, haud æquus fuerit* (6 Co. 52).—He who decides anything, one party being unheard, though he decide rightly, does wrong. (See Maxim 79.)

852. *Qui concedit aliquid concedere videtur et id sine quo concessio est irrita, sine quo res ipsa esse non potuit* (11 Co. 52). —He who concedes anything is considered as conceding that without which his concession would be of no effect, without which the thing itself could not exist. (See Maxims 156, 844.)

15

853. *Quicquid demonstratæ rei additur satis demonstratæ frustra est* (D. 33, 4, 1).—Whatever is added to describe anything already sufficiently described, is without effect.   (See Maxims 263, 1038.)

854. *Quicquid plantatur solo, solo cedit* (Went. Off. of Exec. 58).—Whatever is affixed to the soil belongs to the soil.

But where a man, supposing that he has an absolute title to an estate, builds upon the land with the knowledge of the rightful owner, who stands by, and suffers the erection to proceed, without giving any notice of his own claim, he will be compelled, by a Court of equity, in a suit brought for recovery of the land, to make due compensation for such improvements.   (See Maxims 33, 747.)

855. *Quicquid solvitur, solvitur secundum modum solventis; quicquid recipitur, recipitur secundum modum recipientis* (2 Vern. 606).—Whatever is paid, is paid according to the intention or manner of the party paying; whatever is received, is received according to the intention or manner of the party receiving.

The general rule of law where a debtor has made a payment on account to a creditor to whom he owes several *distinct* debts is, that the debtor may, in the first instance, appropriate the payment; if he omit to do so, the creditor may make the appropriation; but if neither make any appropriation, the law appropriates the payment to the earlier debt.   But where the accounts are treated as *one entire* account the rule does not apply.

856. *Qui cum alio contrahit, vel est, vel debet esse, non ignarus conditionis ejus* (D. 50, 17, 19).—He who contracts with another, either is, or ought to be, acquainted with the condition of that person.

857. *Quid sit jus et in quo consistit injuria, legis est definire* (Co. Litt. 158).—What right is, and in what consists injury, is the business of the law to declare.   (See Maxim 469.)

858. *Qui ex damnato coitu nascuntur inter liberos non computentur* (Co. Litt. 8a).—Those who are born from unlawful intercourse are not counted among the children.

A bastard is reckoned by the law to be *nullius filius*, and thus he has no inheritable blood in him, and cannot take land by succession. Moreover, he can have no heirs but those of his own body, and therefore, if he purchases land and dies seised thereof without issue and intestate, the land shall escheat to the lord of the fee. (See Maxim 326.)

859. *Qui facit per alium facit per se* (Co. Litt. 258).—He who does anything by another does it by himself.

This maxim enunciates the general doctrine on which the law relative to the rights and liabilities of principal and agent depends. Where B employs A to buy goods for him, B is liable in an action for the amount. If a servant do what his master ought to do, it is the same as though the master did it himself; and if a servant do any such thing without the consent of the master, yet if the master subsequently ratify the act of the servant it is sufficient. The maxim applies to everything done by the agent in the scope of his authority, whether the agent be engaged in purchase or sale. It does not apply to the acts of the agent of an agent. (See Maxims 179, 180, 766, 939.)

860. *Qui hæret in literâ hæret in cortice* (Co. Litt. 289).— He who sticks to the letter sticks to the bark; or, he who considers the letter merely, of an instrument, cannot comprehend its meaning.

The law of England respects the effect and substance of the matter, and not every nicety of form or circumstance. The reason and spirit of cases make law, and not the letter of particular precedents. The maxim applies to the interpretation of contracts so as to place the construer in the same position as the party who made the contract, to view the circumstances as he viewed them, and so judge of the meaning of the words and of the correct application of the language to the things

described, and extrinsic evidence for these purposes is
admissible.   (See Maxims 82, 557, 263, 578, 663.)

861. *Qui in jus dominiumve alterius succedit jure ejus uti
debet* (D. 50, 17, 177).—He who succeeds to the right or
property of another ought to be clothed with his right.

> For instance, fee-simple estates are subject, in the hands
> of the heir or devisee, to debts of all kinds contracted
> by the deceased.   (See Maxims 77, 477.)

862. *Qui in utero est, pro jam nato habetur, quoties de ejus
commodo quæritur* (2 Bla. Com.).—He who is in the womb is
now held as born, as often as it is questioned concerning his
benefit.

863. *Qui jure suo utitur neminem lædit* (D. 50, 17, 151).—
He who exercises his right injures no one.

> An action does not lie if a man build a house whereby my
> prospect is interrupted, or open a window whereby my
> privacy is disturbed.

864. *Qui jussu judicis aliquod fecerit non videtur dolo malo
fecisse quia parere necesse est* (10 Co. 76).—He who does
anything by command of a judge will not be supposed to have
acted from an improper motive; because it was necessary to
obey.

> Where a Court has jurisdiction of a cause, and proceeds
> *inverso ordine*, or erroneously, the officer of the Court
> who executes according to its tenor the precept or
> process of the Court is not liable to an action.   But
> when the Court has no jurisdiction of the cause, the
> whole proceeding is *coram non judice*, and actions lie
> against the officer without any regard to the precept or
> process; for in this case it is not necessary to obey one
> who is not judge of the cause, any more than it is to
> obey a mere stranger.   (See Maxim 445.)

865. *Quilibet potest renunciare juri pro se introducto*
(2 Inst. 183).—Every man is able to renounce a right
introduced for himself.

> For instance, a defendant who is sued for a debt barred
> by the Statute of Limitations may waive his right to

rely upon the defence which that statute confers. Similarly, where a person is sued after his coming of age for a debt which he contracted during his infancy, and which, owing to his infancy, was voidable or void, it is generally open to him to waive such ground of defence. But the rule must be applied with this qualification, that, in general, a private compact cannot be permitted to derogate from the rights of third parties. (See Maxim 749.)

866. *Qui non cadunt in constantem virum vani timores sunt æstimandi* (7 Co. 27).—Those fears are to be esteemed vain which do not affect a firm man. (See Maxim 1043.)

867. *Qui non habet in ære, luet in corpore* (2 Inst. 173).— What a man cannot pay with his purse, he must suffer in person.

868. *Qui non habet potestatem alienandi habet necessi-tatem retinendi* (Hob. 336).—He who has no power of alienation must retain. (See Maxims 77, 649.)

869. *Qui non obstat quod obstare potest facere videtur* (2 Inst. 146).—He who does not prevent what he can prevent, is regarded as doing the thing. (See Maxims 130, 289, 870.)

870. *Qui non improbat, approbat* (3 Inst. 27).—He who does not disapprove, approves. (See Maxims 130, 869.)

871. *Qui peccat ebrius, luat sobrius* (Cary's Rep. 133).— Let him who sins when drunk, be punished when sober.
Although drunkenness, as a general rule, is no excuse for crime, yet it may be a circumstance to be taken into consideration where the question is with what intention an act was done; for a person may be so drunk as to be incapable of forming any intention.

872. *Qui per alium facit, per seipsum facere videtur* (Co. Litt. 258).—He who by another does anything, is himself considered to have done it. (See Maxim 859.)

873a. *Qui per fraudem agit, frustrà agit* (2 Rol. Rep. 17).—
What a man does fraudulently, he does in vain.

873b. *Qui prior est tempore potior est jure* (Co. Litt. 14).—
He who is first in time has the strongest claim in law.

> On this maxim may depend the right of property in
> treasure trove, in wreck, derelicts, waifs, and estrays.
> It usually determines the rights of persons who make
> conflicting claims to real property. In accordance with
> the maxim the rule in descents is, that amongst males
> of equal degree the eldest inherits land in preference to
> the others. The law relative to patents and to copy-
> right is referable to this maxim. The finder of a chattel
> lying apparently without an owner may acquire a special
> property therein. (See Maxims 355, 396, 575, 903.)

874. *Qui rationem in omnibus quærunt rationem subvertunt*
(2 Co. Rep. 75a).—They who search for reason in all things
subvert reason. (See Maxim 700.)

875. *Qui sentit commodum sentire debet et onus; et è contra*
(1 Co. 99).—He who enjoys the benefit ought also to bear the
burden; and the contrary.

> This rule applies as well where an implied covenant runs
> with the land, as where the present owner or occupier
> of land is bound by the express covenant of a prior
> occupant; whenever, indeed, Maxim 1020a holds true.
> So, too, where a contract has been entered into by one
> man as agent for another, the person on whose behalf
> it has been made cannot take the benefit of it without
> bearing its burthen. The contract must be performed
> in its integrity.

876. *Qui tacet consentire videtur* (Jenk. Cent. 32).—He
who is silent appears to consent. (See Maxims 130, 295, 336,
869.)

877. *Qui tacet consentire videtur, ubi tractatur de ejus
commodo* (9 Mod. 38).—He who is silent is considered as
consenting, when it is debated concerning his benefit. (See
Maxim 876.)

878. *Qui vult decipi decipiatur* (1 De G. M. & G. 687).—Who wishes to be deceived, let him be deceived.

879. *Quod a quoquo pœnæ nomine exactum est id eidem restituere nemo cogitur* (D. 50, 17, 46).—No one is obliged to restore that which has been exacted by way of penalty.

880. *Quod ab initio non valet, in tractu temporis non convalescit* (4 Co. 2).—That which is bad from the beginning does not improve by length of time.

> When the consideration for a deed is illegal, no lapse of time can cure the defect. The will of an infant is void, and is not rendered available when the infant attains full age, unless there be a new execution. (See Maxims 897, 891.)

881. *Quod approbo non reprobo.*—What I approve I do not reject.

> Where an express condition is annexed to a bequest, the legatee cannot accept and reject, approbate and reprobate, the will containing it. The rule likewise holds where the condition is implied merely. (See Maxim 875.)

882. *Quod ædificatur in areâ legatâ cedit legato.*—That which is built on the ground devised passes to the devisee.

> By the devise of a house all personal chattels annexed to the house and essential to its enjoyment pass to the devisee. As a rule, between the heir and the devisee, the devisee is entitled to all articles which are affixed to the land. (See Maxim 854.)

883. *Quod constat curiæ, opere testium non indiget* (2 Inst. 662).—What appears to the Court needs not the help of witnesses. (See Maxim 709.)

884. *Quod contra legem fit, pro infecto habetur* (4 Co. 31).—What is done contrary to law is considered as not done.

885. *Quod contra rationem juris receptum, non est producendum ad consequentias* (D. 50, 17, 141).—That which is received against the reason of the law is not to be advanced to a precedent.

886. *Quodcunque aliquis ob tutelam corporis sui fecerit, jure id fecisse videtur* (2 Inst. 590).—Whatever anyone does in defence of his person, that he is considered to have done legally. (See Maxim 613.)

887. *Quod dubitas, ne feceris* (Hale P.C. 300).—Where you doubt, do nothing.

888. *Quod est ex necessitate nunquam introducitur, nisi quando necessarium* (2 Rol. Rep. 512).—What is introduced of necessity is never introduced except when necessary.

889. *Quod est inconveniens, aut contra rationem, non permissum est in lege* (Co. Litt. 178).—What is inconvenient, or contrary to reason, is not permitted in law. (See Maxim 1027.)

890. *Quod fieri debet facile præsumitur* (Halk. Max. 153). —What ought to be done is easily presumed.

891. *Quod fieri non debet factum valet* (5 Co. Rep. 38).— What ought not to be done avails when done.
> This maxim will in general be found to apply wherever a form has been omitted which ought to have been observed, but of which the omission is *ex post facto* immaterial. (See Maxims 167, 289, 290, 699.)

892. *Quod in minori valet valebit in majori; et quod in majori non valet nec valebit in minori* (Co. Litt. 260).—What avails in the lesser will avail in the greater; and what does not avail in the greater will not avail in the lesser. (See Maxim 746.)

893. *Quod meum est sine facto meo vel defectu meo amitti vel in alium transferri non potest* (Prest. Abs. 147).—What is mine cannot be lost or transferred to another without alienation or forfeiture.
> Where property in land or chattels has once been effectively and indefeasibly acquired, the right of property can only be lost by some act amounting to alienation or forfeiture by the owner or his representative. (See Maxims 209, 905.)

894. *Quod necessariè intelligitur id non deest* (1 Buls. 71).— What is necessarily understood is not wanting.

895. *Quod necessitas cogit, defendit* (H. H. P.C. 54).—
What necessity forces, it justifies. (See Maxim 616.)

896. *Quod non apparet non est; et non apparet judicialiter
ante judicium* (2 Inst. 479).—That which appears not is not,
and appears not judicially before judgment. (See Maxims 185,
337, 362.)

897. *Quod non habet principium non habet finem* (Co. Litt.
345).—That which has no beginning has no end.

898. *Quod non legitur non creditur* (4 Inst. 304).—What is
not read is not believed.

899. *Quod nostrum est, sine facto sive defectu nostro,
amitti seu in alium transferri non potest* (8 Co. 92).—That
which is ours cannot be lost or transferred to another without
our own act, or our own fault. (See Maxim 893.)

900. *Quod nullius est, est domini regis* (Fleta, 1. 3).—That
which is the property of nobody, belongs to our lord the king.

It is a general rule that whenever the owner or person
actually seised of land dies intestate and without heir,
the law vests the ownership of such land either in the
Crown, or in the subordinate lord of the fee, by escheat.
The Crown is entitled to the undisposed-of personal
estate of any person who happens to die without next-
of-kin.

901. *Quod nullius est id ratione naturali occupanti conceditur* (D. 41, 1, 3).—That which is no one's is granted to
the occupant by natural right.

902. *Quod per me non possum, nec per alium* (4 Co. 24).—
What I cannot do in person, I cannot do by proxy. (See
Maxim 859.)

903. *Quod prius est verius est; et quod prius est tempore
potius est jure* (Co. Litt. 347).—What is first is truer, and what
is first in time is better in law. (See Maxims 355, 396, 575,
873b.)

904. *Quod remedio destituitur ipsâ re valet si culpa absit* (Bac. Max. Reg. 9).—That which is without remedy avails of itself if there be no fault in the party seeking to enforce it.

" The benignity of the law is such that, when, to preserve the principles and grounds of law, it deprives a man of his remedy without his own fault, it will rather put him in a better degree and condition than a worse; for if it disable him to pursue his action, or to make his claim, sometimes it will give him the thing itself by operation of law without any act of his own; sometimes it will give him a more beneficial remedy." The maxim applies in the case of retainer—that is, where a creditor is made executor or administrator to his debtor. (See Maxim 626.)

905. *Quod semel aut bis existit prætereunt legislatores* (D. 1, 3, 6).—Legislators pass over that which happens only once or twice. (See Maxim 93.)

906. *Quod semel meum est amplius meum esse non potest* (Co. Litt. 49b).—What is once mine cannot be more fully mine. (See Maxims 209, 893.)

907. *Quod semel placuit in electione, amplius displicere non potest* (Co. Litt. 146).—Where choice is once made it cannot be disapproved any longer.

A contract induced by fraud is not void, but only voidable at the election of the party defrauded. When once he has elected to abide by the contract, being aware of the fraud, he cannot afterwards rescind it.

908. *Quod subintelligitur non deest* (Ld. Raym. 832).— What is understood is not lacking.

909. *Quod vanum et inutile est, lex non requirit* (Co. Litt. 319).—The law requires not what is vain and useless. (See Maxim 510.)

910. *Quo ligatur, eo dissolvitur* (2 Rol. Rep. 21).—By the same power by which a man is bound, by that he is loosed. (See Maxim 221.)

911. *Quomodo quid constituitur eodem modo dissolvitur* (Jenk. Cent. 74).—In the same manner by which anything is constituted, by that it is dissolved. (See Maxim 221, 961.)

912. *Quotiens idem sermo duas sententias exprimit: ea potissimum excipiatur, quæ rei generandæ aptior est* (D. 50, 17, 67).—Whenever the same language expresses two meanings, that is to be taken which is the better fitted for effecting the proposed end.

913. *Quoties in stipulationibus ambigua oratio est, commodissimum est id accipi quo res de quâ agitur in tuto sit* (D. 41, 1, 80).—Whenever in contracts the expression is doubtful, it is most advantageous that that meaning be accepted by which the safety of the subject-matter may be assured.

914. *Quoties in verbis nulla est ambiguitas ibi nulla expositio contra verba expressa fienda est* (Co. Litt. 147).— When in the words there is no ambiguity, then no exposition contrary to the expressed words is to be made.

> Where an instrument appears on the face of it to be complete, parol evidence is inadmissible to vary or contradict the agreement—*e.g.* to show that the word " and " was inserted by mistake; in such cases the Court will look to the written contract in order to ascertain the meaning of the parties, and will not admit parol evidence to show that the agreement was in reality different from that which it purports to be. The maxim applies equally to the interpretation of an Act of Parliament. (See Maxims 80, 376, 558.)

915. *Quum principalis causa non consistit, ne ea quidem quæ sequuntur locum habent* (D. 50, 17, 129).—When the principal does not hold, the incidents thereof ought not to obtain. (See Maxim 4.)

916. *Ratihabitio mandato comparatur* (D. 50, 17, 60).— Ratification is equivalent to a command.

> " *Ratihabitio* " here means " the act of assenting to what has been done by another in my name." (See Maxim 766.)

917. *Ratio est legis anima, mutata legis ratione mutatur et lex* (7 Co. 7).—Reason is the soul of law; the reason of law being changed, the law is also changed. (See Maxims 102, 103, 524, 918, 1027.)

918. *Ratio legis est anima legis* (Jenk. Cent. 45).—The reason of law is the soul of law. (See Maxims 102, 103, 524, 917, 1027.)

919. *Receditur a placitis juris potius quam injuriæ et delicta maneant impunita* (Bac. Max. Reg. 12).—We dispense with the forms of law rather than that crimes and wrongs should be unpunished.

> This maxim must, at the present day, be understood to apply only to those cases in which the judges are invested with a discretionary power to permit such amendments to be made—*e.g.* in an indictment—as may prevent justice from being defeated by mere legal technicalities; and a distinction must, therefore, still be remarked between the "*placita*" and the "*regulæ*" *juris*, inasmuch as the law will rather suffer a particular offence to escape without punishment, than permit a violation of its fixed and positive rules. (See Maxim 958.)

920. *Regnum non est divisibile* (Co. Litt. 165).—The kingdom is not divisible.

921. *Regula est, juris quidem ignorantiam cuique nocere, facti vero ignorantiam non nocere* (D. 22, 6, 9).—It is the rule, that everyone is prejudiced by his ignorance of law, but is not prejudiced by his ignorance of a material fact. (See Maxims 345, 347.)

922. *Relativorum, cognito uno, cognoscitur et alterum* (Cro. Jac. 539).—Of things relating to each other, one being known, the other is also known.

923. *Remoto impedimento emergit actio* (Wing. 20).—An impediment being removed, an action emerges.

924. *Repellitur à sacramento infamis* (Co. Litt. 158).—The oath of an infamous person is not to be received.

925. *Reprobata pecunia liberat solventem* (9 Co. 79).—Money refused frees the debtor.

A tender of money, to release the debtor, must be made by a person authorised by the debtor, and to the creditor or some one authorised to receive it. The exact sum must be tendered, and in compliance with the terms of the contract.

926. *Rerum ordo confunditur, si unicuique jurisdictio non servetur* (4 Inst. Proem.).—The order of things is confounded if everyone keeps not within his jurisdiction.

927. *Rerum progressu ostendunt multa, quæ in initio præcaveri seu prævideri non possunt* (6 Co. 40).—In the course of events many things arise which at the beginning could not be guarded against or foreseen.

928. *Rerum suarum quilibet est moderator et arbiter* (Co. Litt. 223).—Everyone is the manager and judge of his own affairs.

929. *Res accessoria sequitur rem principalem.*—The accessory follows the principal.

A principal thing is a thing which can subsist by itself, and does not exist for the sake of any other thing. All that belongs to a principal thing, or is in connection with it, is called an accessory thing. (See Maxim 4.)

930. *Rescriptum principis contra jus non valet* (Reg. Civ. Jur.).—The prince's rescript avails not against right.

931. *Resignatio est juris proprii spontanea refutatio* (Godb. 284).—Resignation is a spontaneous relinquishment of one's own right.

932. *Res inter alios acta alteri nocere non debet* (Co. Litt. 132).—One person ought not to be injured by the acts of others to which he is a stranger.

The above rule operates to exclude all the acts, declarations, or conduct of others as evidence to bind a party, either directly or by inference; so that, in general, no declaration, written entry, or affidavit made by a stranger

is evidence against a man; nor can a person be affected,
still less concluded, by any evidence, decree, or judgment to which he was not actually, or, in consideration
of law, privy. (See Maxim 472.)

933. *Res ipsa loquitur.*—The thing speaks for itself.
This maxim is applicable in actions for injury by negligence
where no proof of negligence is required beyond the
accident itself, which is such as necessarily to involve
negligence—*e.g.* where a ship in motion collides with a
ship at anchor. It ought not to be applied unless the
facts proved are more consistent with negligence in the
defendant than with a mere accident; nor ought it to be
applied to evidence of an unexplained accident, if the
evidence is as consistent with the cause of the accident
having been the victim's own negligence, as with its
having been that of the defendant.

934. *Res judicata pro veritate accipitur* (Co. Litt. 103).—
A thing adjudicated is received as true. (See Maxims 633,
412, 440.)

935. *Res per pecuniam æstimatur et non pecunia per res*
(9 Co. 76).—The value of a thing is estimated according to
its worth in money; but the value of money is not estimated
by reference to the thing.

936. *Resoluto jure concedentis resolvitur jus concessum*
(Mackeld. 179).—The grant of a right comes to an end on the
termination of the right of the grantor. (See Maxims 631, 649.)

937. *Res perit suo domino* (Bell Dict. 857).—The loss falls
on the owner.
Where loss, damage, or delay of goods in transit arises
from the act of God, the loss falls upon the owner and
not upon the carrier. (See Maxims 169, 594.)

938. *Respiciendum est judicanti, ne quid aut durius aut
remissius constituatur quam causa deposcit; nec enim aut
severitatis aut clementiæ gloria affectanda est* (3 Inst. 220).—
It is a matter of import to one adjudicating that nothing either
more lenient or more severe than the cause itself warrants

should be done, for the glory neither of severity nor clemency should be affected.

939. *Respondeat superior* (4 Inst. 114).—Let the principal answer.

> This maxim is more usually applied to actions *ex delicto* than to such as are founded in contract. Where, for instance, an agent commits a tortious act, under the direction or with the assent of his principal, each is liable at the suit of the party injured; the agent is liable because the authority of the principal cannot justify his wrongful act, and the person who directs the act to be done is likewise liable under this rule of *respondeat superior*. (See Maxims 179, 859.)

940. *Res sua nemini servit.*—No one can have a servitude over his own property.

941. *Reus læsæ majestatis punitur, ut pereat unus ne pereant omnes* (4 Co. 124).—A traitor is punished that one and not all may perish. (See Maxim 154.)

942. *Reversio terræ est tanquam terra revertens in possessione donatori sive hæredibus suis post donum finitum* (Co. Litt. 142).—A reversion of land is as it were the return of the land to the possession of the donor or his heirs after the termination of the estate granted.

943.   *Re, verbis, scripto, consensu, traditione,*
       Junctura vestes sumere pacta solent
(Plow. Com. 161).—Compacts are accustomed to be clothed by the thing itself, by words, by writing, by consent, by delivery, by connection.

944. *Rex est caput et salus reipublicæ* (4 Co. 124).—The king is the head and guardian of the commonwealth.

945. *Rex est legalis et politicus* (Lane, 27).—The king is both legal and politic.

946. *Rex est major singulis, minor universis* (Bract. lib. 1, c. 8).—The king is greater than any single person : less than all.

> See Maxim 843; but if the claims of the king come in contact with the rights of all the people, he must either yield or revolution will result.

947. *Rex non debet esse sub homine sed sub Deo et lege, quia lex facit regem* (Bract. lib. i. 5).—The king ought not to be under any man, but under God and under the law, for the law makes the king.

> The Case of Prohibitions shows that the king is not above the law, for he cannot in person assume to decide any case, civil or criminal, but must do so by his judges.

948. *Rex non debet judicare sed secundum legem* (Jenk. Cent. 9).—The king ought to govern only according to law.

949. *Rex non potest fallere nec falli* (Jenk. Cent. 48).—The king cannot deceive or be deceived.

950. *Rex non potest gratiam facere cum injuria et damno aliorum* (3 Inst. 236).—The king cannot confer a favour on one subject to the injury and damage of others.   (See Maxim 705.)

951. *Rex non potest peccare* (2 Rol. Rep. 204).—The king can do no wrong.

> It is not to be presumed that the king will do or sanction anything contrary to law, to which he is equally amenable with his subjects (Maxim 947).   But if an evil act be done, though emanating from the king personally, it will be imputed to his ministers, and the king is in no way responsible for their acts.   Upon this principle the Crown cannot be prejudiced by the wrongful acts of its servants nor by errors in letters patent, &c.   (See Maxim 211.)

952. *Rex nunquam moritur* (Branch, Max. 5th ed. 197).—The king never dies.

> The law ascribes to the king, in his political capacity, an absolute immortality; and immediately upon the decease of the reigning prince in his natural capacity, the kingly dignity and the prerogatives and politic capacities of the supreme magistrate, by act of law, without any interregnum or interval, vest at once in his successor, in accordance with Maxim 359.

953. *Rex quod injustum est facere non potest* (Jenk. Cent. 9).—The king cannot do what is unjust.   (See Maxim 951.)

954. *Rex semper præsumitur attendere ardua regni pro bono publico omnium* (4 Co. 56).—The king is always presumed to attend to the business of the realm, for the public good of all.

955. *Sacramentum habet in se tres comites, veritatem, justitiam et judicium: veritas habenda est in jurato, justitia et judicium in judice* (3 Inst. 160).—An oath has in it three component parts—truth, justice, and judgment: truth is requisite in the party swearing, justice and judgment in the judge administering the oath.

956. *Sacramentum si fatuum fuerit, licet falsum, tamen non committit perjurium* (2 Inst. 167).—A foolish oath, though false, does not make perjury.

957. *Sacrilegus omnium prædonum cupiditatem et scelera superat* (4 Co. 106).—Sacrilege transcends the cupidity and wickedness of all other thefts.

958. *Salus populi est suprema lex* (13 Co. 139).—The welfare of the people, or of the public, is supreme law.

This phrase is based on the implied assent of every member of society, that his own individual welfare shall, in cases of necessity, yield to that of the community; and that his property, liberty, and life shall, under certain circumstances, be placed in jeopardy or even sacrificed for the public good. (See Maxims 361, 615.)

959. *Scientia utrinque par pares contrahentes facit* (3 Bur. 1910).—Equal knowledge on both sides makes the contracting parties equal.

960. *Scribere est agere* (2 Rol. Rep. 89).—To write is to act.

961. *Scriptæ obligationes scriptis tolluntur, et nudi consensus obligatio contrario consensu dissolvitur* (Jur. Civ.).—Written obligations are superseded by writings, and an obligation of naked assent is dissolved by naked assent to the contrary. (See Maxims 221, 911.)

962. *Secundum naturam est, commoda cujusque rei eum sequi, quem sequuntur incommoda* (D. 50, 17, 10).—It is

16

natural that the advantages of anything should follow him whom the disadvantages follow. (See Maxim 875.)

963. *Seisina facit stipitem* (Wright, Ten. 185).—The seisin makes the heir. (See Maxim 698.)

964. *Semper in dubiis benigniora præferenda.*—Always in doubtful matters the more liberal construction should be preferred.

965. *Semper in obscuris, quod minimum est sequimur* (D. 50, 17, 9).—Always in obscure matters we should follow that which is the least obscure.

> In interpreting an Act of Parliament the Courts may consider what is its fair meaning, and expound it differently from the letter, in order to preserve the intent. (See Maxims 860, 557.)

966. *Semper præsumitur pro legitimatione puerorum; et filiatio non potest probari* (Co. Litt. 126).—It is always to be presumed that children are legitimate; and filiation cannot be proved. (See Maxims 281, 967b.)

967a. *Semper præsumitur pro negante.*—The presumption is always in favour of the negative.

> When the Lords of Appeal are equally divided in opinion this rule is applied.

967b. *Semper pro matrimonio præsumitur.*—It is always presumed in favour of marriage. (See Maxims 281, 966.)

968. *Semper specialia generalibus insunt* (D. 50, 17, 147).—Specialities are always included in generalities. (See Maxims 312, 988.)

969. *Sententia contra matrimoniam nunquam transit in rem judicatam* (7 Co. Rep. 43).—A sentence against marriage never becomes *res judicata.*

970. *Sententia interlocutoria revocari potest, definitiva non potest* (Bac. Max.).—An interlocutory sentence may be recalled, but not a final.

971. *Sententia non fertur de rebus non liquidis; et oportet quod certa res deducatur in judicium* (Jenk. Cent. 7).— Sentence is not given on things not proven; and something definite ought to be brought to judgment.

972. *Servitia personalia sequuntur personam* (2 Inst. 374). —Personal services follow the person.

973. *Sic utere tuo ut alienum non lædas* (9 Co. 59).—So use your own property as not to injure your neighbour's.

In considering whether a defendant is liable to a plaintiff for damage which the latter has sustained, the question often is, not whether the defendant has acted with due care and caution, but whether his acts have occasioned the damage; and this doctrine is founded on good sense. For when one person in managing his own affairs causes, however innocently, damage to another, it is obviously only just that he should be the party to suffer (*Fletcher* v. *Rylands*, 1 Smith L.C.). (See Maxims 32, 669, 248, 414.)

974. *Sicut natura nil facit per saltum, ita nec lex* (Co. Litt. 238).—In the same way as nature does nothing by a leap, so neither does the law.

975. *Silentium in senatu est vitium* (12 Co. 94).—Silence in the senate is a fault.

976. *Silent leges inter arma* (4 Inst. 70).—The laws are silent amidst arms.

977. *Simonia est voluntas sive desiderium emendi vel vendendi spiritualia vel spiritualibus adhærentia. Contractus ex turpi causâ et contra bonos mores* (Hob. 167).—Simony is the will or desire of buying or selling spiritualities, or things pertaining thereto. It is a contract founded on a bad cause, and against morality.

978. *Simonia est vox ecclesiastica, à " Simone," illo " Mago," deducta qui donum Spiritûs Sancti pecuniâ emi putavit* (3 Inst. 153).—Simony is an ecclesiastical word, derived

from that Simon Magus who thought to buy the gift of the Holy Ghost with money.

979. *Simplex obligatio non obligat.*—A simple commendation of goods, &c., by a vendor, binds not. (See Maxim 212.)

980. *Si quidem in nomine, cognomine, prænomine, legatarii testator erraverit, cum de personâ constat, nihilominus valet legatum* (Inst. 2, 20, 29).—Though a testator may have made a mistake in the proper name or in the surname of the legatee, when it is certain who is the person meant, the legacy is nevertheless valid. (See Maxim 263.)

981. *Si quid universitati debetur singulis non debetur nec quod debet universitas singuli debent* (D. 3, 4, 7, 1).—If anything is owed to an entire body it is not owed to the individual members, nor do the individual members owe what is owed by the entire body.

982. *Si quis unum percusserit, cum alium percutere vellet, in feloniâ tenetur* (3 Inst. 51).—If a man kill one, meaning to kill another, he is held guilty of felony.

983. *Si suggestio non sit vera, literæ patentes vacuæ sunt* (10 Co. 113).—If the suggestion be not true, the letters patent are void.

984. *Socii mei socius meus socius non est* (D. 50, 17, 47).—The partner of my partner is not my partner.

985. *Solo cedit, quicquid solo plantatur* (Went. Off. Ex. 57).—What is affixed to the soil belongs to the soil. (See Maxim 854.)

986. *Solutio pretii emptionis loco habetur* (Jenk. Cent. 56).—The payment of the price stands in the place of the purchase.

987. *Sommonitiones aut citationes nullæ liceant fieri infra palatium regis* (3 Inst. 141).—No summonses or citations are permitted to be served within the king's palace.

988. *Specialia generalibus derogant* (L. R. 1 C.P. 546).—Special words derogate from general ones. (See Maxims 312, 968.)

989. *Spoliatus debet ante omnia restitui* (2 Inst. 714).—
The despoiled ought to be restored before anything else. (See
2 T. R. 753.)

990. *Sponsalia dicuntur futurarum nuptiarum conventio et
repromissio* (Co. Litt. 34).—A betrothing is the agreement and
promise of a future marriage.

991.   *Sponte virum fugiens mulier et adultera facta,*
         Dote suâ careat, nisi sponsi sponte retracta
(Co. Litt. 37).—A woman leaving her husband of her own
accord, and committing adultery, loses her dower, unless her
husband take her back of his own accord.

992. *Stabit præsumptio donec probetur in contrarium* (Co.
Rep. 71b).—A presumption will stand good until the contrary
is proved.

> It is a general rule that, where a person is required to do
> an act, the not doing of which would make him guilty of
> a criminal neglect of duty, it shall be intended that he
> has duly performed it unless the contrary be shown;
> negative evidence rebuts this presumption, that all has
> been duly performed.

993. *Statutum affirmativum non derogat communi legi*
(Jenk. Cent. 24).—An affirmative statute does not take from
the common law. (See Maxim 829.)

994. *Sublato fundamento cadit opus* (Jenk. Cent. 106).—
Remove the foundation, the superstructure falls.

995a. *Sublata causa, tollitur effectus* (2 Bl. Com. 203).—
The cause being removed, the effect ceases. (See Maxim 917.)

995b. *Sublato principali tollitur adjunctum* (Co. Litt. 389).
—The principal being taken away, its adjunct is also taken
away.

> When the estate to which a warranty is annexed is defeated,
> the warranty is also defeated.

996. *Subsequens matrimonium tollit peccatum præcedens*
(Reg. Jur. Civ.).—A subsequent marriage removes the previous
wrong.

997. *Succurritur minori: facilis est lapsus juventutis* (Jenk. Cent. 47).—A minor is to be assisted: a mistake of youth is easy. (See Maxim 577.)

998. *Summa ratio est quæ pro religione facit* (Co. Litt. 341).—The highest rule is that which advances religion.

In deciding doubtful points of law our Courts can give due weight to moral considerations; but where our law is clear, they are bound to administer the law as they find it, irrespective of opinions upon its morality. With regard to foreign laws, however, when they are brought to their notice, our Courts do not feel compelled by what is called the comity of nations to violate our own laws, or the laws of God and nature.

999. *Summum jus, summa injuria* (Hob. 125).—Extreme law is extreme injury.

1000. *Super fidem chartarum, mortuis testibus, erit ad patriam de necessitate recurrendum* (Co. Litt. 6).—The truth of charters is necessarily to be referred to a jury, when the witnesses are dead.

1001. *Superflua non nocent* (Jenk. Cent. 184).—Superfluities hurt not. (See Maxims 1002, 1038.)

1002. *Surplusagium non nocet* (9 H. 6, 26).—Surplusage hurts not.

It is a rule with reference to the construction of written instruments, and in the science of pleading, that matter which is mere surplusage may be rejected, and does not vitiate the instrument or pleading in which it is found. (See Maxims 711, 1038.)

1003. *Talis interpretatio semper fienda est, ut evitetur absurdum et inconveniens, et ne judicium sit illusorium* (1 Rep. 52).—Interpretation is always to be made in such a manner that what is absurd and inconvenient may be avoided, and that judgment may not be illusory.

1004. *Talis non est eadem; nam nullum simile est idem* (4 Co. 18).—What is like is not the same; for nothing similar is the same.

1005. *Tantum bona valent, quantum vendi possunt* (3 Inst. 305).—Things are worth what they will sell for.

1006. *Tenor est pactio contra communem feudi naturam ac rationem in contractu interposita* (Wright, Ten. 21).—Tenure is a compact contrary to the common nature of the fee, put into a contract.

1007. *Tenor est qui legem dat feudo* (Craig, Jus. Feud. 66). It is the tenor of the feudal grant which regulates its effect and extent. (See Maxims 158, 591.)

1008. *Terminus annorum certus debet esse et determinatus* (Co. Litt. 45).—A term of years ought to be certain and determinate.

1009. *Terminus, et feodum non possunt constare simul in una eademque persona* (Plow. Com. 29).—The term and the fee cannot both be in one and the same person at the same time.

1010. *Terra transit cum onere.*—See Maxim 1020a.

1011. *Testamenta, cum duo inter se pugnantia reperiuntur, ultimum ratum est; sic est, cum duo inter se pugnantia reperiuntur in eodem testamento* (Co. Litt. 112).—When two conflicting wills are found, the last prevails; so it is when two conflicting clauses occur in the same will.

1012. *Testamenta latissimam interpretationem habere debent* (Jenk. Cent. 81).—Wills ought to have the broadest interpretation. (See Maxims 413, 421, 1034.)

1013. *Testibus deponentibus in pari numero dignioribus est credendum* (4 Inst. 279).—Where the number of witnesses is equal on both sides, the more worthy are to be believed.

1014. *Testis lupanaris sufficit ad factum in lupanari* (Moor, 817).—A strumpet is a sufficient witness to a happening in a brothel.

1015. *Testis oculatus unus plus valet quam auriti decem* (4 Inst. 279).—One eye-witness is worth more than ten ear-witnesses.

1016. *Testmoignes ne poent testifie le negative, mes l'affirmative* (4 Inst. 279).—Witnesses cannot prove a negative, but an affirmative.

1017. *Thesaurus competit domino regi, et non domino libertatis, nisi sit per verba specialia* (Fitz. Corone, 281).—A treasure belongs to the king, and not to the lord of a liberty, unless it be through special words.

1018. *Thesaurus inventus est vetus dispositio pecuniæ, &c., cujus non extat modo memoria, adeo ut jam dominum non habeat* (3 Inst. 132).—Treasure-trove is an ancient hiding of money, &c., of which no recollection exists, so that it now has no owner. (See Maxims 741, 873b.)

1019a. *Thesaurus non competit regi, nisi quando nemo scit qui abscondit thesaurum* (3 Inst. 132).—Treasure does not belong to the king, unless no one knows who hid it.

1019b. *Traditio loqui chartam facit* (5 Rep. 1).—Delivery makes a deed speak. (See Maxim 424.)

1020a. *Transit terra cum onere* (Co. Litt. 231a).—Land passes with its burthen. (See Maxims 4, 875.)

1020b. *Triatio ibi semper debet fieri, ubi juratores meliorem possunt habere notitiam* (7 Co. 1).—Trial ought to be had always there where the jury can have the best knowledge.

1021. *Turpis est pars quæ non convenit cum suo toto* (Plow. 161).—That part is bad which accords not with its whole.

1022. *Tuta est custodia quæ sibimet creditur* (Hob. 340).—That guardianship is secure which trusts to itself alone.

1023. *Tutius semper est errare acquietando quam in puniendo, ex parte misericordiæ quam ex parte justitiæ* (H. H. P.C. 290).—It is always safer to err in acquitting than in punishing : on the side of mercy, than of strict justice.

1024. *Ubi aliquid conceditur, conceditur et id sine quo res ipsa esse non potest.*—Where anything is granted, that is also granted without which the thing itself is not able to exist. (See Maxim 156.)

1025. *Ubi cessat remedium ordinarium ibi decurritur ad extraordinarium* (4 Co. 93).—Where a common remedy ceases, there recourse must be had to an extraordinary one.

1026. *Ubi damna dantur, victus victori in expensis condemnari debet* (2 Inst. 289).—Where damages are given the losing party ought to pay the costs of the victor.

1027. *Ubi eadem ratio ibi idem jus, et de similibus idem est judicium* (Co. Litt. 191).—Where there is the same reason, there is the same right; and of things similar, the judgment is similar.

> For the first part of this maxim it may be said that law is founded upon reason, and is the perfection thereof, and that what is contrary to reason is contrary to law; and for the second, that where no established precedent can be found exactly in point, whereupon to ground a decision, the case in question may be properly decided by reference to similar cases. (See Maxims 103, 524, 917, 918.)

1028. *Ubi jus ibi remedium* (Co. Litt. 197).—Where there is a right, there is a remedy.

> *Jus* signifies here the legal authority to do or to demand something; and *remedium* may be defined to be the right of action, or the means given by law, for the recovery or assertion of a right. It was held in *Ashby* v. *White* that a man who has a right to vote at an election for Members of Parliament may maintain an action against the returning officer for maliciously refusing to admit his vote, though his right was never determined in Parliament, and though the persons for whom he offered to vote were elected; and Lord Holt observed that "if men will multiply injuries, actions must be multiplied too, for every man that is injured ought to have his recompense (*Ashby* v. *White*, 1 Smith L.C.). (See Maxims 170, 391.)

1029. *Ubi lex aliquem cogit ostendere causam necesse est quod causa sit justa et legitima* (2 Inst. 269).—Where the law compels a man to show cause, it is incumbent that the cause be just and lawful.

1030. *Ubi lex non distinguit, nec nos distinguere debemus* (7 Co. 5).—Where the law distinguishes not, we ought not to distinguish.

1031*a*. *Ubi non est principalis non potest esse accessorius* (4 Co. 43).—Where there is no principal, there cannot be an accessory. (See Maxim 4.)

1031*b*. *Ubi nullum matrimonium, ibi nulla dos est* (Co. Litt. 32).—Where there is no marriage there is no dower. (See Maxim 208.)

1032. *Ubi quid generaliter conceditur inest hæc exceptio si non aliquid sit contra jus fasque* (11 Rep. 78*b*).—Where a thing is conceded generally, this exception arises, that there shall be nothing contrary to law and right.

> If an act which is the subject of a contract may, according to the circumstances, be lawful or unlawful, it will not be presumed that the contract was to do the unlawful act: the contrary is the proper inference.

1033. *Ubi verba conjuncta non sunt sufficit alterutrum esse factum* (D. 50, 17, 110).—Where words are not conjoined it suffices if either be complied with. (See Maxim 377.)

1034. *Ultima voluntas testatoris est perimplenda secundum veram intentionem suam* (Co. Litt. 322).—The last will of a testator is to be fulfilled according to his true intention. (See Maxims 82, 421, 413, 1012.)

1035. *Unumquodque dissolvitur eodem ligamine quo ligatur.* —See Maxim 671.

1036. *Unumquodque eodem modo quo colligatum est dissolvitur* (2 Rolle Rep. 39).—In the same manner in which anything is bound it is loosened. (See Maxim 671.)

1037. *Usucapio constituta est ut aliquis litium finis esset.*— The object of *usucapio* is to put an end to litigation.

1038. *Utile per inutile non vitiatur* (Dyer, 292).—That which is useful is not rendered useless by that which is useless. Where words of known significance are so placed in the context of a deed that they make it repugnant and senseless, they are to be rejected equally with words of no known signification. It is also a rule in conveyancing, that if an estate be granted in any premises, and that grant is express and certain, the *habendum*, although repugnant to the deed, shall not vitiate it. (See Maxims 183, 263, 578, 1002.)

1039. *Utlagatus est quasi extra legem positus: caput gerit lupinum* (7 Co. 14).—An outlaw is, as it were, put out of the protection of the law : he carries the head of a wolf.

1040. *Ut pœna ad paucos, metus ad omnes perveniat* (4 Inst. 6).—Though few are punished, the fear of punishment affects all. (See Maxim 354.)

1041. *Ut res magis valeat quam pereat* (Noy, Max. 50).—It is better for a thing to have effect than to be made void. (See Maxim 82.)

1042. *Uxor non est sui juris sed sub potestate viri* (3 Inst. 108).—A wife has no power of her own, but is under the government of her husband. (See Maxim 758.)

1043. *Vani timores sunt æstimandi qui non cadunt in constantem virum* (7 Rep. 27).—Those fears are to be counted vain which affect not a resolute man. (See Maxim 866.)

1044. *Verba æquivoca ac in dubio sensu posita intelliguntur digniori et potentiori sensu* (6 Co. 20).—Words equivocal, and placed in a doubtful sense, are to be taken in their more worthy and effective sense.

1045. *Verbc aliquid operari debent; debent intelligi ut aliquid operentur* (8 Co. 94).—Words ought to have some effect; they ought to be interpreted in such a way as to give them some effect.

1046. *Verba chartarum fortius accipiuntur contra proferentem* (Co. Litt. 36).—The words of deeds are to be taken
most strongly against him who uses them.

> This maxim ought to be applied only where other rules of
> construction fail; and, indeed, in *Taylor* v. *St. Helen's
> Corporation*, Jessel, M.R., is reported to have said : '' I
> do not see how, according to the now established rules
> of construction as settled by the House of Lords in the
> well-known case of *Grey* v. *Pearson*, followed by *Roddy*
> v. *Fitzgerald* and *Abbott* v. *Middleton*, the maxim can
> be considered as having any force at the present day.
> The rule is to find out the meaning of the instrument
> according to the ordinary and proper rules of construction.
> If we can thus find out its meaning, we do not want
> the maxim.   If, on the other hand, we cannot find out
> its meaning, then the instrument is void for uncertainty,
> and in that case it may be said that the instrument
> is construed in favour of the grantor, for the grant is
> annulled.''

1047. *Verba cum effectu accipienda sunt* (Bac. Max.
Reg. 3).—Words are to be understood according to their effect.
(See Maxim 82.)

1048. *Verba generalia generaliter sunt intelligenda* (3 Inst.
76).—General words are to be generally understood. (See
Maxim 309.)

1049. *Verba generalia restringuntur ad habilitatem rei vel
aptitudinem personæ* (Bac. Max. Reg. 10).—General words are
restricted to the nature of the subject-matter or the aptitude of
the person.

> In accordance with the above maxim, the subject-matter
> of an agreement is to be considered in construing its
> terms, and they are to be understood in the sense most
> agreeable to the nature of the agreement.   If a deed
> relates only to a particular subject, general words in it
> shall be confined to that subject, otherwise they must
> be taken in their general sense.   The words of the
> condition of a bond cannot be taken at large, but must
> be tied up to the particular matters of the recital, unless,

indeed, the condition itself is manifestly designed to be extended beyond the recital. (See Maxim 313.)

1050. *Verba intentioni, non è contra, debent inservire* (8 Co. 94).—Words ought to be made subservient to the intent, not contrary to it. (See Maxims 82, 557, 578.)

1051. *Verba illata inesse videntur* (Co. Litt. 359).—Words inferred are to be considered as incorporated.

1052. *Verba ita sunt intelligenda ut res magis valeat quam pereat.*—See Maxim 82.

1053. *Verba posteriora, propter certitudinem addita, ad priora, quæ certitudine indigent, sunt referenda* (Wing.).— Subsequent words, added for the purpose of certainty, are to be referred to preceding words which need certainty.

> If any section of an Act be intricate, obscure, or doubtful, the proper mode of discovering its true meaning is by comparing it with the other sections, and finding out the sense of one clause by the words or obvious intent of another. Reference should be made to a subsequent section in order to explain a previous clause of which the meaning is doubtful.

1054. *Verba relata hoc maximè operantur per referentiam ut in eis inesse videntur* (Co. Litt. 359).—Words to which reference is made in an instrument have the same effect and operation as if they were inserted in the instrument referring to them.

> It is important to bear in mind, when reading any particular clause of a deed or written instrument, that regard must be paid not only to the language of that clause, but also to that of any other clause which may by reference be incorporated with it. For instance, if a contract or an Act of Parliament refer to a plan, the plan forms part of the contract or Act, for the purpose for which the reference is made.

1055. *Veredictum, quasi dictum veritatis, ut judicium quasi juris dictum* (Co. Litt. 226).—The verdict is, as it were, the *dictum* of truth, as the judgment is the *dictum* of law.

1056. *Veritas, à quocunque dicitur, à Deo est* (4 Inst. 153). Truth, by whomsoever pronounced, is from God.

1057. *Veritas nihil veretur nisi abscondi* (9 Co. 20).—Truth fears nothing but concealment.

1058. *Veritas nimium altercando amittitur* (Hob. 334).—By too much altercation truth is lost.

1059. *Veritas nominis tollit errorem demonstrationis* (Bac. Max. Reg. 24).—See Maxim 813.

1060. *Via trita via tuta* (10 Rep. 142).—The trodden road is the safe one.

> This maxim should be considered in connection with Maxim 167. Courts of law will not sanction a speculative novelty without the warrant of any principle, precedent, or authority. (See Maxims 289, 761.)

1061. *Vicarius non habet vicarium.*—A delegate cannot have a delegate. (See Maxim 179.)

1062. *Vigilantibus, et non dormientibus, jura subveniunt* (Wing. 692).—The vigilant, and not the sleepy, are assisted by the laws.

> In all actions, suits, and other proceedings at law and in equity, the diligent and careful actor is favoured to the prejudice of him who is careless. The Statutes of Limitation, whether as respects real or personal property, persons, or things, are made in furtherance of the principle of this maxim. So the law may deny relief to one who has long and negligently delayed to file a bill for specific performance.

1063. *Violenta præsumptio aliquando est plena probatio* (Co. Litt. 6).—Violent presumption is sometimes full proof.

1064. *Viperina est expositio quæ corrodit viscera textus* (11 Co. 34).—It is a bad exposition which corrupts the text.

1065. *Vir et uxor censentur in lege una persona* (Jenk. Cent. 27).—Husband and wife are considered one person in law.

> The rigidity of this old fiction of the common law has been greatly modified by legislation.

1066. *Vitium clerici nocere non debet* (Jenk. Cent. 23).—An error of a clerk ought not to hurt.

1067. *Vix ulla lex fieri potest quæ omnibus commoda sit, sed si majori parti prospiciat utilis est* (Plow. 369).—Scarcely any law can be made which is applicable to all things; but it is useful if it regard the greater part.

1068. *Volenti non fit injuria* (Wing. Max. 482).—That to which a man consents cannot be considered an injury.

> In actions founded on tort the leave and licence of the plaintiff to do the act complained of usually constitutes a good defence; and as a rule a man must bear loss arising from acts to which he assented. On this principle, when a man connives at or condones the adultery of his wife, he cannot in such a case obtain damages from the seducer, nor sustain a petition for divorce. A railway company usually owes a duty to a passenger to take reasonable care of him, but he cannot demand such care if he expressly agree, in consideration of a free pass, to travel at his own risk. (See Maxims 130, 685.)

1069. *Voluntas donatoris in chartâ doni sui manifestè expressa observetur* (Co. Litt. 21).—The will of the donor, manifestly expressed in his deed of gift, is to be observed.

1070. *Voluntas facit quod in testamento scriptum valeat* (D. 30, 1, 12).—The intention makes the wording of a will effective.

1071. *Voluntas in delictis non exitus spectatur* (2 Inst. 57).—In crimes, the will, and not the result, is looked to. (See Maxims 115, 1072.)

1072. *Voluntas reputabatur pro facto* (3 Inst. 69).—The will is to be taken for the deed.

> This is the old maxim with respect to treasonable offences. To constitute the offence of treason the intent alone was sufficient. Between subject and subject the will is not to be taken for the deed unless there be some external

act which shows that progress has been made in the direction of it, or towards maturing and effecting it. (See Maxims 26, 1071.)

1073. *Voluntas testatoris est ambulatoria usque ad extremum vitæ exitum* (4 Co. 61).—The will of a testator is ambulatory until death. (See Maxim 752.)

1074. *Voluntas testatoris habet interpretationem latam et benignam* (Jenk. Cent. 260).—The intention of a testator has a broad and benignant interpretation.

1075. *Vulgaris opinio est duplex—viz. orta inter graves et discretos, quæ multum veritatis habet, et opinio orta inter leves et vulgares homines, absque specie veritatis* (4 Co. 107).— Common opinion is double—namely, that proceeding from grave and discreet men, which has much truth in it, and that proceeding from foolish and vulgar men, without any semblance of truth in it.

SUBJECT-INDEX TO MAXIMS

17

17*

PART III.—GENERAL VOCABULARY

A.

a or **ab,** prep. w. abl., *from, by.*
abátaméntum,-i, n. *abatement, destroying.*
abáto,-áre,-ávi,-átum, *abate, enter into land, destroy.*
abbréviatúra,-æ, f. *abridgment.*
abétto,-áre,-ávi,-átum, *abet, assist.*
abhórreo,-ére,-ui, ——, *shrink from, be adverse to, abhor.*
abjúro,-áre,-ávi,-átum, *abjure, forswear.*
abóleo,-ére,-évi, or **ui,-ítum,** *abolish, destroy.*
abortívus,-a,-um, adj., *abortive.*
abrogátio,-ónis, f. *repeal, abrogation.*
ábrogo,-áre,-ávi,-átum, *repeal, abrogate, disannul.*
abscóndo,-ere,-di,-ditum, *hide, secrete, conceal.*
ábsens,-ntis, adj., *absent.*
absolútus,-a,-um, adj., *absolute.*
absólvo,-ere,-vi,-solútum, *absolve from, acquit.*
absque, prep., *without.*
absum, abesse, afui, *be absent, wanting.*
absúrdus,-a,-um, adj., *absurd, discordant.*
abúndans,-ntis, adj., *abundant, unusual.*
abúndo,-áre,-ávi,-átum, *overflow, abound.*
abúsus,-us, m. *abuse, using up.*
abutto,-áre,-ávi,-átum, *abut, border upon.*
ac, conj., *and.*
accélero,-áre,-ávi,-átum, *quicken, accelerate, make haste.*
acceptántia,-æ, f. *acceptance.*
acceptátio,-ónis, f. *acceptance.*
accéssio,-ónis, f. *addition, approach.*
accessitor,-óris, m. *accuser.*
accessórium,-ii, n. *accessory, incident.*
accessórius,-a,-um, adj., *accessory.*
áccidens,-ntis, n. *accident.*
áccido,-ere,-cidi,——, *happen, fall to.*
accípio,-ere,-cépi,-céptum, *accept, receive.*
accompliaméntum,-i, n. *accomplishment.*

accrésco,-ere,-évi,-étum, *survive, accrue.*
accusátor,-óris, m. *accuser, plaintiff.*
accúso,-áre,-ávi,-átum, *accuse.*
acquietántia,-æ, f. *acquittance.*
acquíeto,-áre,-ávi,-átum, *acquit, discharge.*
acra,-æ, f. *acre.*
áctio,-ónis, f. *action.*
áctor,-óris, m. *plaintiff, doer.*
áctum,-i, n. *act.*
áctus,-us, m. *act.*
ad, prep. with acc., *based upon, according to.*
adápto,-áre,-ávi,-átum, *suit, adapt.*
áddo,-ere,-didi,-ditum, *add.*
addúco,-ere,-duxi,-ductum, *lead to, adduce.*
adeo, adv., *so, just, moreover.*
adhaéreo,-ére,-si,-sum, *cling to.*
adhíbeo,-ére,-ui,-itum, *give to.*
adímpleo,-ére,-évi,-étum, *fulfil, carry out.*
adjórno,-áre,-ávi,-átum, *adjourn.*
adjournaméntum,-i, n. *adjournment.*
adjúngo,-ere,-nxi,-nctum, *join to, add to.*
administrátio,-ónis, f. *administration.*
admínistro,-áre,-ávi,-átum, *administer.*
admirálitas,-átis, f. *the Admiralty.*
admítto,-ere,-mísi,-míssum, *admit, receive.*
adnullátio,-ónis, f. *nullity, an annulling.*
adnúmero,-áre,-ávi,-átum, *include among, reckon with, pay to.*
adsum, adesse, adfui, *be present.*
adúlter,-i, m. *adulterer.*
adúltera,-æ, f. *adulteress.*
adultérium,-ii, n. *adultery.*
adversárius,-ii, m. *adversary.*
ædífico,-áre,-ávi,-átum, *build.*
æquális,-e, adj., *equal.*
æquálitas,-tátis, f. *equality, uniformity.*
æquipáro,-áre,-ávi,-átum, *put on equality with, equal.*
aéquitas,-átis, f. *equity.*
aequivocus,-a,-um, adj., *equivocal.*
aéquus,-a,-um, adj., *just.*
æs, æris, n. *money.*
æstimátio,-ónis, f. *estimate, value.*
aéstimo,-áre,-ávi,-átum, *estimate, value.*

aétas,-átis, f. *age, majority.*
ætérnus,-a,-um, adj., *eternal.*
afféctus (adf-),-us, m. *intention, desire, disposition.*
afféro (adf-),-férre, áttuli, adlátum, *bring to, allege.*
affício,-ere,-féci,-féctum, *affect.*
affidátio,-ónis, f. *affidavit.*
affirmátio,-ónis, f. *affirmation.*
affirmatívus,-a,-um, adj., *affirmative.*
affírmo (adf-), - áre, - ávi, - átum, *affirm, corroborate, confirm.*
affráia,-æ, f. *affray.*
agens,-éntis, c. *agent.*
ágo,-ere, égi, áctum, *transact, act, perform, bring action.*
álias, adv., *otherwise, on another occasion.*
alienátio,-ónis, f. *alienation, transfer of property.*
aliéno,-áre,-ávi,-átum, *alienate.*
aliénus,-a,-um, adj., *another's.*
aliquándo, adv., *sometimes, formerly.*
áliquis, áliquid, indef. subst. pron., *some one, anything.*
áliter, adv., *otherwise.*
álius,-a,-ud, pron. adj., *other than one, another.*
állegans,-ntis, *one alleging.*
allegátio,-ónis, f. *allegation.*
allegátum,-i, n. *allegation, averment.*
állego,-áre,-ávi,-átum, *allege.*
álloquor,-loqui,-locútus sum, *address, speak to.*
allúvio,-ónis, f. *alluvion.*
álter,-era,-erum, adj., *another, one or other.*
áltercor,-ári,-átus, *dispute.*
alternatívus,-a,-um, adj., *alternative.*
álteruter, alterutra, alterutrum, pron. adj., *either, one of two.*
áltus,-a,-um, adj., *high.*
ambígue, adv., *ambiguously, obscurely.*
ambigúitas,-átis, f. *ambiguity.*
ambíguus,-a,-um, adj., *ambiguous, obscure.*
ambo,-æ,-o, adj., *both.*
ambulatórius,-a,-um, adj., *ambulatory.*
amícus,-i, m. *friend.*
amítto,-ere,-mísi,-míssum, *lose.*
amóveo,-ére,-móvi,-mótum, *remove, steal.*
ámplio,-áre,-ávi,-átum, *enlarge.*
ámplius, adv., *further, again.*

an, conj., *whether, or.*
Anglia,-æ, f. *England.*
angústus,-a,-um, adj., *narrow, restricted.*
angústo,-áre,-ávi,-átum, *restrict, limit.*
ánimal,-ális, n. *animal.*
ánimus,-i, m. *mind, intention.*
annécto,-ere,-néxui,-néxum, *fasten to.*
ánnus,-i, m. *year.*
ánte, prep. w. acc., *before.*
anteá, adv., *formerly, before.*
antecédens,-ntis, n. *antecedent.*
antecéssor,-óris, m. *ancestor.*
anteféro,-férre,-túli,-látum, *prefer.*
antenátus,-i, m. *one born before wedlock.*
antequam, conj., *before that.*
antíquus,-a,-um, adj., *ancient, old.*
apértus,-a,-um, adj., *open.*
appáreo,-ére,-ui,-itum, *appear.*
appellátio,-ónis, f. *title, appeal.*
appéllo,-áre,-ávi,-átum, *appeal, call by name, sue.*
appéto,-ere,-ívi or **ii,-ítum,** *strive after.*
applicátio,-ónis, f. *application.*
appóno,-ere,-pósui,-pósitum, *apply.*
ápprobo,-áre,-ávi,-átum, *approve.*
aptitúdo,-inis, f. *aptitude.*
aptus,-a,-um, adj., *fit, suitable, adapted.*
ápud, prep. w. acc., *among.*
áqua,-æ, f. *water.*
árbiter,-tri, m. *judge, master, controller.*
arbítrium,-ii, n. *award, discretion.*
árbor,-oris, f. *tree.*
árctus,-a,-um, adj., *binding, strict.*
árduus,-a,-um, adj., *high, difficult, troublesome.*
área,-æ, f. *building site.*
arguméntum,-i, n. *argument.*
árma,-órum, n. plur., *arms.*
armátus,-i, m. *an armed person.*
ármo,-áre,-ávi,-átum, *arm.*
arrestátus,-a,-um, adj., *accused, suspected.*
árs, ártis, f. *art, handicraft, calling.*
artículus,-i, m. *article, moment.*
ártifex,-icis, c. *artificer, artist.*
ascéndo,-ere,-scéndi,-scénsum, *ascend.*

asséntio,-íre,-sénsi,-sénsum, *assent to.*
asséntio,-ónis, f. *assent, meeting.*
assignátus,-i, m. *assignee.*
assuetúdo,-inis, f. *usage.*
átque, conj., *and.*
átrox,-ócis, adj., *savage, cruel, violent.*
atténdo,-ere,-téndi,-téntum, *attend, observe.*
aúctor,-óris, m. *assignor, creator, seller.*
auctóritas,-átis, f. *authority.*
aucúpium,-ii, n. *quibbling.*
aúdio,-íre,-ívi,-ítum, *hear.*
aúla,-æ, f. *hall, court.*
aurítus,-i, m. *ear-witness.*
aut, conj., *either,* or *rather.*
aútem, conj., *but, yet, however.*
auxílior,-ári,-átus, *aid, assist.*
auxílium,-ii, n., *help, aid.*

B.

bastárdia,-æ, f. *bastardy.*
bastárdus,-i, m. *bastard.*
béllum,-i, n. *war.*
béne, adv., *well, correctly* (with adj. or adv., *very, extremely*).
beneficiális,-e, adj., *beneficial.*
benefícium,-ii, n. *benefit, advantage.*
benígne, adv., *favourably, liberally.*
benígnus,-a,-um, adj., *favourable, liberal.*
bílla,-æ, f. *bill, writ.*
bis, num. adv., *twice.*
bóna,-órum, n. plur., *goods, property.*
bónus,-a,-um, adj., *good.*
bónus,-i, m. *bonus.*
bréve,-is, n. *writ.*
brévis,-e, adj., *brief, short.*

C.

cádo,-ere, cécidi, cásum, *fail, fall.*
caécus,-a,-um, adj., *hidden, secret, doubtful.*
caédium,-ii, n. *slaughter.*
caéterus,-a,-um, adj., *the other, the rest.*

calámitas,-átis, f. *misfortune, loss, injury.*
cancelária,-æ, f. *chancery.*
cápax,-ácis, adj., *capable of, able to hold.*
cápio,-ere, cépi, cáptum, *be capable of, take, receive, hold.*
cápital,-is, n. *capital crime.*
cáput,-itis, n. *head, leader.*
cárcer,-eris, n. *prison.*
cáreo,-ére,-ui,-itum, *be free from, not have.*
cássis,-idis, f. *helmet.*
cásso,-áre,-ávi,-átum, *quash.*
cásus,-us, m. *event.*
catállum,-i, n. *chattel.*
caúsa,-æ, f. *cause, motive.*
caúso,-áre,-ávi,-átum, *cause, move.*
cautéla,-æ, f. *caution.*
cáveo,-ére, cávi, caútum, *beware.*
cédo,-ere, céssi, céssum, *pass, go, yield.*
céler,-eris,-ere, adj., *swift, quick.*
célo,-áre,-ávi,-átum, *conceal.*
cénseo,-ére,-ui,-sum, *reckon, hold, judge.*
certitúdo,-inis, f. *certainty.*
cértus,-a,-um, adj., *certain.*
césso,-áre,-ávi,-átum, *cease.*
chárta,-æ, f. *writing, instrument, deed.*
chártum,-i, n. *deed.*
chírographum,-i, n. *the document itself.*
círca, prep., *about.*
circúitus,-us, m. *circuitous way.*
circumvéntio,-ónis, f. *circumventing, defrauding.*
citátio,-ónis, f. *citation.*
cíto, adv., *quickly, sooner, rather.*
civílis,-e, adj., *civil, relating to state.*
civíliter, adv., *civilly.*
clandestínus,-a,-um, adj., *secret.*
clárus,-a,-um, adj., *clear, plain.*
claúdico,-áre,-ávi,-átum, *be defective, halt, limp.*
claústrum,-i, n. *bounds, barrier.*
claúsula,-æ, f. *clause.*
cleméntia,-æ, f. *clemency.*
cléricus,-i, m. *clerk, clergy.*
clýpeus,-i, m. *shield.*
coélum,-i, n. *sky.*
coérceo,-ére,-cui,-citum, *confine, restrain.*

cogitátio,-ónis, f. *thought.*
cógito,-áre,-ávi,-átum, *design, purpose, ponder.*
cognátio,-ónis, f. *blood-relationship. .*
cognómen,-inis, n. *surname.*
cognósco,-ere,-nóvi,-nítum, *ascertain, investigate, try (a case).*
cógo,-ere, coégi, coáctum, *compel, drive, force.*
cohábito,-áre,-ávi,-átum, *live or dwell together.*
cohéres,-édis, c., *co-heir.*
cóitus,-us, m. *sexual intercourse.*
collectívus,-a,-um, adj., *collected.*
cólligo,-áre,-ávi,-átum, *bind together, connect.*
cólligo,-ere,-légi,-léctum, *collect.*
cómes,-itis, m. *companion, attendant.*
comítia(pl.)**,-orum,** n. *assembly, parliament.*
comfórto,-áre,-ávi,-átum, *comfort.*
commendátio,-ónis, f. *recommendation.*
comméndo,-áre,-ávi,-átum, *commend, recommend.*
commércium,-ii, n. *commerce, trade.*
commítto,-ere,-mísi,-míssum, *commit a crime.*
commodátum,-i, n. *loan.*
cómmodum,-i, n. *advantage, benefit.*
cómmodus,-a,-um, adj., *suitable, convenient.*
commúnis,-e, adj., *common.*
commúniter, adv., *in common, jointly, commonly.*
cómparo,-áre,-ávi,-átum, *compare, place on same footing with.*
compéto,-ere,-ívi,-ítum, *be suitable, qualified, belong.*
compléctor,-plexus, *comprehend, embrace.*
comprehéndo,-ere,-di,-sum, *comprehend, describe.*
cómprobo,-áre,-ávi,-átum, *sanction, confirm.*
compromissárius,-ii, m. *arbitrator.*
compútus,-i, m. *account.*
conátus,-us, m. *attempt.*
concédo,-ere,-céssi,-céssum, *yield, grant, concede.*
concéssio,-ónis, f. *grant.*
conclúsio,-ónis, f. *conclusion.*
concórdia,-æ, f. *concord.*
concórdo,-áre,-ávi,-átum, *reconcile, agree.*
concúbitus,-us, m. *cohabitation.*
concúrro,-ere,-cúrri,-cúrsum, *concur, conflict.*
condemnátio,-ónis, f. *sentence.*
condémno,-áre,-ávi,-átum, *condemn, sentence.*

condítio,-ónis, f. *condition.*
conféssio,-ónis, f. *confession, acknowledgment.*
conféssus, part. of *confiteor.*
confirmátio,-ónis, f. *confirmation.*
confírmo,-áre,-ávi,-átum, *confirm, corroborate.*
confíteor,-éri,-féssus, *confess, acknowledge.*
confúndo,-ere,-fúsi,-fúsum, *confound, perplex.*
conjúnctus,-a,-um, adj., *connected by birth or marriage, conjoined.*
connúbium,-ii, n. *marriage.*
cónqueror,-i,-quéstus, *complain bitterly.*
consciéntia,-æ, f. *conscience.*
consénsus,-us, m. *consent.*
conséntiens,-ntis, as adj., *agreeing.*
conséntio,-íre,-si,-sénsum, *consent.*
cónsequens,-ntis, adj., *following, suitable.*
consequéntia,-æ, f. *precedent, conclusion.*
cónsequor,-i,-secútus sum, *follow.*
consérvo,-áre,-ávi,-átum, *observe, regard, preserve.*
consídero,-áre,-ávi,-átum, *consider, inspect.*
consílium,-ii, n. *plan, purpose, advice.*
consímilis,-e, adj., *entirely, similar.*
consísto,-ere,-stiti,-stitum, *remain, exist, rest, depend upon.*
cónsonus,-a,-um, adj., *suitable, consonant.*
constans,-ntis, adj., *steadfast, firm, resolute.*
constítuo,-ere,-ui,-útum, *establish, set up.*
constitútio,-ónis, f. *ordinance, law.*
cónsto,-áre,-stiti,-státum, *be consistent with, correspond, exist, endure, be evident, appear.*
constrúctio,-ónis, f. *construction.*
cónstruo,-ere,-strúxi,-strúctum, *construct, create.*
consuetúdo,-inis, f. *custom.*
consúmmo,-áre,-ávi,-átum, *complete, accomplish, consummate.*
contemporáneus,-a,-um, adj., *contemporaneous.*
contíneo,-ére,-ui,-tentum, *include, contain.*
contíngens,-ntis, adj., *touching, contingent.*
contínuus,-a,-um, adj., *continuous.*
cóntra, prep. w. acc., *against;* adv., *on the contrary.*
contráctus,-us, m. *contract.*
cóntraho,-ere,-tráxi,-tráctum, *contract, consummate.*
contrárietas,-átis, f. *opposition, contrariety.*

contrárius,-a,-um, adj., *opposite, contrary.*
contravénio,-íre,-véni,-véntum, *thwart, run counter to.*
contrectátio,-ónis, f. *handling, touching.*
contribútio,-ónis, f. *contribution.*
cóntumax,-ácis, adj., *contumacious, defiant.*
convalésco,-ere,-válui,—, *gather strength.*
convénio,-íre,-véni,-véntum, *coincide, agree.*
convéntio,-ónis, f. *convention, contract, agreement.*
convérsus,-a,-um, *turned about.*
convérto,-ere,-ti,-sum, *transform, convert.*
convínco,-ere,-víci,-víctum, *convict.*
copulátio,-ónis, f. *joining, coupling.*
córam, prep. with abl., *in the presence of.*
Cornélius,-a,-um, adj., *of Cornelius.*
coróna,-æ, f. *crown.*
corporális,-e, adj., *corporeal, bodily.*
córpus,-oris, n. *body, person, gist.*
corréctio,-ónis, f. *amendment, reform.*
corródo,-ere,-si,-sum, *gnaw to pieces.*
corrúmpo,-ere,-rúpi,-rúptum, *destroy, corrupt.*
córtex,-icis, m. and f. *bark.*
créber,-bra,-brum, adj., *frequent.*
credíbilis,-e, adj., *credible.*
créditor,-óris, m. *creditor.*
crédo,-ere,-didi,-ditum, *believe, trust, intrust, lend.*
crésco,-ere, crévi, crétum, *grow, increase.*
crímen,-inis, n. *crime.*
criminális,-e, adj., *criminal.*
criminósus,-a,-um, adj., *slanderous, abusive, blameworthy.*
cújus,-a,-um, pron., *of whom, whose.*
cúlpa,-æ, f. *guilt, crime, fault.*
cúltus,-us, m. *worship.*
cum, prep. w. abl., *with, in company with.*
cum, conj., *when.*
cunctátio,-ónis, f. *delay.*
cupíditas,-átis, f. *avarice, cupidity.*
cúria,-æ, f. *court.*
cúro,-áre,-ávi,-átum, *care for, take care, adjust.*
cúrro,-ere,-cucúrri,-cúrsum, *run.*
cúrsus,-us, m. *practice.*
custódia,-æ, f. *custody, guard.*
custódio,-íre,-ívi, or ii,**-ítum,** *guard, protect, preserve.*
cústos,-ódis, c., *guardian.*

D.

damnátus,-a,-um, adj., *criminal.*
damnificátus,-a,-um, adj., *injured, damnified.*
dámno,-áre,-ávi,-átum, *condemn, sentence.*
damnósus,-a,-um, adj., *injurious, hurtful.*
dámnum,-i, n. *loss, damage.*
de, prep. w. abl., *about, concerning, according to.*
débeo,-ére,-ui,-itum, *ought.*
débilis,-e, adj., *weak.*
débitor,-óris, m. *debtor.*
débitum,-i, n. *debt.*
débitus,-a,-um, adj., *due.*
décem, indecl. adj., *ten.*
decérno,-ere,-crévi,-crétum, *determine, judge, decide.*
decído,-ere,-cídi,-císum, *decide.*
décima,-æ, f. *tithe.*
decípio,-ere,-cépi,-céptum, *deceive, impose upon.*
decísum,-i, n. *decision.*
declarátio,-ónis, f. *declaration, disclosure.*
decláro,-áre,-ávi,-átum, *reveal, explain.*
decrétum,-i, n. *decree.*
decúrro,-ere,-curri,-cursum, *have recourse to.*
dedúco,-ere,-xi,-ctum, *bring.*
deféctus,-us, m. *defect, error.*
deféndens,-ntis, m. *defendant.*
deféndo,-ere,-si,-sum, *defend.*
defénsio,-ónis, f. *defence.*
defício,-ere,-féci,-féctum, *fail.*
definio,-íre,-ívi,-ítum, *define.*
definítio,-ónis, f. *definition.*
definitívus,-a,-um, adj., *final.*
defúnctus,-a,-um, adj., *deceased, dead.*
dégo,-ere, dégi, —, *live, reside.*
delegátus,-a,-um, adj., *conferred, delegated.*
delégo,-áre,-ávi,-átum, *delegate, assign.*
deliberátio,-ónis, f. *deliberation, consideration.*
delíbero,-áre,-ávi,-átum, *deliberate, determine.*
delicátus,-i, m. *dainty person.*
delíctum,-i, n. *offence, crime.*
delínquo,-ere,-líqui,-líctum, *be wanting, offend.*
demándo,-áre,-ávi,-átum, *intrust, commit.*
demonstrátio,-ónis, f. *proof, indication, description.*

demónstro,-áre,-ávi,-átum, *indicate.*
depóno,-ere,-pósui,-pósitum, *depose.*
depósco,-ere,-popósci, —, *demand (for punishment).*
derivatívus,-a,-um, adj., *derived.*
derívo,-áre,-ávi,-átum, *derive, divert.*
derogatórius,-a,-um, adj., *derogatory.*
dérogo,-áre,-ávi,-átum, *detract from.*
descéndo,-ere,-di,-sum, *descend.*
desidérium,-ii, n. *desire.*
designátio,-ónis, f. *marking out, designation.*
désino,-ere,-sívi,-situm, *cease, stop.*
déstino,-áre,-ávi,-átum, *appoint, elect, intend.*
destítuo,-ere,-ui,-útum, *abandon, abrogate.*
destrúctio,-ónis, f. *destruction, refutation.*
déstruo,-ere,-xi,-ctum, *destroy.*
désum,-ésse,-fui, —, *be wanting.*
detégo,-ere,-téxi,-téctum, *uncover, reveal.*
deténtio,-ónis, f. *detention.*
detérior,-us, adj., *worse, poorer.*
deterióro,-áre,-ávi,-átum, *make worse, deteriorate.*
detérmino,-áre,-ávi,-átum, *determine, limit.*
detórqueo,-ére,-torsi,-tortum, *twist, distort.*
detriméntum,-i, n. *loss, damage.*
déus,-i, m. *God.*
devénio,-íre,-véni,-véntum, *relate to, arrive at.*
diábolus,-i, m. *devil.*
díco,-ere, díxi, díctum, *say, affirm, assert.*
dictámen,-inis, n. *dictate.*
díctum,-i, n. *saying.*
díes,-éi, m. *day.*
differo,-férre,-distuli, dilátum, *differ, postpone.*
dígnitas,-átis, f. *merit, authority, worth.*
dígnus,-a,-um, adj., *worthy, suitable.*
dilátio,-ónis, f. *delay.*
dimíssio,-ónis, f. *lease, discharge.*
diréctus,-a,-um, adj., *direct.*
dírimo,-ere,-émi,-émptum, *remove, destroy.*
discérno,-ere,-crévi,-crétum, *divide, ascertain.*
dísco,-ere, dídici, —, *learn.*
discrétio,-ónis, f. *discretion.*
discrétus,-a,-um, adj., *discreet, prudent.*
disjunctivus,-a,-um, adj., *disjunctive.*
displiceo,-ére,-ui,-itum, *displease, be dissatisfied.*

dispóno,-ere,-pósui,-pósitum, *dispose.*
disposítio,-ónis, f. *disposition, disposal, arrangement.*
dísputo,-áre,-ávi,-átum, *discuss, dispute.*
díssipo,-áre,-ávi,-átum, *scatter, publish.*
dissolútio,-ónis, f. *dissolution, abolition, refutation.*
dissólvo,-ere,-sólvi,-solútum, *unloose, discharge, abrogate.*
distínguo,-ere,-nxi,-nctum, *distinguish, separate.*
diú, adv., *for a long while.*
diutúrnitas,-átis, f. *long duration (of time).*
divérsus,-a,-um, adj., *different, diverse.*
divinátio,-ónis, f. *divination.*
divíno,-áre,-ávi,-átum, *prophesy, foretell, forecast.*
divínus,-a,-um, adj., *divine.*
divisíbilis,-e, adj., *divisible.*
divísio,-ónis, f. *division.*
divítiæ,-arum, f. pl., *riches, wealth.*
do, dáre, dédi, dátum, *give, furnish.*
dolósus,-a,-um, adj., *crafty, deceitful.*
dólum,-i, n. *device.*
dólus,-i, m. *deceit* (**dolus malus,** *fraud*).
domésticus,-a,-um, adj., *private, domestic.*
domínicus,-a,-um, adj., *of the lord.*
domínium,-ii, n. *lordship, right of ownership.*
dóminus,-i, m. *lord, master, owner.*
dómus,-i,[-us], f. *house.*
donatárius,-ii, m. *donee.*
donátio,-ónis, f. *donation, gift.*
donátor,-is, m. *donor.*
donec, conj., *while, until.*
dóno,-áre,-ávi,-átum, *give.*
dónum,-i, n. *gift.*
dórmiens,-ntis, c. *a sleeping or negligent person.*
dórmio,-íre,-ívi,(-íi),-ítum, *sleep.*
dos, dótis, f. *dower.*
dubitátio,-ónis, f. *doubt.*
dúbito,-áre,-ávi,-átum, *be in doubt, doubt.*
dúbius,-a,-um, adj., *doubtful, ambiguous.*
dúco,-ere, dúxi, dúctum, *lead.*
dúctor,-óris, m. *leader, guide.*
dum, conj., *while.*
dúo,-æ,-o, num. adj., *two.*
dúplex,-icis, adj., *twofold.*
dúrus,-a,-um, adj., *hard, harsh, stern, burdensome.*

E.

ebríetas,-átis, f. *drunkenness.*
ébrius,-a,-um, adj., *intoxicated.*
ecclésia,-æ, f. *church.*
ecclesiásticus,-a,-um, adj., *ecclesiastical.*
efféctum,-i, n. *effect.*
efféctus,-us, m. *effect, consequence.*
effício,-ere,-féci,-féctum, *accomplish, produce, show.*
effúndo,-ere,-fúdi,-fúsum, *shed.*
égo, pers. pron., *I.*
ejúro,-áre,-ávi,-átum, *renounce, abjure.*
eléctio,-ónis, f. *election.*
eméndo,-áre,-ávi,-átum, *correct, amend, improve.*
emérgo,-ere,-si,-sum, *emerge, appear.*
émo,-ere, émi, émptum, *buy, acquire.*
émptio,-ónis, f. *purchase.*
émptor,-óris, m. *buyer.*
énim, conj., *for, in fact.*
éo, íre, ívi, ítum, *go.*
epíscopus,-i, m. *bishop.*
equipólleo,-ére, *be of equal avail, prevail equally.*
erro,-áre,-ávi,-átum, *be mistaken, be in error.*
érror,-óris, m. *mistake, error.*
esséntia,-æ, f. *essence.*
essentiális,-e, adj., *essential.*
ét, conj., *and, also.*
étiam, conj., *even, also.*
evénio,-íre,-véni,-véntum, *result, happen.*
evéntus,-ús, m. *event, result.*
evíto,-áre,-ávi,-átum, *avoid, shun.*
ex, prep. w. abl., *by virtue of, from.*
exaúdio,-íre,-ívi,-ítum, *regard, heed.*
excédo,-ere,-céssi,-céssum, *exceed.*
excelléntia,-æ, f. *excellence, superiority.*
excéptio,-ónis, f. *exception.*
excessivum,-i, n. *prolixity, excess.*
excéssus,-us, m. *digression, departure.*
excípio,-ere,-cépi,-céptum, *except, receive.*
exclúdo,-ere,-clúsi,-clúsum, *exclude, explain.*
exclúsio,-ónis, f. *exclusion.*
excúso,-áre,-ávi,-átum, *excuse, condone.*
excútio,-cútere,-cússi,-cússum, *examine, search.*

execútio,-ónis, f. *execution*.
exémplum,-i, n. *example, copy, precedent*.
éxeo,-íre,-ii,-itum, *depart*.
exérceo,-ére,-cui,-citum, *exercise, administer, preside over*.
exercitátio,-ónis, f. *exercise, practice*.
exércitus,-us, m. *army*.
exhíbeo,-ére,-ui,-itum, *mete out, dispense, give*.
exhórreo,-ére, *tremble exceedingly, dread*.
éxigo,-ere,-égi,-áctum, *exact, demand, enforce*.
éximo,-ere,-émi,-émptum, *get rid of, remove*.
exísto,-ere,-stiti,-stitum, *exist, appear, happen*.
éxitus,-ús, m. *end, close, death*.
éxpedit, *it is profitable, expedient*.
expénsum,-i, n. *expense, money paid, costs*.
experiéntia,-æ, f. *experience*.
exposítio,-ónis, f. *construction, exposition*.
expréssio,-ónis, f. *expressing*.
éxprimo,-ere,-préssi,-préssum, *express, describe*.
exténdo,-ere,-di,-sum(-tum), *extend, prolong*.
exténsio,-ónis, f. *extension*.
exténsus,-a,-um, adj., *extensive*.
exténuo,-áre,-ávi,-átum, *extenuate, palliate*.
extérior,-óris, comp. adj., *outer, external*.
extérmino,-áre,-ávi,-átum, *destroy*.
extínguo,-ere,-stinxi,-stinctum, *extinguish, abolish*.
exto (exsto),-áre, *exist*.
extráho,-ere,-tráxi,-tráctum, *drag forth*.
extráneus,-i, m. *stranger, foreigner*.
extráordinárius,-a,-um, adj., *extraordinary*.
extrémus,-a,-um, adj., *dire, extreme, urgent*.
éxuo,-úere,-ui,-útum, *lay aside, divest oneself of*.

F.

fácilis,-e, adj., *easy*.
fácinus,-óris, n. *crime*.
fácio,-ere, féci, fáctum, *do, make, commit*.
fáctum,-i, n. *fact, deed, action*.
fácultas,-átis, f. *opportunity, capability*.
fállo, fállere, fefélli, fálsum, *deceive, escape*.
fálsus,-a,-um, adj., *false*.
fáma,-æ, f. *reputation, character, rumour*.
famósus,-a,-um, adj., *notorious, infamous, slanderous*.
fas, n. indecl., *divine law, right, lawful*.

fáteor,-éri, fássus sum, *confess.*
fatígo,-áre,-ávi,-átum, *weary, fatigue, vex.*
fátuus,-a,-um, adj., *foolish, silly.*
fáveo,-ére, fávi, faútum, *favour.*
fávor,-óris, m. *boon, favour.*
favorábilis,-e, adj., *in favour, popular.*
félix,-ícis, adj., *fortunate, happy.*
félleus,-a,-um, adj., *like gall, malignant.*
félo,-ónis, m. *felon.*
felónia,-æ, f. *felony.*
fémina,-æ, f. *woman.*
feódum or **feudum,-i,** n. *fee.*
feódum simplex, *fee simple.*
feódum taliátum, *fee tail.*
féro, férre, túli, látum, *bear, carry.*
festinátio,-ónis, f. *haste.*
fíctio,-ónis, f. *fiction.*
fídes,-ei, f. *faith, credit.*
filiátio,-ónis, f. *affiliation, copulation.*
fílius,-i, m. *son.*
fingo,-ere, finxi, fictum, *make, imagine, feign.*
fínis,-is, c. *end, limit, final.*
fío, fíeri, fáctus sum, *to be made, become, be produced.*
fírmo,-áre,-ávi,-átum, *strengthen.*
fírmus,-a,-um, adj., *firm, solid, strong.*
físcus,-i, m. *money, revenue.*
fíxus,-a,-um, adj., *fixed.*
flúmen,-inis, n. *river.*
fons,-ntis, m. *fountain-head, origin.*
fórma,-æ, f. *form.*
fórmula,-æ, f. *rule, principle, form of procedure.*
fórtis,-e, adj., *powerful, strong.*
fortúitus,-a,-um, adj., *fortuitous.*
fórum,-i, n. *forum, court.*
fráctio,-ónis, f. *fraction.*
fráter,-tris, m. *brother.*
fraudúlentus,-a,-um, adj., *fraudulent.*
fraudulósus,-a,-um, adj., *fraudulent.*
fraus,-dis, f. *fraud.*
fréquens,-ntis, adj., *frequent.*
frequéntia,-æ, f. *frequency.*
frústra, adv., *in vain, uselessly.*
frúctus,-us, m. *fruit.*

fucátus,-a,-um, adj., *painted*.
fúgio,-ere, fúgi, fúgitum, *fly from, run away*.
fúlcio,-íre, fúlsi, fúltum, *uphold, support*.
fundaméntum,-i, n. *foundation*.
fundus,-i, m. *bottom, guarantor, security*.
fúngor,-i, functus, *perform, discharge*.
furiósus,-i, m. *madman*.
fúror,-ári,-átus sum, *steal*.
fúror,-óris, m. *madness*.
fúrtum,-i, n. *theft*.
futúrum,-i, n. *future*.
futúrus,-a,-um, adj., *future*.

G.

generális,-e, adj., *general*.
generáliter, adv., *generally*.
género,-áre,-ávi,-átum, *create, beget*.
géns, géntis, f. *race, mankind, nation*.
génus,-eris, n. *descent, origin, descendant, sort, kind*.
géro,-ere, géssi, géstum, *transact, bear, administer*.
glória,-æ, f. *glory, renown*.
grádus,-ús, m. *step, degree*.
grammática,-æ, f. *grammar*.
grátia,-æ, f. *grace, favour*.
grávis,-e, adj., *severe, grave, eminent, venerable*.
grávo,-áre,-ávi,-átum, *burden, oppress, annoy*.

H.

hábeo,-ére,-ui,-itum, *have, hold, consider*.
hábilis,-e, adj., *capable*.
habílitas,-átis, f. *aptitude, ability*.
hæréditas,-átis, f. *heirship, inheritance*.
haéreo,-ére, haési, haésum, *cling to, stick, adhere*.
haéres,-édis, m. *heir*.
haud, adv., *not at all, by no means*.
hic, hæc, hoc, demons. pron., *this*.
homicídium,-ii, n. *homicide, manslaughter*.
hómo,-inis, m. *man*.
honéstus,-a,-um, adj., *proper, honest*.
honóro,-áre,-ávi,-átum, *honour, respect*.
hóstis,-is, c. *enemy*.
humánus,-a,-um, adj., *human*.

I.

íbi, adv., *there.*
ídem, éadem, ídem, demons. pron., *the same.*
idéntitas,-átis, f. *identity.*
ídeo, adv., *on that account.*
ignárus,-a,-um, adj., *ignorant, unacquainted with.*
ignóbilis,-e, adj., *low-born, unknown.*
ignórans,-ntis, adj., *ignorant.*
ignorántia,-æ, f. *ignorance.*
ignóro,-áre,-ávi,-átum, *not know, fail to heed, overlook.*
illícitus,-a,-um, adj., *illicit, forbidden.*
illusórius,-a,-um, adj., *illusory.*
illústro,-áre,-ávi,-átum, *illuminate, illustrate, explain.*
ímitor,-ári,-átus, *represent, imitate.*
ímmemor, adj., *unmindful.*
immísceo,-ére,-míscui,-míxtum, *meddle with.*
immóbilis,-e, adj., *immutable, immovable.*
immortális,-e, adj., *immortal.*
immutábilis,-e, adj., *unchanging, immutable.*
impediméntum,-i, n. *impediment, incumbrance.*
impédio,-íre,-ívi,-ítum, *hamper, impede, impair.*
imperítia,-æ, f. *inexperience.*
impérium,-i, n. *sovereignty, authority, jurisdiction.*
ímpero,-áre,-ávi,-átum, *command, order, hold authority.*
ímplico,-áre,-ávi,-átum, *imply, implicate, be associated.*
impóno,-ere,-pósui,-pósitum, *place, put, impose.*
impossíbilis,-e, adj., *impossible.*
impoténtia,-æ, f. *inability, impotence.*
imprímo,-ere,-préssi,-préssum, *impress.*
ímprobo,-áre,-ávi,-átum, *disapprove.*
ímprobus,-a,-um, adj., *wicked.*
impúgno,-áre,-ávi,-átum, *impugn, assail, oppose.*
impúne, adv., *safely, with impunity.*
impúnitas,-átis, f. *impunity.*
impunítus,-a,-um, adj., *unpunished, secure.*
in, prep. w. acc., *into, to, against*—i.e. *motion;* w. abl., *in, on*—i.e. *rest.*
inaédifico,-áre,-ávi,-átum, *build upon.*
inaudítus,-a,-um, adj., *unheard, untried.*
incéndo,-ere,-di,-sum, *illuminate, inflame, excite.*
incéptus,-us, m. *beginning.*
incértus,-a,-um, adj., *uncertain.*
inchoátus,-a,-um, adj., *incomplete, imperfect.*

18

incípio,-cípere,-cépi,-céptum, *begin.*
incivílis,-e, adj., *uncivil, unjust.*
inclúsio,-ónis, f. *inclusion.*
incómmodum,-i, n. *disadvantage, injury.*
incóngruus,-a,-um, adj., *incongruous.*
inconsuétus,-a,-um, adj., *unusual.*
inconvéniens,-ntis, adj., *unlike, dissimilar, inconvenient.*
incorporális,-e, adj., *incorporeal.*
incúmbo,-ere,-cúbui,-itum, *rest upon.*
índe, adv., *thence.*
indefinítus,-a,-um, adj., *indefinite.*
índex,-icis, c., *indication, sign.*
índico,-áre,-ávi,-átum, *indicate, show.*
indígeo,-ére,-ui, —, *to be in want of.*
indígnus,-a,-um, adj., *unworthy.*
indivisíbilis,-e, adj., *indivisible.*
indúbito,-áre,-ávi,-átum, *doubt about.*
indúco,-ere,-dúxi,-dúctum, *bring in, introduce.*
indúlgeo,-ére,-dulsi,-dultum, *give, grant.*
ineo,-íre,-ii,-itum, *begin, originate.*
inestimábilis,-e, adj., *inestimable.*
infámis,-e, adj., *of ill repute, infamous.*
inféctus,-a,-um, adj., *not done.*
infero,-férre,-túli, illátum, *infer, inflict, cause.*
ínferus,-a,-um, adj., *belonging to the Lower World, lower.*
inficiátio,-ónis, f. *denial.*
infício,-fícere,-féci,-féctum, *infect, spoil, instruct in.*
infinítum,-i, n. *endless number, want of finality.*
infírmus,-a,-um, adj., *not strong, weak.*
informátus,-a,-um, adj., *informed.*
infórmo,-áre,-ávi,-átum, *inform.*
infortúnia,-æ, f. *misfortune.*
infortúnium,-i, n. *misfortune, disaster.*
ínfra, adv., *beneath, below.*
ingrátus,-a,-um, adj., *ungrateful.*
inhábilis,-e, adj., *incapable.*
inhabílito,-áre,-ávi,-átum, *incapacitate.*
inhonéstus,-a,-um, adj., *dishonourable.*
iníque, adv., *unjustly.*
iníquus,-a,-um, adj., *unfair, unjust, injurious.*
inítium,-i, n. *beginning.*
injúria,-æ, f. *injury, wrong.*
injústus,-a,-um, adj., *unjust.*

ínnocens,-ntis, c. *an innocent person.*
innocéntia,-æ, f. *innocence.*
innovátio,-ónis, f. *innovation.*
ínnovo,-áre,-ávi,-átum, *introduce.*
inobediéntia,-æ, f. *disobedience.*
inopinátum,-i, n. *unexpected event.*
inopinátus,-a,-um, adj., *unexpected.*
inquisítio,-ónis, f. *inquisition.*
ínsero,-ere,-sérui,-sértum, *insert, introduce.*
insérvio,-íre,-íi(-ivi),-ítum, *be subservient to.*
insípidus,-a,-um, adj., *insipid, tasteless.*
inspício,-ere,-spéxi,-spéctum, *look into, examine.*
instans,-ntis, adj., *instant, present, urgent.*
instánter, adv., *instantly.*
instítuo,-ere,-ui,-útum, *institute, appoint.*
instruméntum,-i, n. *instrument.*
insufficiénter, adv., *insufficiently.*
insum,-esse,-fui, *be contained in, belong to.*
ínteger,-tegra,-tegrum, adj., *whole, perfect.*
intélligo,-ere,-léxi,-léctum, *understand, interpret.*
inténdo,-ere,-di,-tum(-sum), *intend, extend, maintain.*
inténtio,-ónis, f. *intention.*
ínter, prep. w. acc., *among.*
interesse, *interest.*
interlocutárius,-a,-um, adj., *interlocutory.*
interpóno, - ere, - pósui, - pósitum, *put among, insert, introduce.*
intérpres,-pretis, c. *interpreter, expounder.*
interpretátio,-ónis, f. *interpretation, signification.*
interpretátor,-óris, m. *interpreter, explainer.*
intérpretor,-ári,-átus, *explain, interpret, decide.*
interrégnum,-i, n. *interregnum.*
interrúptio,-ónis, f. *interruption.*
intérsum,-ésse,-fui, *be of interest, important to.*
intervénio,-íre,-véni,-véntum, *happen, come between.*
intestínus,-a,-um, adj., *internal.*
intolerábilis,-e, adj., *unbearable.*
introdúco,-ere,-dúxi,-dúctum, *introduce, assert, institute.*
inútilis,-e, adj., *useless, injurious.*
inválidus,-a,-um, adj., *invalid.*
invénio,-íre,-véni,-véntum, *meet with, find out, discover, invent.*
invérsus,-a,-um, adj., *reversed, inverted.*

invíto,-áre,-ávi,-átum, *invite, attract.*
invítus,-a,-um, adj., *unwilling, against one's will.*
invóco,-áre,-ávi,-átum, *invoke, designate.*
ípse,-a,-um, demons. pron., *himself, herself, itself.*
íra,-æ, f. *anger.*
irrídeo,-ére,-rísi,-rísum, *laugh at, mock.*
írritus,-a,-um, adj., *invalid, of no effect.*
ís, éa, id, demons. pron., *he, she, it, this.*
íste,-a,-ud, demons. pron., *such.*
it, *see* **eo.**
íta, adv., *in such a way, so.*
íterum, adv., *again, repeatedly.*

J.

jam, adv., *now.*
júbeo,-ére,-jússi,-jússum, *command.*
júdex,-icis, m. *judge.*
judicátio,-ónis, f. *judicial investigation.*
judicátus,-us, m. *office of judge.*
judiciális,-e, adj., *judicial.*
judiciáliter, adv., *judicially.*
judiciárius,-a,-um, adj., *belonging to the courts of justice, judicial.*
judícium,-ii, n. *judgment, decision, sentence, the court.*
júdico,-áre,-ávi,-átum, *judge, adjudicate, condemn, decide.*
junctúra,-æ, f. *connection, joining.*
junctus,-a,-um, adj., *united, near.*
jungo,-ere, junxi, junctum, *join.*
juraméntum,-i, n. *oath.*
jurátor,-óris, m. *juror.*
jurídicus,-a,-um, adj., *legal.*
jurisdíctio,-ónis, f. *jurisdiction.*
júrisprudéntia,-æ, f. *jurisprudence.*
júro,-áre,-ávi,-átum, *swear, take an oath.*
jus, júris, n. *law, right, justice, equity.*
jusjurándum,-i, n. *oath.*
jussum,-i, n. *command, decree.*
justiciárius,-ii, m. *a justice.*
justítia,-æ, f. *justice.*
jústus,-a,-um, adj., *just.*
juvo,-áre, júvi, jútum, *help, benefit, assist.*
juxtá, adv., *by the side of;* prep., *along with.*

L.

labor,-óris, m. *labour, hardship.*
laédo,-ere,-si,-sum, *injure* (**laedere majestatem,** *to commit treason*).
láicus,-i, m. *layman.*
lánguidus,-a,-um, adj., *weak, sick.*
látens,-ntis, adj., *hidden, secret.*
láteo,-ére,-ui, *lie hid, lurk.*
látus,-a,-um, adj., *broad, wide.*
laúdo,-áre,-ávi,-átum, *praise, commend.*
legális,-e, adj., *legal.*
legatárius,-ii, m. *legatee.*
legátum,-i, n. *legacy.*
legátus,-i, m. *ambassador.*
legislátor,-óris, m. *legislator.*
legitimátio,-ónis, f. *legitimacy.*
legítimus,-a,-um, adj., *legitimate, lawful.*
légo,-ere, légi, lectum, *read, select, choose.*
levis,-e, adj., *light, trivial, unreliable.*
léx, légis, f. *law.*
libéllus,-i, m. *libel.*
líber,-era,-erum, adj., *free, independent.*
líbero,-áre,-ávi,-átum, *absolve, discharge.*
líbertas,-átis, f. *liberty.*
libertínus,-i, m. *freedman.*
libet,-ére,-uit or **-itum est,** *it pleases.*
licéntia,-æ, f. *freedom, liberty, licence.*
lícet,-ere,-cuit and **-citum est,** *it is lawful, permitted, one may or can.*
licet, conj., *though, even if.*
lícitus,-a,-um, adj., *lawful, legal.*
ligámen,-inis, n. *band, bond.*
lígeantia,-æ, f. *allegiance.*
lígnum,-i, n. *wood, lumber.*
ligo,-áre,-ávi,-átum, *tie, bind.*
límes,-itis, m. *boundary, path.*
limitátio,-ónis, f. *limitation, restriction.*
límito,-áre,-ávi,-átum, *limit.*
línea,-æ, f. *line, limit.*
liqueo,-ére, líqui, *to be clear, evident* (**non liquet,** *it is not proven*).
líquidus,-a,-um, adj., *liquid, clear, proven.*

lis, lítis, f. *suit.*
lítera,-æ, f. *letter.*
locuplés,-étis, adj., *wealthy, rich.*
locupléto,-áre,-ávi,-átum, *enrich.*
lócus,-i, m. *place.*
lóngus,-a,-um, adj., *long.*
loquéla,-æ, f. *cause, complaint, plaint.*
lóquor,-i, locútus sum, *speak.*
lúcror,-ári,-átus, *gain, acquire.*
lúctus,-us, m. *mourning.*
lúo,-ere, lúi, lútum, *expiate, pay.*
lupánar,-áris, n. *brothel.*
lupínus,-a,-um, adj., *of a wolf.*
lux, lúcis, f. *light.*

M.

magis, adv., *rather.*
magíster,-tri, m. *master.*
magístra,-æ, f. *mistress.*
magistrátus,-us, m. *magistracy, government.*
majéstas,-átis, f. *majesty.*
májor,-us, adj., *greater.*
majóres,-um, m. pl. *ancestors.*
mále, adv., *badly, wrongly.*
maledíctus,-a,-um, adj., *cursed.*
malefícium,-ii, n. *crime, wrong, evil deed.*
malítia,-æ, f. *malice.*
málum,-i, n. *evil, misfortune, wrong.*
málus,-a,-um, adj., *bad, evil.*
mandatárius,-ii, m. *mandatory.*
mandátum,-i, n. *command, order.*
mándo,-áre,-ávi,-átum, *command, commit, consign.*
maneo,-ére,-si,-sum, *remain, continue.*
manérium,-ii, n. *manor.*
maniféste, adv., *manifestly.*
maniféstus,-a,-um, adj., *manifest, evident.*
manumítto, - ere, - mísi, - míssum, *emancipate, free, affranchise.*
mánus,-us, f. *hand, custody* (**manus mortua,** *mortmain*).
máre,-is, n. *sea.*
máter,-ris, f. *mother.*
matrimónium,-ii, n. *marriage, matrimony.*

maturésco,-ere,-rui, *ripen, come to maturity.*
matúrus,-a,-um, adj., *mature, speedy, timely.*
máximè, adv., *especially.*
máximus,-a,-um, adj., *greatest, highest.*
mélior,-óris, adj., *better.*
melióro,-áre,—,-átum, *make better, improve.*
memória,-æ, f. *memorial, memory.*
mendácium,-ii, n. *falsehood.*
méns,-ntis, f. *intent, mind.*
ménsa,-æ, f. *board, table.*
mensúra,-æ, f. *measure.*
méntior,-íri, mentitus sum, *lie.*
mercátor,-óris, m. *merchant, purchaser.*
mére, adv., *merely.*
méreor,-éri, méritus sum, *deserve.*
mérito, adv., *deservedly.*
mérus,-a,-um, adj., *mere.*
méta,-æ, f. *boundary, limit.*
métus,-us, m. *fear.*
mílito,-áre,-ávi,-átum, *wage war.*
mína,-æ, f. *threat.*
minimè, adv., *least of all, very little, by no means.*
mínimus,-a,-um, adj., *very little, trifling.*
ministeriális,-e, adj., *ministerial.*
mínor,-ári, minátus sum, *threaten.*
mínor,-us, adj., *lesser, inferior, younger, minor.*
mínuo,-ere,-ui,-útum, *diminish.*
mínus, adv., *less.*
mísceo,-ére, míscui, míxtum, *mix, assemble, unite.*
míser,-era,-erum, adj., *wretched.*
misericórdia,-æ, f. *mercy, pity.*
móbilis,-e, adj., *movable.*
moderátor,-óris, m. *manager.*
módus,-i, m. *agreement, custom, bound, limit, mode.*
moméntum,-i, n. *importance, moment.*
móneto,-áre,-ávi,-átum, *coin, money.*
monopólium,-ii, n. *monopoly.*
mónstro,-áre,-ávi,-átum, *point out.*
monuméntum,-i, n. *monument.*
móra,-æ, f. *delay.*
mórior, mori, mórtuus sum, *die.*
mórs, mórtis, f. *death.*
mórtuus,-a,-um, adj., *dead.*

mos, móris, m. *custom, moral.*
mótus,-ús, m. *motion.*
móveo,-ére, móvi, mótum, *move, remove.*
múlier,-éris, f. *woman, wife.*
múltiplex,-icis, adj., *multiplex, numerous.*
multitúdo,-inis, f. *multitude.*
múltus,-a,-um, adj., *many, much.*
múndus, m. *world.*
mutábilis,-e, adj., *changeable.*
múto,-áre,-ávi,-átum, *change.*

N.

nam, conj., *for.*
narrátio,-ónis, f. *narration, count.*
náscor,-i, nátus sum, *arise, be born.*
natúra,-æ, f. *nature.*
naturális,-e, adj., *natural.*
ne, adv. and conj., *lest, not.*
nec, adv., *not.*
necessárie, adv., *necessarily.*
necessárius,-a,-um, adj., *necessary, unavoidable.*
necésse, adj. indecl., *unavoidable, necessary.*
necéssitas,-átis, f. *necessity.*
necessitúdo,-inis, f. *necessity.*
negátio,-ónis, f. *negation, denial, negative.*
negatíve, adv., *negatively.*
negatívus,-a,-um, adj., *negative.*
negligéntia,-æ, f. *negligence.*
négligo,-ere,-lexi,-lectum, *neglect, disregard.*
négo,-áre,-ávi,-átum, *refuse, deny.*
negótium,-ii, n. *business, matter.*
némo,-inis, c. *no one.*
nequáquam, adv., *in no wise, not at all.*
néque, adv., *not, neither . . . nor.*
néscio,-íre,-ívi(-íi),-ítum, *not know, be unable.*
neúter,-tra,-trum, adj., *neither.*
níhil, nil, indecl. n. *nothing.*
nihilóminus, conj., *nevertheless.*
nímius,-a,-um, adj., *excessive.*
nísi, conj., *unless.*
nóbilis,-e, adj., *excellent, famous, noble.*
nobílitas,-átis, f. *nobility.*

nócens,-ntis, c. *wrongdoer, guilty person.*
nóceo,-ére,-ui,-itum, *harm, do injury.*
nómen,-inis, n. *name.*
non, adv., *not.*
nondum, adv., *not yet.*
nórma,-æ, f. *rule.*
nósco,-ere, nóvi, nótum, *recognise, acknowledge.*
nóster,-tra,-trum, poss. pron., *our, of us.*
notítia,-æ, f. *knowledge, acquaintance.*
novátio,-ónis, f. *novation.*
novérca,-æ, f. *stepmother.*
nóvitas,-átis, f. *novelty.*
nóvus,-a,-um, adj., *new.*
núbes,-is, f. *cloud.*
núbilis,-e, adj., *marriageable.*
núbo,-ere,-psi,-ptum, *be married to.*
núdus,-a,-um, adj., *naked.*
núllus,-a,-um, adj., *no (one).*
númen,-inis, n. *deity.*
número,-áre,-ávi,-átum, *count.*
núnquam, adv., *never.*
nupta,-æ, f. *bride, wife.*
núptiæ,-árum, f. plur., *marriage.*

O.

obligátio,-ónis, f. *bond, obligation.*
óbligo,-áre,-ávi,-átum, *bind.*
oblíquus,-a,-um, adj., *sideways, indirect.*
oblívio,-ónis, f. *oblivion.*
obscúrus,-a,-um, adj., *obscure.*
observántia,-æ, f. *observance.*
obsérvo,-áre,-ávi,-átum, *observe.*
óbsto,-áre,-stiti,-státum, *prevent, oppose.*
óbstruo,-ere,-xi,-ctum, *impede, obstruct.*
obtémpero,-áre,-ávi,-átum, *comply with, obey.*
obtíneo,-ére,-ui,-téntum, *obtain, acquire.*
occído,-ere,-cídi,-císum, *kill, slay.*
occísio,-ónis, f. *slaughter.*
occultátio,-ónis, f. *concealment.*
occupo,-áre,-ávi,-átum, *occupy.*
occúrro,-ere,-curri,-cursum, *lie in the way.*
oculátus,-a,-um, adj., *seeing.*

odiósus,-a,-um, adj., *odious, hateful.*
ódium,-ii, n. *odium.*
offero,-férre, obtúli, oblátum, *offer, adduce.*
offício,-ere,-féci,-féctum, *obstruct, be hurtful.*
offícium,-ii, n. *office, duty.*
omíssio,-ónis, f. *omission.*
omítto,-ere,-mísi,-míssum, *omit.*
omníno, adj., *altogether, wholly.*
ómnis,-e, adj., *all.*
ónero,-áre,-ávi,-átum, *burden, aggravate.*
ónus,-eris, n. *incumbrance, burden.*
operátio,-ónis, f. *operation.*
óperor,-ári,-átus, *operate.*
opínio,-ónis, f. *opinion.*
opórtet,-ére,-uit, *it behoves, one must or ought.*
optáto, adv., *according to one's own desire.*
óptimus,-a,-um, sup. adj., *best.*
ópus,-eris, n. *superstructure, work, assistance.*
ópus ésse, *to be necessary.*
orátio,-ónis, f. *speech, language, mode of speech.*
ordinárius,-a,-um, adj., *ordinary, regular.*
órdo,-inis, m. *order, course.*
órigo,-inis, f. *birth, origin, family.*
órior,-íri, órtus sum, *arise, accrue.*
orthográphia,-æ, f. *spelling.*
ós, óris, n. *mouth, language.*
osténdo,-ere,-di,-sum, *exhibit, expose, show, declare.*
óstium,-ii, n. *door.*

P.

páctio,-ónis, f. *agreement, contract.*
páctum,-i, n. *agreement.*
pálam, adv., *plainly, openly.*
palátium,-ii, n. *palace.*
pár, páris, adj., *equal.*
párco,-ere, pepérci (pársi), párcitum (pársum), *spare, preserve.*
párens,-éntis, c. *parent.*
páreo,-ére,-ui,-itum, *obey, submit to.*
pário,-ere, péperi, páritum, *produce, bring about.*
Parliaméntum,-i, n. *Parliament.*
páro,-áre,-ávi,-átum, *prepare.*

paróchia,-æ, f. *parish.*
párs,-rtis, f. *part, side, party.*
particéps,-cipis, m. *partner.*
partícula,-æ, f. *little bit, particle.*
pártus,-us, m. *offspring.*
párum, adv., *not enough.*
pátens,-ntis, adj., *patent.*
páteo,-ére,-ui, *extend, be allowable, stand open.*
páter,-tris, m. *father.*
patérnus,-a,-um, adj., *paternal.*
pátiens,-entis, adj., *patient.*
pátior, pati, passus, *allow, suffer.*
pátria,-æ, f. *country, jury.*
patrocínium,-ii, n. *defence, protection.*
patrócinor,-ári,-átus, *furnish defence or protection.*
paúci,-órum, m. plur., *few.*
pax,-cis, f. *peace.*
peccátum,-i, n. *fault, error.*
pécco,-áre,-ávi,-átum, *do wrong, err.*
pecúnia,-æ, f. *money.*
pecúniárius,-a,-um, adj., *pecuniary.*
pécus,-oris, n. *cattle.*
péndeo,-ére, pepéndi, *depend upon, be in suspense.*
per, prep. w. acc., *through, by.*
perágo,-ere,-égi,-áctum, *carry through, accomplish.*
percípio,-ere,-cépi,-céptum, *perceive, understand.*
percútio,-ere,-cússi,-cússum, *kill.*
pérdo,-ere,-didi,-ditum, *destroy.*
perénnis,-e, adj., *perpetual.*
péreo,-íre,-ívi(-ii),-itum, *fail, fall, perish, be lost.*
perféctio,-ónis, f. *completing, perfection.*
perféctus,-a,-um, adj., *complete, perfect, excellent.*
perfício,-ere,-féci,-féctum, *accomplish, perfect.*
perículósus,-a,-um, adj., *dangerous.*
perículum,-i, n. *risk, action at law, trial.*
périmo,-ere,-émi,-émptum, *destroy, prevent, extinguish.*
perímpleo,-ére,-évi,-étum, *carry out, execute.*
perínde, adv., *just as.*
perítus,-a,-um, adj., *skilful, experienced.*
perjúria,-æ, f. *perjury.*
perlégo,-ere,-légi,-léctum, *read through, view all over.*
permítto,-ere,-mísi,-míssum, *allow, permit.*
pérperam, adv., *wrongly.*

perpétro,-áre,-ávi,-átum, *perpetrate, accomplish.*
perpétuus,-a,-um, adj., *continuous, perpetual.*
persóna,-æ, f. *person.*
personális,-e, adj., *personal.*
perspício,-ere,-exi,-ectum, *look at, examine.*
pertíneo,-ére,-ui, *concern, pertain to.*
pertúrbo,-áre,-ávi,-átum, *disarrange, throw into confusion.*
pervénio,-íre,-véni,-véntum, *reach, attain, fall to the possession of.*
pes, pédis, m. *foot.*
petítio,-ónis, f. *petition, suit.*
petítor,-óris, m. *plaintiff.*
péto,-ere,-ívi or **-ii,-ítum,** *seek, request, sue for.*
píscor,-ári,-átus, *fish.*
pláceo,-ére,-cui and **-citus sum,-citum,** *please, be agreeable, intend, satisfy.*
plácito,-áre,-ávi,-átum, *sue, litigate.*
plácitum,-i, n. *plea, maxim, principle.*
plánto,-áre,-ávi,-átum, *affix, annex.*
plécto,-ere, *punish.*
pléne, adv., *fully, especially.*
plénus,-a,-um, adj., *complete, full.*
plus, plúris, adj., *more, several.*
poéna,-æ, f. *punishment, penalty.*
pœnális,-e, adj., *penal.*
polítia,-æ, f. *policy, civil government.*
políticus,-a,-um, adj., *political, civil.*
póndero,-áre,-ávi,-átum, *weigh.*
póno,-ere, pósui, pósitum, *place, appoint.*
pópulus,-i, m. *people.*
pórrigo,-ere,-réxi,-réctum, *extend.*
pórtus,-ús, m. *harbour, port.*
posítio,-ónis, f. *position.*
positívus,-a,-um, adj., *positive.*
posséssio,-ónis, f. *possession.*
posséssor,-óris, m. *possessor.*
possíbilis,-e, adj., *possible.*
possídeo,-ére,-sédi,-séssum, *own, possess.*
póssum, pósse, pótui, —, *be able.*
póst, prep. w. acc., *after, since, behind.*
postérior,-ius, comp. adj., *later.*
postéritas,-átis, f. *posterity.*

pótens,-ntis, adj., *powerful.*
poténtia,-æ, f. *power.*
potéstas,-átis, f. *power, sovereignty.*
pótior,-ius, comp. adj., *better, more important.*
pótis,-e, adj., *powerful, able.*
pótius, adv., *rather, more.*
praébeo,-ére,-ui,-itum, *offer, present, occasion, furnish.*
præcáveo,-ére,-cávi,-caútum, *guard against beforehand.*
præcédens,-ntis, n. *precedent.*
præcédo,-ere,-céssi,-céssum, *precede, excel.*
præcéptum,-i, n. *precept, maxim, order.*
prædíctus,-a,-um, adj., *aforesaid.*
prædo,-ónis, m. *plunderer, robber.*
præfátus,-a,-um, adj., *aforesaid.*
præféro,-férre,-tuli,-látum, *prefer, show, offer.*
præjúdico,-áre,-ávi,-átum, *prejudge, be prejudicial.*
prælátus,-i, m. *bishop, prelate.*
præmíssio,-ónis, f. *premiss.*
praémium,-ii, n. *reward.*
prænómen,-inis, n. *individual name.*
præparatórius,-a,-um, adj., *preparatory.*
præscríbo,-ere,-psi,-ptum, *prescribe, order.*
præscríptio,-ónis, f. *prescription.*
praésens,-ntis, adj., *present.*
præséntia,-æ, f. *presence.*
præsértim, adv., *especially.*
praésto,-áre,-stiti,-státum and -stitum, *warrant, show.*
præsúmo,-ere,-súmpsi,-súmptum, *presume.*
præsúmptio,-ónis, f. *presumption.*
præsuppóno,-ere,-pósui,-pósitum, *presuppose.*
praéter, adv., *except, unless;* prep., *before, against, besides.*
prætéreo,-íre,-ii,-itum, *pass over.*
prætérita,-órum, n. pl., *things gone by, the past.*
prætéritus,-a,-um, adj., *past.*
prævénio,-íre,-véni,-véntum, *prevent, anticipate.*
prævídeo,-ére,-vísi,-vísum, *foresee.*
praxis,-eos, f. *practice.*
prémo,-ere, pressi, pressum, *restrain, check, stop.*
prétium,-ii, n. *price.*
primitívus,-a,-um, adj., *original.*
prímo, adv., *at first, firstly.*
prímum, adv., *at first, in the first place.*
prínceps,-ipis, m. *prince, sovereign.*

principális,-is, m. *principal.*
princípium,-ii, n. *beginning, first principles.*
príor,-us, gen. **-óris,** adj., *former, previous.*
pristínus,-a,-um, adj., *original.*
príus, comp. adv., *before, first.*
priúsquam, conj., *before.*
privátio,-ónis, f. *privation, taking away.*
privátus,-a,-um, adj., *private.*
privilégium,-ii, n. *privilege.*
prívo,-áre,-ávi,-átum, *deprive of, deliver, supersede.*
pro, prep. w. abl., *for, in behalf of.*
probábilis,-e, adj., *credible, probable.*
probátio,-ónis, f. *proof.*
próbo,-áre,-ávi,-átum, *approve, prove, manifest.*
procéssus,-ús, m. *process, course.*
prodítio,-ónis, f. *treason.*
próditor,-óris, m. *traitor.*
pródo,-ere,-didi,-ditum, *record, disclose, betray.*
prodrómus,-i, m. *forerunner.*
prodúco,-ere,-xi,-ctum, *bring forward, introduce.*
prófero,-férre,-tuli,-látum, *mention, offer, reveal, quote.*
profício,-ere,-féci,-féctum, *profit, accomplish, contribute.*
progréssus,-us, m. *advance, progress.*
prohíbeo,-ére,-ui,-itum, *prevent, forbid.*
promíscue, adv., *promiscuously, indifferently.*
prómissor,-óris, m. *promisor* (Maxim 275).
pronúncio,-áre,-ávi,-átum, *pronounce.*
proposítio,-ónis, f. *resolution, representation, statement.*
propósitum,-i, n. *purpose, intention.*
propríetas,-átis, f. *a special nature or property.*
próprius,-a,-um, adj., *one's own, peculiar, proper.*
própter, prep. w. acc., *on account of.*
próspere, adv., *favourably, prosperously.*
prospício,-ere,-spéxi,-spéctum, *look forward, provide for.*
prósum, prodésse, prófui, —, *do good, benefit.*
protéctio,-ónis, f. *protection.*
provénio,-íre,-véni,-véntum, *originate, happen.*
provísio,-ónis, f. *provision, foresight, prevention.*
próximus,-a,-um, sup. adj., *nearest, next, following.*
públicus,-a,-um, adj., *public.*
púdor,-óris, m. *virtue, chastity.*
púer,-eri, c. *child.*
púgno,-áre,-ávi,-átum, *conflict, fight, contradict.*

púnio,-íre,-ívi(-ii),-ítum, *punish.*
púrgo,-áre,-ávi,-átum, *cleanse, remove, justify.*
púrus,-a,-um, adj., *pure.*
púto,-áre,-ávi,-átum, *regard, consider.*

Q.

qua, adv., *where, as far as, anywhere.*
quaéro,-ere,-sívi(-ii),-sítum, *inquire into, seek, ask.*
quaéstio,-ónis, f. *question, inquiry, investigation.*
quaéstus,-us, m. *gain, advantage.*
quam, adv., *than.*
quamvis, adv., *ever so;* conj., *although, however much.*
quándo, adv., *when.*
quántitas,-átis, f. *quantity.*
quántus,-a,-um, adj., *how great, as, such as.*
quási, adv., *as if, as it were.*
quatuor, *four.*
que, encl. conj., *and.*
queréla,-æ, f. *complaint.*
qui, quæ, quod, rel. pron., *who, which.*
quía, conj., *because.*
quícunque, quaécunque, quódcunque, rel. pron., *whoever, whatever, all.*
quídam, quaédam, quoddam, indef. pron., *certain, somebody, something.*
quidem, adv., *indeed, certainly, for example.*
quílibet, quaélibet, quódlibet, indef. pron., *any kind of, no matter who, anyone.*
quin, conj., *but that.*
quis, quæ, quid, interrog. pron., *what.*
quisquam, quæquam, quidquam, indef. pron., *any, anyone.*
quisque, quæque, quodque, indef. pron., *each, every, everyone.*
quísquis, quaéquæ, quícquid, pron., *whoever, whatever.*
quóad, adv., *until, as far as, as to.*
quodammódo, adv., *in a certain manner.*
quomodo, adv., *in what manner.*
quóties(-iens), adv., *as often as, how often.*

R.

ráro, adv., *seldom.*
ratihabítio,-ónis, f. *ratification.*
rátio,-ónis, f. *reason, rule.*
rationábilis,-e, adj., *reasonable.*
rátus,-a,-um, adj., *confirmed, valid, established.*
rebéllio,-ónis, f. *rebellion.*
recédo,-ere,-céssi,-céssum, *depart.*
recépto,-áre,-ávi, *receive habitually.*
recípio,-ere,-cépi,-céptum, *receive, be capable of, admit.*
recórdum,-i, n., *record.*
récreo,-áre,-ávi,-átum, *renew, restore.*
rectátus,-a,-um, adj., *accused.*
récte, adv., *rightly.*
réctum,-i, n. *right, truth.*
réctus,-a,-um, adj., *right, just, lawful.*
récurro,-ere,-curri, *return, revert.*
réddo,-ere,-didi,-ditum, *give, make.*
rédigo,-ere,-égi,-actum, *drive back, reduce to.*
rédimo,-ere,-émi,-émptum, *redeem, rescue, gain.*
réditus,-us, m. *rent.*
reféllo,-ere,-felli, *disprove, refute.*
referéntia,-æ, f. *reference.*
reféro,-ferre, réttuli, relátum, *refer, relate.*
refert,-ferre,-tulit, *it concerns, it matters.*
refréno,-áre,-ávi,-átum, *restrain, curb.*
refúgium,-ii, n. *refuge.*
refutátio,-ónis, f. *refutation.*
regális,-e, adj., *regal, kingly.*
régius,-a,-um, adj., *royal, regal.*
régnum,-i, n. *kingdom.*
régo,-ere, réxi, réctum, *control, rule.*
regrédior,-grédi,-gréssus, *recall, return.*
régula,-æ, f. *rule.*
rejício,-ere,-jéci,-jéctum, *refuse, reject.*
relátio,-ónis, f. *report, motion, proposition.*
relatívus,-a,-um, adj., *having reference or relation.*
rélevo,-áre,-ávi,-átum, *be relevant to, relieve.*
relígio,-ónis, f. *religion.*
relínquo,-ere,-líqui,-líctum, *leave, abandon.*
remáneo,-ére,-mánsi, *remain, continue.*
remédium,-ii, n. *remedy.*

remíssus,-a,-um, adj., *indulgent, lenient, remiss.*
remótus,-a,-um, adj., *remote, separate.*
remóveo,-ére,-móvi,-mótum, *remove.*
renúncio,-áre,-ávi,-átum, *renounce, refuse, revoke.*
repéllo,-ere, réppuli, repúlsum, *reject, repel, disdain.*
repério,-íre, repperi *or* **reperi, repertum,** *find, obtain.*
repræsentátio,-ónis, f. *representation.*
réprobo,-áre,-ávi,-átum, *refuse, disallow, reprehend.*
repromíssio,-ónis, f. *counter-promise.*
réputo,-áre,-ávi,-átum, *take, compute, meditate.*
requíro,-ere,-sívi(-ii),-sítum, *ask, require.*
res, réi, f. *thing, affair, matter.*
rescíndo,-ere,-scidi,-scíssum, *disregard.*
rescríptum,-i, n. *rescript.*
resíduus,-a,-um, adj., *remaining, outstanding;* subst.,
residue, remainder.
resignátio,-ónis, f. *resignation.*
resisto,-ere,-stiti, *oppose, resist.*
resólvo,-ere,-solvi,-solútum, *annul, release, loosen.*
respício,- ere,- spéxi,- spéctum, *look backward, regard,*
respect.
respóndeo,-ére,-di,-spónsum, *answer to, respond.*
respónsio,-ónis, f. *reply.*
respública,-éi,-æ, f. *republic, state.*
restítuo,-úere,-ui,-útum, *correct, restore, reverse.*
restitútio,-ónis, f. *restoring, restitution.*
resto,-áre,-stiti, *remain, resist.*
restringo,-ere,-nxi,-íctum, *confine, restrict.*
retíneo,-ére,-ui,-téntum, *hold, retain.*
retráho,-ere,-xi,-ctum, *call back, bring back.*
retrotráhor, *be retrospective.*
réus,-a,-um, adj., *criminal, guilty.*
réus,-i, m. *defendant, guilty person, prisoner.*
revélo,-áre,-ávi,-átum, *reveal.*
revérsio,-ónis, f. *reversion.*
revérto,-ere,-verti, *return, revert to.*
revocátio,-ónis, f. *revocation.*
révoco,-áre,-ávi,-átum, *recall.*
rex, régis, m. *king.*
ríte, adv., *duly, rightly.*
rívulus,-i, m. *little stream.*
Románus,-a,-um, adj., *Roman.*
rúmor,-óris, m. *rumour.*
rúo,-ere, rúi, rútum, *fall.*

19

S.

sacerdótium,-ii, n. *priesthood.*
sacraméntum,-i, n. *oath, civil suit, affidavit.*
sacrilégium,-ii, n. *sacrilege.*
sacrilégus,-i, m. *a sacrilegious person.*
saépe, adv., *often.*
sæpenúmero, adv., *again and again, repeatedly.*
sal,-is, m. *salt.*
sáltus,-us, m. *leap, bound.*
sálus,-útis, f. *welfare, preservation.*
sánctio,-ónis, f. *oath, sanction.*
sánctus,-a,-um, adj., *sacred.*
sánguis,-inis, m. *blood, consanguinity, offspring.*
sáno,-áre,-ávi,-átum, *heal, correct, repair.*
sápiens,-ntis, adj., *wise, judicious.*
sapiéntia,-æ, f. *wisdom, discernment.*
sárcio,-íre, sarsi, sarsum, *restore.*
scélerus,-a,-um, adj., *wicked.*
scéna,-æ, f. *court.*
scéptrum,-i, n. *sceptre.*
sciénter, adv., *knowingly, with knowledge.*
sciéntia,-æ, f. *knowledge.*
scío,-íre, scívi, scítum, *know.*
scríbo,-ere, scrípsi, scríptum, *write.*
scríptum,-i, n. *deed.*
scriptúra,-æ, f. *writing, composition.*
scrútor,-ári,-átus sum, *scrutinise.*
se, reflex. pron., *himself, herself, itself, themselves.*
secrétum,-i, n. *secret.*
séctor,-ári,-átus, *pursue.*
seculáris,-e, adj., *secular.*
secúndum, prep. w. acc., *according to.*
sed, conj., *but, yet.*
sédes,-is, f. *seat, residence, situation.*
seísina,-æ, f. *seisin.*
sémel, adv., *once.*
sémper, adv., *always.*
senátus,-us, m. *senate.*
sénsus,-ús, m. *sense.*
senténtia,-æ, f. *opinion, decree, judgment, sentence, purpose, meaning.*
séntio,-íre,-si,-sum, *perceive, bear, feel, deem.*

separátus,-a,-um, *separate, distinct.*
séquor,-qui, secútus sum, *follow, result, strive for.*
sermo,-ónis, m. *speech, conversation, language.*
servio,-íre,-ii (or **-ívi**),**-ítum,** *serve, be subject to.*
servítia,-órum, n. plur., *services.*
sérvitus,-útis, f. *servitude, subjection, liability.*
sérvo,-áre,-ávi,-átum, *keep, preserve, uphold.*
servus,-a,-um, adj., *subject.*
servus,-i, m. *servant, slave.*
seu, conj., *or.*
sevére, adv., *severely.*
sevéritas,-atis, f. *severity.*
sex, indecl. num., *six.*
sí, conj., *if.*
sic, adv., *so, in such a manner.*
sicárius,-ii, m. *assassin.*
sicut, adv., *as, like, as if.*
significátio,-ónis, f. *signification, indication, expression.*
significo,-áre,-ávi,-átum, *signify, mean.*
sígnum,-i, n. *sign.*
sílentium,-ii, n. *silence, inaction.*
síleo,-ére,-ui, —, *be silent, remain inactive, rest, cease.*
símilis,-e, adj., *like, similar.*
simónia,-æ, f. *simony.*
símplex,-icis, adj., *simple, plain.*
simplícitas,-átis, f. *simplicity, honesty.*
simul, adv., *at the same time, together.*
síne, prep. w. abl., *without.*
singuláris,-e, adj., *single, alone, particular.*
sínguli,-æ,-a, plur. adj., *individual, separate.*
síno,-ere, sívi, sítum, *permit.*
síve, conj., *or.*
sóbrius,-a,-um, adj., *sober.*
sócius,-ii, m. *partner, associate.*
solénniter, adv., *solemnly, according to usage.*
sóleo,-ére,-itus, *be wont.*
solíditas,-átis, f. *solidity, substance.*
sólidus,-a,-um, adj., *entire.*
sólium,-ii, n. *throne.*
sólum,-i, n. *soil.*
solum(modo), adv., *only, alone.*
sólus,-a,-um, adj., *single, alone.*
solútio,-ónis, f. *payment.*

sólvo,-ere,-i, solútum, *free, release, discharge, pay.*
soror,-óris, f. *sister.*
sórtior,-íri,-ítus, *distribute, choose, obtain.*
speciális,-e, adj., *special.*
speciáliter, adv., *specially.*
speciátim, adv., *specially, in particular.*
spécies,-ei, f. *semblance, shape.*
spécto,-áre,-ávi,-átum, *look at, regard, pertain.*
spéro,-áre,-ávi,-átum, *hope, anticipate, foresee.*
spirituália, n. pl., *spiritualities.*
spoliátor,-óris, m. *wrongdoer, robber.*
spoliátus,-a,-um, adj., *deprived, despoiled.*
sponsália,-ium, n. pl., *betrothal.*
sponsus,-i, m. *betrothed, bridegroom.*
sponsus,-us, m. *engagement, bail, suretyship.*
sponte, *of his own accord.*
stábilis,-e, adj., *firm.*
státuo,-ere,-ui,-útum, *establish, resolve, decree.*
státus,-us, m. *state, estate.*
statútum,-i, n. *statute.*
stípes,-itis, m. *root, stock.*
stipulátio,-ónis, f. *covenant, stipulation.*
stipulátor,-óris, m. *stipulator, party using.*
stípulor,-ári,-átus, *bargain, covenant.*
sto,-áre, stéti, státum, *stand, abide.*
strictè, adv., *strictly.*
stríctus,-a,-um, adj., *strict.*
súbditus,-i, m. *subject.*
subjectio,-ónis, f. *subjection.*
subintélligo,-ere,-éxi,-éctum, *understand.*
súbsequens,-ntis, adj., *subsequent.*
súbsequor,-sequi,-secútus, *follow, ensue.*
subsísto,-ere,-stiti, *stop, resist, pause, cease, subsist.*
substántia,-æ, f. *essence, substance.*
subsúm,-esse, *underlie, be under.*
subtílitas,-átis, f. *subtilty, refinement.*
subvénio,-íre,-véni,-véntum, *assist, come to the aid of.*
subvérto,-ere,-ti,-sum, *overturn, destroy.*
succédo,-ere,-céssi,-céssum, *succeed, enter.*
succéssio,-ónis, f. *succession.*
succéssor,-óris, m. *successor.*
succúrro,-ere,-cúrri,-cúrsum, *come to the aid of.*
suffício,-ere,-féci,-féctum, *suffice.*

suggéstio,-ónis, f. *suggestion, intimation.*
súi, gen. of reflex. pron., *of himself, herself, etc.*
sum, esse, fui, *be, exist, happen.*
súmma,-æ, f. *principal matter, amount, sum.*
summonítio,-ónis, f. *summons.*
súmmus,-a,-um, sup. adj., *highest, supreme.*
súmo,-ere, súmpsi, súmptum, *bring forward, put on, take up, apply.*
supérfluus,-a,-um, adj., *superfluous.*
supérior,-óris, m. *principal ;* comp. adj., *higher, greater.*
súpero,-áre,-ávi,-átum, *surpass, exceed.*
supervácuum,-i, n. *superfluity.*
supervénio,-íre,-véni,-véntum, *come to.*
súppleo,-ére,-évi,-étum, *supply.*
supplícium,-ii, n. *punishment, penalty.*
suppréssio,-ónis, f. *suppression.*
suprémus,-a,-um, sup. adj., *highest, last, closing.*
surpluságium,-ii, n. *surplusage.*
suspéctus,-a,-um, adj., *suspected.*
suspício,-ónis, f. *suspicion.*
suspiciósus,-a,-um, *suspicious.*
súus,-a,-um, poss. pron., *his, her, its.*

T.

táceo,-ére,-cui,-citum, *be silent.*
tácite, adv., *silently, impliedly.*
tácitus,-a,-um, adj., *unmentioned, implied, silent.*
tális,-e, adj., *such.*
tam, adv., *so.*
támen, conj., *yet, however.*
tamétsi, conj., *although.*
tamquam (tanquam), adv., *as it were, just as.*
tango,-ere, tétigi, tactum, *touch.*
tántum,-i, *so much, so far.*
tantummódo, adv., *only, alone.*
tántus,-a,-um, adj., *of such size, so great.*
témere, adv., *rashly, by chance.*
témpus,-oris, n. *time.*
teneméntum,-i, n. *tenement.*
ténens,-ntis, m. *tenant.*
téneo,-ére,-ui, téntum, *regard, hold, bind.*
tenor,-óris, m. *tenor, tenure.*
términus,-i, m. *term, bound, limit.*

térra,-æ, f. *land.*
territórium,-ii, n. *territory, domain.*
tértius,-a,-um, num. adj., *third.*
testaméntum,-i, n. *will, testament.*
testátor,-óris, m. *testator.*
téstis,-is, c. *witness.*
téstor,-ári,-átus sum, *testify, make a will.*
textus,-us, m. *text.*
thesaúrus,-i, m. *treasure.*
thórus,-i, m. *bed, couch.*
tímor,-óris, m. *fear, apprehension.*
títulus,-i, m. *title.*
tólero,-áre,-ávi,-átum, *permit, bear, endure, tolerate.*
tóllo,-ere, sústuli, sublátum, *remove, annul, cancel.*
tótus,-a,-um, adj., *all, whole.*
tracto,-áre,-ávi,-átum, *investigate, discuss, touch, conduct.*
tractus,-us, m. *course, progress.*
tradítio,-ónis, f. *delivery.*
trádo,-ere,-didi,-ditum, *deliver, transmit.*
tráho,-ere, tráxi, tráctum, *draw (to it).*
tranquíllitas,-átis, f. *tranquillity.*
tránseo,-íre,-ívi(-íi),-itum, *pass.*
tránsfero,-férre,-tuli,-látum, *transfer.*
transgrédior,-gredi,-gressus, *step over, exceed.*
transversális,-e, adj., *collateral.*
trés, tria, num. adj., *three.*
triátio,-ónis, f. *trial.*
tríbuo,-ere,-ui,-útum, *give, allow, bestow.*
tripartítus,-a,-um, adj., *threefold.*
trítus,-a,-um, adj., *beaten, frequented.*
tunc, adv., *then.*
túrpis,-e, adj., *base.*
turpitúdo,-inis, f. *baseness, infamy.*
tute, adv., *safely.*
tutéla,-æ, f. *defence, guardian, guardianship.*
tútus,-a,-um, adj., *safe.*
túus,-a,-um, poss. pron., *your.*

U.

úbi, adv., *where.*
ullus,-a,-um, adj., *any, anyone.*
últimus,-a,-um, adj., *final, last.*
unde, adv., *whence, from which.*

únitas,-átis, f. *unity.*
universális,-e, adj., *universal.*
univérsitas,-átis, f. *company, corporation, society.*
univérsus,-a,-um, adj., *everybody, whole, entire.*
únus,-a,-um, num. adj., *one.*
únusquisque, adj., *each one.*
usitátus,-a,-um, adj., *wonted, customary.*
úsque, adv., *all the way up to, until.*
usucápio,-ónis, f. *acquisition of ownership by long use.*
úsus,-us, m. *custom, use.*
ut, conj., *in order that.*
uterínus fráter, *a brother born of the same mother.*
úterus,-i, m. *womb.*
útilis,-e, adj., *useful.*
utílitas,-átis, f. *utility.*
utlagátus,-i, m. *outlaw.*
utlago,-áre,-ávi,-átum, *outlaw.*
útor, úti, úsus sum, w. abl., *resort to, use, enjoy, adopt.*
utrínque, adv., *on both sides.*
úxor,-óris, f. *wife.*

V.

vácuum,-i, n. *empty space, vacuum.*
vácuus,-a,-um, adj., *void.*
vágus,-a,-um, adj., *uncertain, ambiguous.*
váleo,-ére,-ui, —, *stand, be able, avail.*
válor,-óris, m. *value.*
vánus,-a,-um, adj., *vain, groundless.*
várius,-a,-um, adj., *various.*
vástum,-i, n. *waste.*
vel, conj., *or, either . . . or.*
vélo,-áre,-ávi,-átum, *cover, veil.*
venális,-e, adj., *venal, for sale.*
vendítio,-ónis, f. *sale.*
vénditor,-óris, m. *seller.*
véndo,-ere,-didi,-ditum, *sell.*
vénia,-æ, f. *pardon.*
vénio,-íre, véni, véntum, *go, come.*
vénter,-tris, m. *belly, dam.*
vérbum,-i, n. *word.*
vére, adv., *really, truly, rightly.*
veredíctum,-i, n. *verdict.*
véreor,-éri,-itus, *respect, fear.*
verificátio,-ónis, f. *proof.*

verifico,-áre,-ávi,-átum, *verify.*
véritas,-átis, f. *truth.*
véro, adv., *but, in fact, surely.*
vérsor,-ári,-átus, *occupy oneself with, be engaged in.*
vérsus, prep. w. acc., *against.*
vérus,-a,-um, adj., *true.*
véstis,-is, f. *clothing, clothes.*
véteres,-um, m. pl., *our forefathers, the ancients.*
véto,-áre,-ui,-itum, *forbid.*
vétus,-eris, adj., *old, ancient.*
vetústas,-átis, f. *antiquity, posterity.*
vexo,-áre,-ávi,-átum, *vex, molest, injure.*
vía,-æ, f. *way, road.*
vicárius,-ii, m. *delegate, proxy.*
vicínus,-i, m. *neighbour.*
vícis (gen., no nom.), *place, office.*
victor,-óris, m. *victor.*
vídeo,-ére, vídi, vísum, *see, perceive.*
vídeor,-éri, vísus sum, *seem, appear, be regarded as.*
vígilans,-ntis, c. *watchful person.*
vigínti, adj., *twenty.*
vínco,-ere, víci, víctum, *overcome, defeat, win.*
vínculum,-i, n. *bond, chain, link.*
violéntus,-a,-um, adj., *forcible.*
víolo,-áre,-ávi,-átum, *violate, break.*
viperínus,-a,-um, adj., *serpent-like.*
vír, víri, m. *husband, man, manhood.*
vírtus,-útis, f. *virtue.*
vis, vis, f. *force.*
víscus,-eris, n. *flesh, carcass, bowels.*
visitátio,-ónis, f. *visit.*
víta,-æ, f. *life.*
vítio,-áre,-ávi,-átum, *vitiate, make void.*
vítium,-ii, n. *fault, defect, offence.*
vívens,-ntis, m. *a living person.*
vívo,-ere, víxi, víctum, *live.*
vívus,-a,-um, adj., *living.*
vix, adv., *hardly, scarcely.*
vólo, vélle, vólui, —, *wish.*
volúntas,-átis, f. *will.*
vótum,-i, n. *wish, vow.*
vox,-cis, f. *voice, expression, sentence.*
vulgáris,-e, adj., *common, ordinary, usual.*

Lightning Source UK Ltd.
Milton Keynes UK
UKOW02f2023120915

258511UK00004B/192/P

9 781616 193706